The General Education Class in the Secondary School

Other Secondary Education titles from the Holt, Rinehart and Winston list

ALEXANDER AND HALVERSON · *Effective Teaching in Secondary Schools*

ALEXANDER AND SAYLOR · *Modern Secondary Education: Basic Principles and Practices*

BURNETT · *Teaching Science in the Secondary School*

BURTON · *Literature Study in the High Schools*

COLE · *Psychology of Adolescence*, Fifth Edition

FRENCH, HULL, AND DODDS · *American High School Administration: Policy and Practice*, Revised Edition

GILCHRIST, DUTTON, AND WRINKLE · *Secondary Education for American Democracy*, Revised Edition

GRAMBS, IVERSON, AND PATTERSON · *Modern Methods in Secondary Education*, Revised Edition

KINNEY AND PURDY · *Teaching Mathematics in the Secondary School*

LEONARD · *Developing the Secondary School Curriculum*, Revised Edition

The General Education Class in the Secondary School

LOUISE E. HOCK • **THOMAS J. HILL**

New York University *University of Florida*

A HOLT-RINEHART BOOK

Holt, Rinehart and Winston, Inc., New York

Contents

Foreword

By William Van Til

One of the perennial plaints of readers of books on education is that their authors do not use enough specific illustrations. "It sounds all right in theory. But what do the authors mean in concrete, practical terms?"

I predict that *The General Education Class in the Secondary School* will be singularly exempt from this query. Professor Louise E. Hock and Professor Thomas J. Hill have supplied abundant and rich illustration of how education goes on in the general education class. They tap not only the growing volume of case studies reported by successful teachers of the core curriculum in American secondary schools; again and again they reach into seemingly inexhaustible personal archives and utilize experiences they have had in teaching the general education class in Maryland, Ohio, Georgia, and Florida.

The result is a book by authors who obviously know whereof they speak. Their introduction to teaching the general education class is based on tested experience, both their own and that of others.

The general education class in secondary education is one of the exciting developments of twentieth-century education. As described by the authors, the core of the curriculum is much more than a methodological device. The general education class is an approach to vital content growing out of the social realities of our times, our democratic values, modern psychological theory, and what we know of the adolescent and his needs. The purpose is no less than "the maximum development of each young person as an intelligent individual in his own right and as a mature citizen in his relationships with his fellow man."

Challenge to complacency and to retreat rings through the volume. In a time of educational crisis the authors are no summer soldiers or sunshine patriots. They believe in the general education class and they make a strong case for it.

As authors Hock and Hill set forth definitions and bases, then concentrate on how to teach the general education class, retrospect carried me back to my first encounter with the general education class. Loaded with liberal arts content, yet abysmally ignorant of the teaching craft, I came in 1934 to the Ohio State University School to teach adolescents in one of the pioneer general education courses. Would that the present book were available to me then! But perhaps the tribulations of those of us who trod the trail early have contributed to the path so well charted by the authors. Yet if some Wellsian time machine replaces retrospect and transports me back to my first core teaching, I plan to carry aboard with me *The General Education Class in the Secondary School!*

New York University
February, 1960

Acknowledgments

Giving credit where credit is due is difficult when so many people have contributed to one's thinking. It would be impossible to list the many individuals who, over the years, have played a part in the development of our ideas about general education and the general education class. We are indebted, of course, to the hundreds and hundreds of secondary school students in various parts of the country whom we have taught and who have, as a consequence, shared in the development of promising learning experiences. To our many colleagues in secondary schools and colleges we are grateful for the help they have given in the clarification of our thinking regarding the nature of the general education class. Also, we would like to express our appreciation to the many, many teachers and prospective teachers with whom we have worked in our college classes and through our field contacts. Their shrewd questioning and probing have given us pause on many occasions and have led to further analysis of our beliefs and the reasons underlying them.

To this large anonymous group, however, we would like to add the names of several individuals whose specific illustrations of classroom practices contribute much to an understanding of ways of working in the general education class. We are grateful to the following persons for their kindness in permitting us to use examples from their own experience: Miss Gladys Baxter, Dean of Girls, Murphy High School, Mobile, Alabama; Dr. Leslee J. Bishop, Chairman, Combined Studies Department, Evanston Township High School, Evanston, Illinois; Mrs. J. N. Bivona, Teacher, Murphy High School, Mobile, Alabama; Mrs. Madolyn Brown, Supervisor of Social Studies, Dade County Public Schools, Florida; Miss Roberta M. Cogley, Teacher, Southern Garrett County Junior-Senior High School, Oakland, Maryland; Miss Dorothy Knappenberger, Supervisor of Language Arts in

Secondary Schools, Tulsa, Oklahoma; Dr. Sylvan Mikelson, College of Education, Wayne State University, Detroit, Michigan; Mr. William L. Paden, Jr., Teacher, P. K. Yonge Laboratory School, University of Florida, Gainesville, Florida; Mrs. C. L. Scarborough, Teacher, Murphy High School, Mobile, Alabama; Mr. Adrian Stilson, Assistant Professor, University School, Ohio State University, Columbus, Ohio; Miss Martha Ann Wells, Dean of Girls, Hillcrest High School, Springfield, Missouri; Mr. Roy R. Wilkie, Teacher, Murphy High School, Mobile, Alabama; Miss Margaret Willis, Associate Professor, University School, Ohio State University, Columbus, Ohio.

We are indebted to several schools for permission to quote materials relevant to their general education programs: to Evanston Township High School, Evanston, Illinois; to Pennsbury School in Yardley, Pennsylvania; to the P. K. Yonge Laboratory School, University of Florida, Gainesville, Florida; and to University School, Ohio State University in Columbus, Ohio. To Dr. Helen Halter Long, Assistant Superintendent of the Mamaroneck Public Schools, and to Dr. Robert E. Krebs, Audio-Visual Director of the P. K. Yonge School, we are grateful for the photographs from these schools.

Because much of the material and many of the ideas in this book were developed several years ago in connection with her doctoral study, one of the authors would like to give a warm word of thanks to Dr. Gordon N. Mackenzie of Teachers College, Columbia University, New York. His encouragement and helpful guidance at that time were—and are—greatly appreciated.

We would like to express special appreciation to Dr. Gordon F. Vars, New York State College for Teachers, Plattsburgh, New York, whose valuable critical reading of the manuscript in its early stages helped us revise our writing in the direction of greater clarity and consistency. Finally, we wish to thank Miss Ella Playwin for her helpful assistance in the necessary details of manuscript preparation and her personal interest in the successful completion of this publication.

L.E.H.
T.J.H.

Introduction

General Education and

the Contemporary Scene

Only a cursory glance at the daily newspapers or a casual hearing of the radio-television news is enough to remind Americans of the twentieth century that this is not yet the best of all worlds. Even as we allocate time, energy, strength, and money to the pursuit of outer space, we are painfully aware that we have not yet solved the problems of our own planet, our own nation, our own communities. What is even more painful, perhaps tragic, is that we are not at all certain that we have the minds capable of meeting contemporary issues head-on and coming to grips with alternative solutions.

If ever a people engaged in self-examination or felt the need of it, we are such a people today. The questions we are raising are pointed and challenging, the answers still uncertain and uncomfortable.

How are we to deal with the manifold problems posed by the headlong and frightening advances of automation and technology? Who is to come to grips with ensuing problems of unemployment, the potential development of a class society, an increase of leisure time demanding productive and satisfying outlets?

Who can grasp the import of the current struggles in the eternal seesaw of war and peace? How will we rationally resolve the armaments race? When will we learn to live side by side as peoples in intelligent, self-respecting co-existence?

How are we to conquer outer space, and why? How will we control it, when we, the members of the earth's human race, do not know yet how to control ourselves and our neighbors?

Who is to untangle the knotty web of maladjustment in human relationships and guide us toward maturity? Whence will come the insight to deal with marital relationships to bring about a decline in divorce rates and numbers of broken homes? How will we manage our family relationships to prevent youth delinquency or adult, as the case may be? How are we to achieve integrity and ethical standards in government, business, labor, all manner of public life? What is to be done to prevent the tragic numbers of individual breakdowns, the widespread mental health problem—all the sources of which we have not yet fathomed?

How are we to deal with the fundamentals of existence—the simple essentials of adequate food, clothing, shelter? In what ways is our economy to be handled for the greatest benefit to the greatest number?

How are we to develop in people the insights, understandings, knowledges, and moral fiber with which to face questions like these and to arrive at satisfactory answers?

Issues like the above—and many more—have become in this century the common problems of all the people. They must be faced by each of us—strong or weak, rich or poor, laborer or professional, brilliant or dull. All of us participate in decisions affecting these issues —some very directly, most of us indirectly through our use of the ballot, by which we clearly, though not always so consciously as one would wish, express our beliefs on and take a stand on problem after problem. The specialist no longer can assume the sole responsibility for decisions in his small bailiwick. For one thing, the lines formerly separating the specializations are becoming more and more blurred. The economist must deal with political realities, the diplomat with financial frames of reference, the artist with propaganda implications, the scientist with military alignments. For another, the problems and their potential decisions have become too great to be encompassed within the minds of a few, however brilliant. We have finally begun to recognize the need for vast quantities of quality among the human resources of our nation and its neighbors.

In our dilemma it is not surprising to find that we turn to education in our hour of need, believing now, as in the past, that the educated man is the resourceful, dependable, thoughtful man upon who we can rely. As a consequence, our educational systems—for plural they are —are being scrutinized through the eye of the microscope, telescope, and all manner of magnifying equipment, albeit occasionally from the wrong end, it would seem.

Fortunately there are many so engaged in educational evaluation who have begun to recognize that if issues like those mentioned above are to be dealt with intelligently, there must be developed in all our citizenry a fundamental grasp and awareness of those common learnings necessary for dealing with these problems, that all of us must have some essential familiarity with the common problems of mankind in the twentieth century. And so it becomes the task of general education to prepare our youth to be the wise citizens and members of the human race who can and will save us from catastrophe.

The role of general education in our public schools has always been an important one. As we re-examine it now, it is all too easy to fall into the usual habit of playing the numbers game in our efforts to require so many courses in the disciplines generally accepted to be part of general education, to speak in terms of years of study, credit hours, or the usual numerical paraphernalia of curriculum revision. Or to use another analogy, we easily find ourselves rearranging the cafeteria offerings, placing some of them earlier in the line than heretofore, eliminating others, adding an occasional one or two.

For several decades now there have been many of us who have been concerned by this uninspiring and basically unintellectual approach to modifying our educational programs. We have said, and are saying with even more conviction today, that what is really needed is a breakthrough in our educational thinking that will help us to recognize sacred cows for what they are and to face the realities of life with firmness of purpose and imaginative planning. As is true in other fields, a breakthrough can occur at various points on the educational front and can take several directions.

One direction that many of us believe holds rich promise for future dividends is a curriculum pattern that would include a concept of general education from kindergarten through college, varying in relative proportions to more specialized education as one proceeds in educational maturity. Such a pattern would see this general education as an important part of the school day with a content, a purpose, a process even that are peculiarly its own, though not necessarily exclusively. In this part of the school program the focus would be on developing the method of intelligence that can be used in all areas of living and working—the method that involves actual problem solving, critical thinking, analytical research. The content of this class in our curriculum would consist of those studies that give students intelligent foundations to deal with broad issues facing them as youth and as future adults. This content would emphasize concept development, breadth of understanding, acquisition of the tools of intelligent action needed in our society today. The purpose of such a course would be a vast one and a vastly important one—the maximum development of each young person as an intelligent individual in his own right and as a mature citizen in his relationships with his fellow man.

Nothing less can be expected of our educational program today; but we *have* settled for much less in our mistaken belief that patterns of thinking and teaching and organization that sufficed fifty years ago, five hundred years ago, and indeed two thousand years ago, will continue to suffice for generations that have already been projected out of the twentieth century with startling force and clarity while still chained to physical existence in it.

The idea of a general education class that we, the authors, suggest and describe in the following chapters is not revolutionary or even startling. The bases for it have been in the research literature for many years; classes similar to it have been in existence here and there, off and on for several decades; the effectiveness of the idea has been demonstrated in many ways in many places at various times. However, for some curious reason, the idea has not become an essential part of educational practice on as widespread a basis as it deserves to be. Now, perhaps, the time is ripe, the need is great, and the rewards self-evident for all of us to work even harder to close the gap that has existed too long between proven idea and widespread practice.

It is our profound hope that much thought will be given by all persons concerned with the education of our young people and the consequent future of our nation to the ideas and practices herein described. Surely our young people deserve the best of what we know and believe; our country requires the best of which we are capable.

*The General Education Class
in the Secondary School*

Part One

Becoming Acquainted with General Education

1

A Matter of
Definition

In that unique institution, the American high school, we have in attendance nearly nine million teen-age boys and girls, each differing from all the others. Some of these differences are very obvious—age, sex, size, facial characteristics, skin color, personal mannerisms, and the like. Other differences are much less noticeable but equally if not more important—native ability, cultural background, emotional stability, educational achievement and potential, personal hopes and aspirations. It is the duty of a school in a democratic society to respect all individuals and their unique personalities, cherishing some of the differences which exist among them yet minimizing other differences.

Along with the general recognition of this responsibility of the public high school to respect individual personality and to help each person develop to a level which approximates his capacity, there is also a concomitant responsibility to the society which establishes and supports the school for the purpose of educating our youth. In the final analysis a school is established by a society so that the social order itself may be perpetuated and improved. In our American democracy it is imperative that the school develop within each individual an allegiance to the core of commonly held values that give strength and permanence to our way of life.

Even a casual observer of the American high school would be able to note that many schools do not live up to the expectations indicated by the above commitments. There has not been a great deal of change since the following statement was made by the Educational Policies Commission [1] in 1938.

[1] Educational Policies Commission. *Policies for Education in American Democracy* (Washington, D.C.: National Education Association, 1946), p. 271.

3

Here is a scene for the pen of a satirist. *Time:* 1938. *Place:* An American high school. *Setting:* a democracy struggling against strangulation in an era marked by confused loyalties in the political realm, by unrest and deprivation, by much unnecessary ill health, by high-pressure propaganda, by war and the threats of war, by many broken or ill-adjusted homes, by foolish spending, by high crime rates, by bad housing, and by a myriad of other urgent, real human problems. And what are the children in this school, in this age, in this culture, learning? They are learning that the square of the sum of two numbers equals the sum of their squares plus twice their product; that Millard Fillmore was the thirteenth President of the United States and held office from January 10, 1850, to March 4, 1853; that the capital of Honduras is Tegucigalpa; that there were two Peloponnesian Wars and three Punic Wars; that Latin verbs meaning command, obey, please, displease, serve, resist, and the like take the dative; and that a gerund is a neuter verbal noun used in the oblique cases of the singular and governing the same case as its verb.

Let there be no misunderstanding. The items of information just listed are entirely suitable for study by some children. But for the great majority of the boys and girls who now attend American schools such learning is transitory and of extremely little value.

However, there are hopeful signs on the horizon as more and more educators, pupils, parents, and other lay people are coming to recognize the need to provide for some place in the school program where boys and girls can study directly those things everyone needs in order to be a responsible and self-directive individual who is also a productive, contributing member of his society.

School after school is finding it important to ask, "Where in our program do we help boys and girls make intelligent vocational choices; deal with persistent personal problems connected with growing up socially, emotionally, and physically; face the responsibilities of citizenship and meet the challenges which confront all citizens in the dynamic age in which we live?" The present curriculum-development movement in the schools of the nation shows that those concerned with public education are actively and diligently seeking answers to these questions and solutions to these very real problems which face the schools in providing an adequate education for tomorrow's citizens.

A. Major Dissatisfactions with Present Programs

As parents, teachers, and students look at their schools they find many shortcomings of many different types. The physical difficulties of housing, staffing and equipping our schools represent one category of problems, but an even more fundamental group of problems centers in the school program itself. As people study the organization of the school program and the school day they arrive at the conclusion that the situation is somewhat paradoxical. Certain practices and patterns perpetuated in the curriculum seem to stand in the way of the school's successful fulfillment of its assigned tasks, those related both to the youth in the school and to the social order maintaining the school. Four major criticisms seem to be repeatedly leveled by those who take time to study their school programs.

1. EXTREME DEPARTMENTALIZATION

Under the present organization of most secondary school programs into numerous subject areas it is often found that little or no relationship exists between what is taught in one class and what is taught in another. If there is little or no correlation between the *teaching* in any two classes, then there is little likelihood that there is any correlation between the *learning*. There is a growing recognition by many professional people that a vast chasm lies between what is supposedly taught and what is actually learned. Similarly educators are coming to realize that the expectancy of transfer of understanding from one subject discipline to another has been for the most part unwarranted. As a result much thought has been given to ways of breaking down the barriers between classes, either through teaching for the understanding of relationships between subjects or through bringing together the subject areas into a more functional relationship in the school program.

2. FAILURE TO DEVELOP SKILLS OF CRITICAL AND INDEPENDENT THINKING

One of the most telling criticisms of secondary education focuses on its failure to teach young people to make wise choices, to use a problem-solving approach to the situations of life, to think critically and independently. While there is no evidence to support the position that the youth of today are any less capable of making intelligent decisions than were their counterparts of previous generations, it is evident that we can no longer afford the luxury of a citizenry which does not act from carefully thought-out premises and positions. There is also evidence that we do not trust our eighteen-year-old youth enough to allow them to share in making certain decisions that vitally affect their participation in the defense of our country. At the same time, however, we welcome them into the armed forces. Such a position seems to be another way of saying that young people are capable of taking orders and executing them faithfully but incapable of responsible decision in vital matters.

At any rate, many people have questioned the ability of young people today to think judiciously, to decide wisely, to act on principle and thought. In the opinion of some educators such lack of skill and perception is not surprising, for it is difficult to locate many instances to show how such skills are being developed. As one observer has pointed out, after following a young student for an entire day, she found only one occasion when he could exercise the right of choice, and then it was the selection of a ham or cheese sandwich in the school cafeteria at lunchtime. The rest of his school experiences were so planned that he had no choice concerning them. No wonder many people have become alarmed at an approach to education that, if not authoritarian, at least inhibits the very development being sought. A re-examination and revision of current ways of teaching might lead to a greater consistency between actual practices and education's professed goals of developing citizens for democratic living.

3. FAILURE TO PROVIDE FOR REAL NEEDS AND PROBLEMS OF ADOLESCENTS IN TODAY'S WORLD

It is not difficult for an observer in our junior or senior high schools today to find classrooms where the teacher's focus on specific content reveals little recognition or understanding of the young people who are supposedly learning the content. Such a disparity is well illustrated by the seventh-grade teacher who conscientiously drills the eight parts of speech and requires the memorization of innumerable prepositions, but who is completely oblivious to the fact that the boys and girls in his room face some immediate and serious concerns and problems.

With just a little thought and time the teacher could discover what these students actually are thinking and wishing, as another junior high school teacher did. Through various approaches he found youngsters expressing themselves as follows:

At home my parents are thinking of separating and they both want me (I don't know which side to take).

I wish that our family could move into a new modern home.

I would wish first for my mother's sight and my father's health.

(In reply to the question, "What are your difficulties?") My whole family, my father's health and my mother's condition and my oldest brother is in a mess right now. That's one reason why I don't like school, because when I get home I have so much to do, by the time I get done it's too late to go out, and if I didn't go to school I'd have more time to have fun.

I wish that I would be cured of heart trouble because I have it.

Where in the program for these youngsters was some attention being given to simple principles of interior decorating that might have made the low-rent-project homes of these youngsters more endurable? Who feels responsible for building a functional health program for boys and girls with such immediate family health problems and concerns? Who is helping with the emotional development of these boys and girls? How is the impact of the local steel strike on the lives of those youngsters realized and dealt with? Who, indeed, is aware that problems and needs such as these exist? How many schools try to relate their educational offerings to the peculiar nature of the immediate community, whether it be highly industrialized, residential, or rural? Or to the concerns of the specific group of boys and girls who present a composite need cluster very different from the group across town, only ten miles away in distance but perhaps generations apart in background and experiences?

While educational offerings have remained static and sterile, the lives of young people have become dynamic and demanding as they interact with a society that is mobile, changing, and challenging. Somehow the gap which young people see between school and society must be bridged.

4. LACK OF OPPORTUNITY FOR EACH STUDENT TO BE WELL KNOWN BY AT LEAST ONE FACULTY MEMBER

In the highly departmentalized programs so prevalent today it is not unusual to find that teachers meet two hundred or more students each day. In such circumstances it is almost impossible for the teacher to get to know these students. If there is a counselor or guidance specialist in the school, he often has responsibility for several hundred young people. With a large part of his job revolving around testing programs and record keeping, there is little time left for the personal guidance so much needed by adolescents.

The net result of this organization and instructional pattern of the secondary school is that, in most of our high schools, few students are really known and understood by even one teacher, and many students are not really sympathetically understood by any adult. This is a highly disturbing commentary on the very institution which is charged with responsibility for the development of the individual child. There is, then, a growing feeling that somewhere in the school program provision should be made for students to have prolonged contact with a teacher who will be concerned with understanding and guiding them in all aspects of their growth and development.

The dissatisfaction represented by these four criticisms, coupled with the intense concern for the failure of the school to deal realistically with the problems ever present in contemporary society, has led more than one student of the educational scene to advocate a direct offering in the school program that will provide for the general education considered essential for our young people. It is with this kind of offering, the general education class, that we are concerned in this volume, and it is to its definition that we now turn our attention.

B. The General Education Class

In an age when words are used to wage war and achieve peace, to sell products and influence minds, to becloud issues and persuade, confuse, clarify, or entertain, we have all become conscious of the science of semantics in a way that was unfamiliar to our forebears. We realize more and more the inadequacies of written and spoken communication, and what at one time seemed to be the most specific of all communicative arts, namely, language, is now recognized to have as many variants of meaning and shades of interpretation as those other arts of communication—music, the dance, fine arts, and the like.

In many fields, we are faced with the problem of certain words having different meanings for different people in different places. The medical profession, for example, is aware of the need to standardize terminology so that names of drugs will be the same throughout the world, if confusion is to be avoided and research facilitated. In the same way education has its problems of semantics, and educators often find themselves using words that can have several meanings.

It is desirable, therefore, before proceeding further, to attempt to define what we mean when we refer to the general education class. For in the past several decades various terms have evolved to describe several kinds of curriculum offerings, some of which are more or less vaguely related to the concept of general education developed in these pages. In order to avoid confusion and misinterpretation, then, let us state clearly that, to us, the general education class is *that block of time in the school day in which those needs, problems, and concerns of our adolescents and our society that are common to all individuals are directly dealt with through a process of co-operative pupil-teacher planning without regard to the usual subject-discipline lines.*[2]

[2] Other names have been given to classes such as this and to other classes that bear some resemblance to this kind of class—core, common learnings, block-time classes, and the like. It seems to the writers that since the content of the class is general education and since it has application to all adolescents, the designation of "general education class" is appropriate and descriptive.

It is important to note the essential aspects of the general education class as indicated in this definition: (1) a block of time; (2) a content of common learnings; (3) a problem-solving process; (4) freedom from traditional discipline boundaries. If the general education class is to achieve the purposes claimed for it and demanded of it, all of these elements must be present.

In addition, it must be recognized that underlying the concept of a general education class are certain fundamental assumptions to which we must be committed, if we are to be successful. Some of these assumptions are:

1. The school should be concerned with teaching the adolescent here and now as a valuable member of contemporary society.

2. Learning is a function of the total individual, and the student must be seen as a total personality.

3. Education should result, among other things, in self-direction and the development of those skills and insights necessary for further self-education.

4. Recognition must be given to the existence of concomitant learnings, an awareness that more than one thing is learned at a time; for example, while facts are being taught, attitudes are being formed.

5. Education should guide students toward the integration and reorganization of their experience.

6. Individual differences must be respected and provided for within a framework of democratic living.

Acceptance of these assumptions makes it possible for teachers to work with students in the general education class in ways consistent with our goals. Some of these ways might be mentioned at this point, since they give a more descriptive view of the nature of a general education class.

1. Students work with problems that are significant to them and socially significant in our contemporary democratic society, utilizing a wide range of materials in their study.

2. Teachers and students plan together in the identification of and investigation of the problems.

3. In studying each problem every student takes part in a program of broad reading, and has a wide range of opportunity for written, oral, and other creative expression.

4. The right of each person to be heard and to express himself is maintained, and each student is afforded the opportunity to make a contribution to the group.

5. All students engage in a wide variety of activities that are con-

sistent with the students' present development and that will enable them to realize the goals that have been established by teachers and pupils.

6. Students and teachers develop standards of value for each experience in the learning process and continually evaluate their learning.

7. Students and teachers measure progress in terms of actual performance and in relation to their ability and past performance. There is a continuous focus on *growth*.

The general education class, then, becomes part of a total curricular program which has the following characteristics.

1. The curriculum provides for general education and specialized education. General education (the center of which is the general education class) is given the larger portion of the school day in the junior high grades, decreasing in time to the senior year of high school. At the same time, specialized education increases in the amount of time devoted to it and is dual in nature, providing for the development of special competencies needed in the world of work and also encouraging the discovery and development of individual interests for personal enjoyment and satisfaction.

2. The general education class becomes the genuine center of the curriculum and constitutes the major part of the general educational aspect of the program.

3. Guidance becomes an integral part of instruction, and the general education teacher assumes the primary guidance responsibility for the students in his class.

4. Individual differences are provided for within the general education class by drawing on the strengths of everyone in a truly interactive way through students' living and working together. In addition, opportunities are present in the rest of the school program for wide choice in special areas of need and interest.

C. Relationship of General Education and Specialized Education

The relationship that exists between general education and specialized education is subject to many different interpretations. However, for the purpose of this discussion, we will assume that general education is the phase of schooling that deals with the skills, concepts, and knowledge which are needed by all people, as a minimum, for effective participation in society. Regardless of what a person plans to do or to be—a doctor, a lawyer, a truck driver, a schoolteacher or a farmer—there are certain things that will be of importance to him. Among them will be:

1. The ability to use his native language so that he may communicate effectively with others around him and understand the environment in which he lives.
2. The ability to manage his personal finances wisely. This involves a reasonable knowledge of our number system.
3. The ability to work effectively and live peacefully with whomever he comes in contact.
4. The ability to make decisions based upon evidence rather than emotions and prejudices.
5. The ability to assume full responsibility for his own actions.
6. The ability to spend his time wisely and wholesomely.

General education should, throughout the school, concern itself with helping people become increasingly competent in the above mentioned abilities.

On the other hand, there are many areas of competency that are not equally applicable to all people. For example, in a certain type of endeavor, a high degree of proficiency may be very necessary, whereas in some other type of endeavor this proficiency may not be needed at all, or perhaps just a passing acquaintance with it would be sufficient. Let us look at some specifics to illustrate the point.

1. All people do not need to be highly skilled in solving problems involving trigonometry. However, one would be a poor electrical engineer if he did not possess this skill.
2. All people do not need a thorough, detailed understanding of the mechanical operation of the motor car. However, one who did not have this understanding would be an inferior auto mechanic.
3. A poet or journalist would certainly need a greater competence in the technical aspects of language than would a farmer.

For the sake of relationships, let us say that in some cases specialized education is an extension of general education areas, whereas in other cases it deals with certain specific needs of individuals which may not be touched on in general education.

Another distinction that must be pointed out is that existing between the general education class and the other general education aspects of the school program. For there are some learnings needed by all young people that are frequently handled more effectively in separate fashion from the problem-oriented focus of the general education class. For example, at the junior high school level, especially in the seventh and eighth grades, no one would question the general education nature of fundamental mathematical skills. However, these skills are seldom taught as part of the general education class, but constitute a separate course offering in the school schedule. Such an approach, however, does not eliminate the need for youngsters to utilize their mathematical skills and understandings in dealing with problem areas in the general education class. One frequently finds meaningful application of such skills in the use of statistics, the making of charts and graphs, and similar activities in the broader framework of the general education class.

Another instance that might be cited is that of physical education. Again, no one will question its place as part of general education. Usually it is taught as a separate subject, however. It is interesting to note, though, that some schools have experimented with scheduling math and physical education as part of the general education block in an effort to correlate more effectively all those learnings considered common and general for effective individual development and desirable citizenship growth. These experiments have met with varying degrees of success.

In another direction we might mention the intricate relationships existing between the general education class and the more specialized aspects of the school program. At the senior high school level a general education class will be responsible for continuous attention to skills of effective speaking, writing, reading, listening—the fundamental communication skills. However, as students mature and individual differences widen in terms of interests and future goals, there might also be offerings in the school of courses in journalism or in drama, or a workshop in creative writing. These classes provide opportunities for individual students to delve more deeply into specialized areas of communication in a way that is not essential to the "common education" of all young people.

In summary, then, we find a secondary school program consisting of the general education class, other general education offerings, and specialized course offerings that meet the needs of highly developed interest and skills on the part of students and of differences in future goals and directions. It is our belief that the closer the relationship among all these elements and the greater the degree of correlation of learning, the better will be the resultant education of the adolescent learner.

D. General Education in the Daily Time Schedule

Scheduling of general education classes can be done in several ways. However, it should always involve a block of time which will enable activities to take place that require more than the usual fifty or fifty-five-minute periods. Perhaps the general education class should not be less than two fifty-minute periods in length. It is desirable, if possible, that all general education sections be scheduled at the same time of the day. However, this is not imperative. Scheduling all general education classes at the same time will provide the following advantages.

1. All special subject teachers are available for resource purposes.

2. There is a common time for school-wide activities, such as assemblies.

3. All sections of any given grade may hold class meetings and other joint activities or functions at that time.

In terms of the proportion of the school day devoted to general education in the junior and senior high school, the following plan is offered for a typical school which may be operating on the basis of six fifty-five-minute periods per day.

	Grade 7	Grade 8	Grade 9	Grade 10	Grade 11	Grade 12
8:30–10:30	Gen. Ed.	Gen. Ed.	Gen. Ed.	Gen. Ed.	Gen. Ed.	Gen. Ed.
10:35–11:30	Gen. Ed.	Gen. Ed.	Elective	Elective	Elective	Elective
11:35–12:30	Gen. Ed.	Science	Elective	Elective	Elective	Elective
Lunch						
1:15–2:10	Math	Math	Elective	Elective	Elective	Elective
2:15–3:10	Phys. Ed.	Phys. Ed.	Elective	Elective	Elective	Elective

Some of the time that is labeled "elective" will, in effect, be required classes for certain individuals, depending upon the requirements for graduation in a given situation and upon the needs of the students with regard to entrance to a particular college or university.

E. Subject Matter in the General Education Class

The school's part in meeting the needs of pupils and society is accomplished best through the solution of the problems that face pupils as they live in and out of school and by projected solutions of common, persistent social problems. In the general education class, projected solutions are made after all available information is brought to bear on the problem, after known sources of information have been thoroughly explored and studied.

With respect to subject matter, science may contribute, or history,

English, language, art, music, or perhaps all of these may have a contribution to make concerning a given problem. Life is not divided into economic, political, historical, and other distinct segments. Rather it consists of attempts to solve the ever-recurring problems arising from the effort to attain a happier and more satisfying existence.

This concept of the place of subject matter is one which denies the value of subject-matter acquisition as an end in itself and insists that subject matter has value only as it contributes to the solution of one's problems. In effect, it places subject matter in the category of a tool to be used as needed, rather than something to be memorized for its own sake or something to which one becomes a slave. This problem approach to the acquisition and use of subject matter is one that enhances meaning and promotes lasting impressions upon participants.

Perhaps a specific example of how subject matter contributes to and is used in a general education class will be helpful. The following is a description of a general education project carried on by a ninth-grade group at the P. K. Yonge Laboratory School, University of Florida, during February and March of 1958. The project is here described by Mrs. Huguette Parrish, as it appeared in the *P. K. Yonge Tidal Wave,* which is the school newspaper.

The most unusual thing about the firing of a rocket by six P. K. Yonge Laboratory School ninth graders is that this project did not originate from a science class, but from a general education class. General education is practiced at P. K. Yonge at the junior high and senior high school levels. It consists, in the ninth through twelfth grades, of a two-hour block of time in which the students elect to work on a particular project or problem for a certain number of weeks. The solution of this problem, or the satisfactory carrying-on of the selected project, includes all sorts of research and studies in the subject-matter areas, English, Social Studies, Mathematics, Sciences, Humanities, etc. The final goal of the students is the solution of the problem stated. The academic areas are treated *as means* to the solution and not *as ends* in themselves. This, in short, is the general education program.

Under the supervision of the ninth-grade general education teacher at the P. K. Yonge Laboratory School, the 9A general education class selected rocketry as a project. The class divided itself into committees. Six students volunteered to serve on a "Firing a Rocket" Committee.

Many persons were asked for advice: One of the science teachers at the P. K. Yonge Laboratory School furnished magazines showing actual plans for rockets, gave many suggestions and ideas, and helped at the launching site. A student at the University of Florida, with a P. K. Yonge student, helped make the fins, loaded the rocket with fuel, and also helped at the launching rack. A professor of the Department of Aeronautical Engineering of the University of Florida gave ideas on fin construction and launching practice. A person from the Electronics Laboratory at the University of Florida machined the parts.

After about a month's work (day work, evening work, night work), all was ready for the launching. Official permissions were obtained. Result: success. . . . Question: Where did the rocket go?

Actually, whether the rocket is found or not does not really matter. The important thing is that this firing was part of a general education class project. Science and mathematics were used extensively *as means* in the construction and launching of the rocket, as well as the ability of youngsters and specialists to work together. But the "after-firing" period includes questions as to the place of rockets in our technological society, ethical questions raised by the building and firing of rockets, its implications in national and international politics, and many others. These questions are at the heart of the general education program.

This is just one example of how subject matter contributes to the general education class.

• **The idea of a general education class in our secondary school program, then, involves a commitment on our part to a problem approach to content and process, to a direct study of those skills, attitudes, understandings, appreciations, and knowledges deemed essential for all adolescents, and to a block of time that makes meaningful study possible. The assumptions underlying a commitment to such a class in our secondary schools are important and inescapable ones, and we will now turn our attention to them in the following chapter.**

2

Bases for the
General Education Class

In examining the need for and the nature of a general
education class in our secondary schools one will find firm bases for
support in four foundational areas whose research findings point the
way to meaningful content and purposeful process in the kind of class
many of us consider desirable: (1) the nature of society and its needs;
(2) the democratic base of our society and its ideals; (3) modern
psychological theory; (4) the nature of adolescence and the adolescent's
role in today's society. An understanding of these bases will be helpful to all those concerned with the development of an effective general education class.

A. Societal Needs and the General Education Class

Not too many years ago, the educational objectives of a given community were reasonably clear because the school served a fairly homogeneous population from the standpoint of occupation and interest.
However, geographic communities no longer coincide with communities of interest. This means that in practically any classroom there will
be children from homes which represent a wide variety of interest
groups. This also means that a wide diversity of viewpoints on religious, economic, social, and political issues will be encountered. It
is highly important that children be afforded an opportunity to come to
grips with these important issues which play a large part in shaping
their lives. It is highly important that children be helped and encouraged in developing a method by which they may, with some degree
of objectivity, examine these issues.

The American way of life demands a dynamic, changing society. Any democracy, if it is to remain a democracy, must expect, anticipate, and welcome orderly change—political, social, and economic. History has shown that if such change is not possible through the processes of open discussion and free ballot, it will then come by violent revolution. Democracy, therefore, must recognize that controversy regarding proposed or developing change will arise, and it must provide the skills and machinery for the people to think intelligently on these issues and to express their collective judgment.

In our democracy, the school is looked upon as the chief agency for the development of a skilled, well-informed citizenry and for the reconstruction of values. A well-ordered school, where partisanship and bias are at a minimum, offers an individual the best possible introduction to controversial issues. Here scientific and democratic techniques of attack on social, political, and economic problems can be both taught and practiced. Basic to the American way of life is the use of discussion, arbitration, and appeal to reason, rather than the use of force, to settle controversies. It is an obligation of the school, therefore, to provide specifically and carefully for the realistic induction of our future citizens into the methods of arriving at rational decisions on the tough problems which must be determined by popular will or consent. No other agency of society even approaches the school in capability, opportunity, or responsibility for performing this function, which does not exist in a totalitarian social order.

A dynamic school will, by its very nature, bring students face to face with some issues which are yet unresolved. The teachers of such a school will help students to make use of the great reservoir of established values, accepted principles, and proved facts in considering unsolved problems. Students will be led to see that much of our great body of accepted values is based upon the solved problems of the past. They can proceed with the assurance that most problems of today will have commonly accepted answers in the future. They will recognize that the consideration of controversial issues is essential to continuing orderly change.

Of the various issues which involve conflict with affiliations or loyalties, there is only one type of study which is clearly beyond the legal mandate of the public school. The teaching of sectarian religious beliefs is not a function of the public school. This qualification, however, does not mean that important social issues are to become taboo in the schools whenever any religious group takes a stand concerning them. The determination of whether a given issue is properly classified as involving "sectarian religious beliefs" must rest with the school.

The curriculum may be defined as consisting of the organized pattern of activities provided by the school to achieve the aims of education. Since one of the responsibilities of the school is to prepare students for participation in civic affairs, any *desirable* means to that end may properly be employed. It is important that schools cultivate in students the skills and attitudes needed to deal with controversial problems which constantly arise in any democratic society.

In many schools today, no provision is made for the consideration of society's unsolved problems. The schools tend to place the emphasis in the curriculum on the learning of facts, accepted principles, and the issues which already have largely been settled. Such a curriculum needs reappraisal in terms of its contribution to citizenship education. To be effective, the curriculum should help to meet the personal and social needs of the students. It should stress training for citizenship. The accomplishment of these ends requires the study of some of the controversies inherent in our gradually changing social order. The general education class affords an excellent opportunity for citizenship education because children from all interest groups are involved, and because there are no strict subject-matter boundaries to constrict investigation.

Unsolved issues may be said to have a high priority in the curriculum because they provide motivation, are in keeping with sound learning theory, and give vitality to the curriculum. A good curriculum, however, makes use of a proper balance of "heritage" and of "contemporary" content. It must be recognized that when any contemporary problem is discussed, the element of controversy is almost sure to enter.

And for that reason consideration of controversial questions calls for the establishment of a suitable classroom climate. The teacher must first look to his own part in creating the atmosphere necessary for a proper approach to possibly disturbing discussions. At the same time, the wise teacher will consider outside factors which may affect the objective approach so desirable when controversial problems are being examined.

A detailed account of the ideas that influence any classroom would require extended observation and analysis. There are, however, several assumptions which can reasonably be made for any classroom in the United States:

1. It is almost certain that pupils will bring with them into the classroom a number of strong convictions which will largely determine their views on current issues.

2. It is likely that for the most part these convictions will have been picked up uncritically, often in the home or in their neighborhood.

3. It is highly probable that in most cases pupils will not have en-

countered or considered much evidence bearing upon the soundness of the views they have come to accept.

4. Except in homogeneous communities, we may expect that students will differ widely with respect to the particular convictions they have happened to pick up.

Some teachers wrongly see in this set of conditions a challenge to find out what views the children hold and then to "correct" those which seem unwarranted. They overlook the fact that any view which has never been examined by its holder is unwarranted in the sense that it rests upon no evidence. The attempt by the teacher to give students the "right" view on controversial questions, if successful, generally represents no more than the replacing of one set of unexamined opinions by another.

The teacher who is quite properly disturbed because his pupils have accepted blindly the views of their parents or associates can scarcely make a case for asking them, instead, to accept his views. Such an approach leads to a competition for the uncritical loyalty of the child, a competition which the community cannot reasonably be expected to pay for, sponsor, or even tolerate.

That students need to ground their views on evidence is hardly a matter for debate. Nor is there any use in refusing to recognize that carrying this process forward will result in the student's modifying or abandoning some part of what he has picked up. The teacher ought therefore to keep steadily in mind the difficulties encountered in an attempt to deal thoughtfully with controversial questions in the classroom:

1. Parents do not ordinarily send their children to school in the expectation that their basic ideas will be modified. The school must, at the very least, keep the parents informed and steadily reassure them as to what is going on.

2. Every community includes a number of groups, often quite powerful, which do not want certain topics to be opened up to scrutiny.

3. Parents who encounter a marked change in the views of their children are likely to suspect that the school or the teacher has deliberately sought that particular change, and that the new view is a result of deliberate indoctrination or propaganda.

Because of these inherent difficulties, the teacher should have a clear understanding of what he is about so that he can deal with the objections or protests of parents and pressure groups as opportunities for making clear exactly what he is trying to do, rather than as attacks to be fought off or met by appeasement. The teacher should be able to point out that:

1. He is not seeking to "teach" a point of view on any controversial issue; rather, he is creating a situation within which the pupil can clarify, refine, and extend the range of his own understanding.

2. He is trying to establish an atmosphere of inquiry. This means that he must deliberately cause the student to question or wonder about the adequacy of the opinions he has picked up, for doubt is an indispensable condition of inquiry. Even the teacher's opinions, whose soundness he may be able to prove, should be challenged to provide the stimulus for seeking out additional evidence either to remove the uncertainty or render the opinions untenable.

3. He is trying to maintain a permissive atmosphere, within which students may talk freely without fear of ridicule or reprisal. The student must feel confident that any relevant hypothesis he cares to advance will be entertained seriously, that any relevant information from his experience or reading will be welcomed, and that neither his grades nor the esteem in which he is held by teacher and classmates will be injured by any opinion he may express. Obviously, no teacher can guarantee to maintain this last condition; but a steady effort to do so will provide a great measure of reassurance.

B. Democratic Ideals and the General Education Class

Democracy is a way of living together which embodies various concepts, values, and beliefs by different people. One of the strong points of democracy is its flexibility and all-inclusiveness. As an ideology, democracy is perhaps the most revolutionary and far reaching of all. Yes, even religion places certain restrictions upon what a person may believe, whereas democracy, in its fullest sense, provides for no restrictions upon the individual so long as his activities do not infringe upon the freedom and rights of others.

Due to the nature of the personal and social problems dealt with in the general education class, an excellent opportunity for an excursion into the realm of democratic living is made available. Since the general education class is freed from conventional subject-matter boundaries and restrictions, teachers and pupils feel free to explore into areas of living which have not previously been examined in the schools. These are the areas that have been "closed" because of value conflicts or emotional associations—the areas which contribute so heavily to the shaping of personality and character, the areas which have been left largely in the hands of chance in our modern civilization, the areas of understanding upon which we pattern our way of life. We refer to our relationships to other human beings which are largely determined by our values, beliefs, and attitudes. What, then, are some of the democratic ideals and how can the general education class contribute to their realization through its unique organization and orientation?

In a democracy, education functions for the welfare of *all* the people. In the general education class, the community becomes a very integral part of the school activities through the utilization of community resources, community opinion, and thorough study of community problems. The method of problem solving used in the general education class emphasizes the importance of putting conclusion, reached through reflective study, to actual test, thereby making available to *all* citizens the fruits of conclusions reached after thorough investigation. In this way the school can contribute to making the community a better place in which to live by developing young people who are ready to examine their community problems in the light of what seems best for all concerned.

In a democracy, education attempts to provide equal educational opportunity for all, regardless of intelligence, vocational plans, social status, economic status, race, or religion. In the general education class heterogenous grouping which attempts to approximate life situations is used. The rich and the poor, the genius and the slow learner, the banker's son and the ditch digger's son, the attractive and the unattractive, the leader and the follower all have an opportunity to contribute what they can to the solution of persistent human problems, and thereby secure a feeling of worth and belonging which is so important to a sense of well-being.

In life it is necessary to enter into relationships with people from all walks of life in problem-solving situations, and the general education class attempts to give young people experiences which will help them make these relationships the most effective possible.

In a democracy, education attempts to clarify the meanings of basic civil liberties through study and to respect them in practice. In the general education class, the Bill of Rights would be entirely acceptable as an area for investigation and study, and through positive leadership on the part of the teacher may result in the formulation of a "Bill of Responsibilities." Children may be encouraged to express the things which they feel to be their rights and helped to see that these can be preserved only through assuming the responsibility to see that others are also entitled to these rights. For example, most children will say that they have a right to be heard and to express their opinion. However, upon examination it is very obvious that this right cannot be preserved unless someone assumes the responsibility of listening.

In a democracy, education attempts to examine and help youth determine those political, social, and economic concepts and conditions which are needed for the propagation and continuation of freedom. (For purposes of this discussion, freedom is defined as the power of "effective choice" and "effective choice" is defined as a choice that will lead to further freedoms for the individual making the choice, as well as for others.) These have been the "closed" areas in the schools, the controversial areas which people have been unable or unwilling to examine reflectively or scientifically. The general education class makes a deliberate attempt to bring problems in these areas up for deliberation in the light of the evidence that might exist concerning a given problem. Prejudices, misconceptions, and myths have been passed on from generation to generation largely because people have refused to examine values and attitudes in these controversial areas.

In a democracy, education employs democratic methods in the classroom, in student activities, and in administration. In the general education class, teacher-pupil planning is carried on constantly. The general education class portrays democratic procedure from the establishment of goals and objectives all the way through the process of reflective and scientific problem solving to a co-operative evaluation of what has been accomplished. The teacher is a member of the group, an influential member by virtue of his training and experience which help him provide effective leadership at times and to encourage the effective utilization of leadership which may exist within any group. The general education class insists that pupils participate in decision making in areas that directly affect them, and further insists that they assume responsibility for the consequences, good or bad, that follow the making of decisions. This is the democratic method in action—the method which trains youth who will not readily be indoctrinated by an idea or ideal that cannot stand the test of reflective investigation, youth who can preserve the democratic way of life.

The intent of this discussion is not to imply that democratic methods cannot be used in classes other than general education; however, general education classes more readily lend themselves to such methods because they can operate in a much broader framework than classes which are further limited by specific subject-matter content.

C. Modern Psychology and the General Education Class

Learning is a continuous process of selecting and interacting with experiences that tend to satisfy the learner's motives. It might further be said that the learning process involves the selection and/or rejection of information and activities in so far as they have personal meaning for the learner. Therefore, the learner learns what is taught to the extent that the teachings have personal meaning for him. For example, driver training would result in different degrees and types of learning for a student who has immediate access to an automobile and a student who has no possibility of getting an automobile in the foreseeable future.

Here is another example concerning the personal meaning of information:

1. You are listening to a news broadcast on the radio and hear that a tornado has hit some distant city causing extensive property damage. This information is not likely to have much influence on your behavior and action; in fact, it may not even register with you if you are thinking of something else.

2. You hear on the radio that a tornado has struck some distant city causing extensive property damage and loss of life. Since you are a human being and human life has become involved, this information becomes more personalized and you are likely to discuss it with your friends and family. You may even suggest what a terrible thing this is and feel sorry for the survivors of the dead.

3. You hear in a special radio bulletin that a tornado has struck your neighboring town causing considerable damage and loss of life, and further, that it seems headed in your direction. At this point the information becomes highly personalized and you spring into action, making plans how you can best protect your family and loved ones.

The kind of learning we in the public schools are seeking is what we might call "effective" learning, or learning that results in changed behavior on the part of the learner. We are aware that behavioral changes may be in an undesirable direction as well as in a desirable one, and this means that the teacher needs to know in what direction a student's learnings are taking him. It also means that teaching must be personalized to the highest degree attainable within the realistic restriction under which we operate, such as teacher load, class size, heterogeneity of groups, and limited finances.

How then does the general education class fit in with this modern philosophy or psychology of learning, which is one of the end products we are seeking? One of the contributions of the general education class is a block of time longer than the fifty-five minutes normally allotted to a class period in the usual subject areas. This means that the teacher has more opportunity to recognize and understand the student's interests, drives, needs, and limitations. The teacher sees the student in a more varied scope of activities and situations and is thereby in a better position to personalize the educative process as well as provide for individual and group counseling and guidance. The block of time also reduces by at least one the number of different groups that a given teacher will need to know well and be closely associated with, and here again is a provision for a more thorough study and understanding of the group.

Another condition for effective learning seems to be the absence of fear. Modern psychology tells us that fear or threat causes a person's vision to narrow, and therefore he is not able to see all of the alternatives in a given situation or problem. It is further said that if this fear or threat becomes severe enough a person may develop "tunnel vision," which may cause him to consider only one course of action. Fear and threat may also cause a person to withdraw into his psychological shell and concentrate only upon his own defense. Information does not have effective meaning if a person is concerned only with his own defense.

We know that people are more likely to consider as a threat or as an object of fear things that are unknown or strange to them. In other words, they fear things with which they are unfamiliar.

In the general education class, information is used in such a way that it relates to the experiences of young people. This gives it personal meaning for the student and in turn fosters effective learning which leads to a lessening of the fear and threat that the classroom may hold for the student. A reduction in fear and threat then leads to a more open and comprehensive investigation of a problem, which allows the student to examine his values and beliefs in light of the available evidence. This appears to be a circle with one step strengthening the other until people become able to make value judgments with which they can live.

Another principle deserving consideration is that the discovery of meaning, which leads to effective learning, is to a high degree a social process. This social process, which involves open discussions where everyone is heard, does not occur in a highly structured situation nor in a situation where the teacher stands before the class and lectures most of the time. There must be interaction between students and teacher and among students themselves. Teacher-pupil planning and organization, as well as open discussions in the general education class, afford an excellent opportunity for this social process to take place.

D. The Nature of Adolescence

The adolescent in this country suddenly finds himself in a position where he is no longer considered a child and is, at the same time, refused adult status. He finds himself in a society which largely maintains a double standard of values—one standard to which it pays lip service and another which seems to direct the actions of its people. For example, a parent will say smoking is harmful yet continue to smoke two packs of cigarettes a day, or he will say that alcohol is an evil yet continue to have his cocktail before dinner. At this critical time of rapid mental and physical development the adolescent finds that he is an "in between."

He finds himself in a society that seems to go from one crisis to another. Will he have to go to war? Will he be able to afford college? Will his parents, teachers, and friends ever understand him? Will he be accepted by his peers? What's all this about sex? Am I normal? How about all these pimples on my face? These and many other personal and social questions dominate the day-to-day life of the adolescent at a time when he desperately needs acceptance and understanding but gets less than he has ever had.

He finds himself in a society where "all men are created equal," but he is sure that some are more nearly equal than others. He finds that whether or not he is accepted by others is determined in part by what his parents do and are, and their position in the socioeconomic structure. He finds that his values do not agree with others' and he wonders who is right. The needs of adolescents, aside from food, clothing, and shelter, are based upon the nature of our society and more specifically upon the foregoing questions they may wonder about. Where in the school program are questions of this nature explored? Where in the normal existence of the adolescent are these questions even discussed with any degree of objectivity? Where and when are young people helped to make decisions in social problem areas on the basis of available information rather than on an uninformed emotional basis?

Living in a highly mobile society such as ours requires that people, young and old, be more self-directive than ever before. Two decades ago communities were more accurately defined in a geographical sense and most of the activities and recreation of the young were carried on within their own community. With this type of community organization most people in a given neighborhood knew each other. For example, everyone knew Tom Brown's son Joe, and for that reason, pressures controlled Joe's behavior to a great extent because the community expected certain things of him. Very little self-direction was needed for Joe to behave himself because if he did not, it would be known all over the community.

In this mid-twentieth century, conditions are quite different. Joe needs only to hop on his motorcycle, get into his automobile or the family car and, within a matter of minutes, he can be where no one knows him. With this lessening of social pressures it becomes necessary for Joe to be in a position of behaving in certain ways because it is right or wrong, not because he is being observed by someone who knows him. This rapidly moving society desperately needs people who can assume the full responsibility for their actions.

• A closer examination of these four areas—the nature of adolescence, of learning, of society, and of our democratic commitment—would reveal even more reasons to support the idea of a general education class than we have cited. As we look more closely at the nature and functioning of general education classes in the secondary school, we shall see how teachers and others are attempting to build sound programs and procedures on the basis of these recognized guides to effective education.

3

Some Points of View

and Some Programs

Acceptance of the four fundamental bases for a sound general education class that were described in the preceding chapter is but a prerequisite to a more searching analysis and examination. For within the broad framework provided by these assumptions there is opportunity for various points of view regarding the particular emphasis a general education program should take and the way in which the content should be organized. This chapter presents the views of various curriculum leaders on these problems.

A. Varying Points of View

In some instances the point of view of a general education program is expressed in terms of purposes to be achieved in a general education class; in others attention is focused on the identification of broad problem areas that should constitute the content of general education. There are, of course, many similarities among the various positions; on the other hand, some highly individualistic emphases are suggested by some authorities.

An important stand on purposes has been taken by the Educational Policies Commission, which advocates a common learnings course that would provide most of the experiences "all young people should have in common in order to live happily and usefully during the years of youth and grow into the full responsibilities of adult life." [1] According to the

[1] Educational Policies Commission, *Education for All American Youth—A Further Look* (Washington, D.C.: National Education Association, 1952), p. 237.

Commission there would be six distinctive aims for this "common learnings" course: [2]

1. To help all youth grow in knowledge of their community, their nation, and the world of nations; in understanding of the rights and duties of citizens of the American democracy; and in diligent and competent performance of their obligations as members of the community and as citizens of the state and nation.
2. To help all youth grow in knowledge of the operations of the economic system and in understanding of the human relations and problems in economic activities, particularly of the relations between management and employees.
3. To help all youth grow in understanding of personal relations within the family, of the conditions which make for successful family life, and of the importance of the family in society.
4. To help all youth grow in ability to purchase and use goods and services intelligently, with accurate knowledge of values received by the consumer and with understanding of the economic consequences of one's acts.
5. To help all youth grow in appreciation and enjoyment of beauty in literature, art, music, and nature.
6. To help all youth grow in ability to listen and read with understanding and to communicate their thoughts with precision and clarity.

In a similar vein a "personal-social problems core" has been advocated by Caswell, a core that would consist of "a continuous, carefully planned series of experiences which are based on significant personal and social problems and which involve learnings of common concern to all youth." [3]

Caswell cites the following as important features of such a class: [4]

1. The student should receive understanding and helpful counsel on his personal and educational problems.
2. The student should be afforded opportunities which will aid him to meet the common demands of civic participation.
3. The student should be afforded opportunities which will aid him to maintain sound health, both physical and mental.
4. All youth are members of families and a large majority will establish homes. . . . Help in the basic areas of family life . . . should be seized upon as an important area of emphasis in the core program.

[2] *Ibid.*, p. 238.
[3] H. L. Caswell and Others, *The American High School* (New York: Harper & Brothers, 1946), p. 143.
[4] *Ibid.*, pp. 143–150.

5. There are certain common skills of communication and computation which are of general significance.

Various curriculum makers [5] have attempted to identify in more detail certain centers of experience that would serve as the basis for problem areas in the general education class. Van Til [6] calls attention to fifteen such areas:

1. Choosing, Buying, and Using Goods and Services
2. Keeping Healthy
3. Home, School, and Friends
4. Ways of Living of Other Lands
5. Recreation and Leisure
6. Getting an Education
7. Racial, Religious, Ethnic, and Social-Economic Relationships
8. Personal Development and Psychological Understanding
9. Proposed Roads for the Domestic Economy
10. War
11. Organization of the Peace
12. Propaganda and Public Opinion
13. Labor, Management, and Government
14. Vocations and Jobs
15. World Views

An interesting focus for a general education class is suggested by Smith, Stanley, and Shores,[7] who see it centered in social values:

> The universal elements of a culture give the society its stability and unity. . . . The values that make up the stable and vital aspects of the universals constitute the heart of the core curriculum. In short, the core of the curriculum consists in large part of the socio-moral rules comprising the core of the culture. In the society of the United States, these rules are chiefly those that constitute the democratic value-system. The core curriculum, therefore, places considerable emphasis upon the deliberate study of the moral content of the culture—especially as this content bears upon the resolution of the social issues that divide the people and thereby prevent effective social action.

[5] For a detailed description of a study resulting in the identification of problem areas, see Lucile L. Lurry and Elsie J. Alberty, *Developing a High School Core Program* (New York: The Macmillan Company, 1957), pp. 58–89.

[6] William Van Til, *A Social Living Curriculum for Post-War Secondary Education.* Unpublished doctoral dissertation (Columbus: Ohio State University, 1946), p. 217.

[7] B. O. Smith, W. O. Stanley, and J. H. Shores, *Fundamentals of Curriculum Development* (Yonkers: World Book Company, 1950), pp. 468–469, 471–472.

The structure of the core curriculum is fixed by broad social problems or by themes of social living. . . . The core curriculum in its pure form is a refinement and simplification of the basic elements of those aspects of the culture that all members of the society share. These elements consist of formative rules, methods of thinking, points of view, and so on.

We could not leave a discussion of diverse rationales for general education content without calling attention to the work of Stratemeyer and her associates.[8] They conceive of the curriculum as focusing on persistent life situations which provide a continuing thread throughout the school experience. They have analyzed these situations into three general categories:

I. Situations Calling for Growth in Individual Capacities
   A. Health
   B. Intellectual power
   C. Responsibility for moral choices
   D. Aesthetic expression and appreciation

II. Situations Calling for Growth in Social Participation
   A. Person-to-person relationships
   B. Group membership
   C. Intergroup relationships

III. Situations Calling for Growth in Ability to Deal with Environmental Factors and Forces
   A. Natural phenomena
   B. Technological resources
   C. Economic-social-political structures and forces

This approach has relevance for all those interested in the development of a general education class, since these are life situations faced by all people and they have a certain continuity to them. As such they could serve as fruitful sources of general education content.

While each of the above points of view has its own distinct focus, there are obvious areas of similarity. The particular emphasis that any program takes will depend upon several factors existing in a particular school situation—factors relating to the community setting and to the nature of the student body. At the same time, relative emphasis will depend upon larger forces existing on the national and international scene at any particular time.

However, regardless of what focus one general education class will have, it is important to keep in mind that certain characteristics

[8] F. B. Stratemeyer, H. L. Forkner, M. G. Mckim, and A. H. Passow, *Developing a Curriculum for Modern Living* (2nd ed., rev.; New York: Bureau of Publications, Teachers College, Columbia University, 1957), pp. 149–150.

must be evident if our fundamental bases are to be effectively implemented.

1. There must be a problems approach to content and process.
2. Content must have meaning for *all* youth in today's societal setting.
3. An important goal is the development of self-direction and self-discipline in the learner.
4. The learner must be deeply involved in the total learning process—planning, organizing, carrying out, and evaluating his learning experiences.
5. Provision must be made for individual differences to be respected, utilized, and developed in constructive ways.

B. Examples of General Education Programs

Thus far we have been speaking in broad conceptual terms about the nature of the general education class and the need for it in our secondary school program. In order to give greater clarity and specificity to this idea of a general education class let us now look at four specific programs as they have developed in four different school situations. After each description there will be a brief example of a unit, illustrating content and ways of learning.

1. P. K. YONGE SCHOOL, UNIVERSITY OF FLORIDA

The P. K. Yonge School is a campus school at the University of Florida in Gainesville. Because of its laboratory nature it has an opportunity to experiment with the implementation of ideas and to discover their effectiveness in actual practice. Because the school is responsible for the education of youngsters from a particular community in the county, in addition to those students it accepts through application, it has an excellent opportunity to work with a diversified student body. This student body has widely differing socioeconomic backgrounds, a wide range of native ability, and varying goals for the future. In this respect the school approximates closely the situation to be found in our public schools. As a result the kinds of programs and procedures that the school finds effective have practical application in other settings.

The P. K. Yonge Laboratory School has a general education program throughout the school, grades kindergarten through twelve. In grades kindergarten through six, the general education program occupies the entire school day. However, it is the secondary school, grades seven through twelve, with which this report is concerned.

The P. K. Yonge School chooses to call the general education program "core." Aside from state requirements for graduation, the school requires that every student take the general education part of the program each year. The stated objectives of the general education classes are:

1. To assist in the maximum development of each individual through:
    a. providing experiences in democratic living
    b. providing effective personal, social, vocational, and educational guidance
    c. providing training and experiences in an acceptable method of problem solving (critical thinking)
    d. developing effective communication (written and oral)
    e. developing effective methods of group process
    f. developing functional understanding of our number system
    g. developing a sense of personal responsibility
    h. developing a social sensitivity toward the rights and needs of others
    i. developing an understanding of and appreciation for our cultural heritage and the democratic way of life
    j. developing an understanding of and appreciation for other cultures of the world, and
    k. stimulating and encouraging creativity.
2. To enhance teaching through:
    a. teacher-pupil planning
    b. close personal relationships with students, and
    c. a healthy respect for the worth and dignity of the individual.

The length of the school day at the P. K. Yonge School is six hours. In the seventh grade four of the six hours are devoted to general education. In the eighth grade three of the six hours are devoted to general education and in grades nine through twelve two of the six hours in the school day are devoted to general education.

The seventh-grade general education class consists of those common learnings that would more usually be found in English, social studies, and science classes, along with guidance responsibilities and exploratory activities. The remaining two hours are spent with specialists in math and physical education. In the eighth grade the focus is the same except that science joins math and physical education as special areas in the curriculum, rather than as part of the general education class. In grades nine through twelve the focus is on those learnings more usually associated with English, social studies, and guidance; the rest of the student's schedule consists of electives in the various subject areas.

In grades nine through twelve the general education class operates in a framework which designates broad areas for each grade level. For example, the ninth-grade general education class is responsible for local, state, and regional social studies; the tenth-grade general education class is responsible for national social studies and government; the eleventh-grade general education class is responsible for world social studies, including studies of how various countries operate and govern themselves; and the twelfth grade is where a study is made of how the individual relates to the various aspects of culture and government.

Here is a description by an eighth-grade teacher of the ways in which the class arrived at understandings of our American heritage through literature.

UNDERSTANDING OUR WESTWARD GROWTH THROUGH LITERATURE
Eighth Grade Unit

Wishing to make a different approach to the history and geography of the Middle West in the period following the Revolution, we decided that "the literature of a people is the reflection of how they live, feel and think."

We selected two novels, *The Adventures of Tom Sawyer* and *The Adventures of Huckleberry Finn,* to read, around which we might build our unit of study.

In order to understand the setting we:

1. Drew maps of the Mississippi River showing chief tributaries, major cities, and bordering states.
2. Drew maps showing the land area drained by the river.
3. Read and made written reports on the importance of the river.
4. Made written reports on river traffic in the Steamboat Era and compared this to traffic in the modern period.
5. Discussed early life in the river towns and changes to 1865.
6. Studied the history of the discovery, exploration, and mapping of the river.
7. Read accounts of the Civil War actions on the river.
8. Discussed the importance of New Orleans and St. Louis as major river cities.
9. Made drawings of river craft—flatboats, steamboats, rafts, barges and tugs.
10. Made copies of songs about the river:
    a. "Ole Man River"
    b. "Levee Song"
11. Studied the construction of levees and their importance.
12. Made illustrations and studied the formations of deltas.
    a. special emphasis on "Birdfoot" or Mississippi Delta.
13. Located and read "tall tales" and folk stories originating on the river.
14. Read poems, sang folksongs, and other materials about the river.

15. Located other rivers of the world, comparable to the Mississippi in size and (or) economic importance to the nation in which they are located.

We read a biography of Samuel Langhorne Clemens and summarized it in our own words. We also

1. Studied the meaning and found examples of
   a. pseudonym
   b. nom de plume
   c. pen names
2. Tried to determine why authors sometimes write under an assumed name.
3. Made a special study of "Mark Twain" to determine its meaning and reasons Clemens chose and used it as a pseudonym.
4. Read short stories by the same author.
5. Tried to determine why the two books we read were written.
6. Compared experiences from the author's life with incidents in our reading to discover some autobiographical content.

We read the books chosen in class. For experience and interest we

1. Dramatized sections of both books.
2. Listed the characters as they appeared in the story.
3. Listed words to be used in spelling lessons and vocabulary exercises.
4. Listed superstitions we discovered during our reading.
5. Made drawings and illustrations on incidents and things mentioned in the stories.
6. Discussed the meanings of literary terms suggested by the story:
   a. setting
   b. folklore
   c. point of view
   d. humor and types of humor
   e. comedy
   f. tragedy
   g. literature
7. Noted philosophical statements which reflected the attitudes of the author and people of the period in history.
8. Studied descriptive writing as found in the books.
9. Wrote character sketches of principal characters.
10. Discussed history as it was presented in the stories.
11. Wrote a synopsis of each book.

We kept a record of our study in notebooks which contained accounts of the above activities and other materials which were accumulated on an individual basis. We

1. Studied the parts of a book.
2. Used the dictionary.
3. Used the encyclopedia.
4. Used the library.
5. Wrote letters to chambers of commerce for information and materials.
6. Saw films on the subject.
7. Made a bibliography.

We had experiences in working together:

1. a. as a class
   b. in small groups
   c. as individuals
2. a. in research
   b. reporting
   c. organizing for work
   d. evaluating

2. EVANSTON TOWNSHIP HIGH SCHOOL

The Evanston Township High School has been widely known for many years. It was an early pioneer in the development of the general education concept; and the New School at Evanston became well known through its description in New Schools for a New Culture.[9] The most helpful brief description of its program is found in a leaflet published by the school itself.[10] We quote from it.

Core Studies Is the Name of a Course. It has been offered by the Evanston High School since 1937. The name "Core" comes from the objectives of the course which is to give each pupil who elects it a *core* of

1. basic subject matter fundamentals that should be a part of the education of every American child;
2. experiences in democratic living that will develop the skills and attitudes appropriate for citizenship in our American democracy.

Core Studies Is a Personal Approach to Education. Whatever the subject matter considered, emphasis is placed on the development of each pupil in terms of his own needs, abilities, and aspirations. The Core method emphasizes maturity in behavior and the growth of self-discipline. It develops those personal, social, and academic skills that will contribute to further education and successful living with others. As counselor, the Core teacher is always available for help and guidance.

[9] C. M. McConnell, E. O. Melby, C. O. Arndt, and L. Bishop, *New Schools for a New Culture* (rev. ed.; New York: Harper & Brothers, 1953).
[10] Evanston Township High School, *Core Studies* (Evanston, Ill., n.d.).

Core Is a Daily Two-Period Class. It receives the two credits of English and Social Studies and replaces these subjects in the program of the pupils who elect it. The remaining six periods of the pupil's school day are spent in the regular science, mathematics, language, and physical education classes of the high school.

Core Is Reading, Writing, Speaking, and Listening. It is subject matter as well as varied activities. Core involves theme assignments, book reports, class discussions, functional grammar, and examinations. Pupils in Core learn to give individual and group reports, to participate in panels and group discussions, and to use various techniques of presenting materials, such as the tape recorder, board drawings, and the opaque projector. They learn to work on committees, to plan and organize subject matter units and social activities, and to do research and present their findings in oral or documented form.

Core Is a Program of General Education. It is English and Social Studies plus phases of art, music, science, and other subject areas when they contribute to a better understanding of the topic being studied. Special periods are organized and committees established to encourage appreciation and participation in these fields.

Core Offers to Its Pupils a Well-Rounded Program. For instance, in the course of a week a pupil in Core will have

1. reporting and discussions on the chosen unit;
2. time devoted to reading, writing, and English skills;
3. individual reports or panel discussions on current news;
4. some experience with literature and the fine arts; and
5. a Core business meeting, perhaps a speaker or field trip.

The Subject Matter of Core Is Very Similar to the English and Social Studies Courses It Replaces. However, there is a difference in the manner of planning and presenting the materials of study and in the objectives sought. For illustration, in four years of Core a pupil would have a sequence similar to the following:

Freshman—Orientation
Our High School and Community
Choosing a Career
New Horizons in Literature
The U.S. and World Affairs

Sophomore—World Mindedness
Drama through the Ages
War and Peace
The Atomic Age
The Development of Law and
 Justice

Junior—U.S. Life and Culture
America in Literature
Our Economic System
The American People
Our Government; its structure and
 development

Senior—Life Adjustment
Marriage and Family Living
Our Literary Heritage
College and Careers
Consumer Education

Core Is a Program of Life Adjustment. In Core, consideration is given to the real-life situations which pupils now face and which will continue to confront them, such as problems of personality adjustment, group relations, and the personal factors in success and progress. Since the Core teacher is the counselor to the pupils in his Core, counseling is an integral part of the program. The use of the *Personalized Evaluation* helps each pupil to understand himself and others. Known and latent interests are developed in the process of the pupil-teacher planning. Pupil committees such as the Planning or News Committees help determine the nature and type of units to be studied.

Core Is a Program of Citizenship Education. In Core, the pupils not only study our democratic tradition, they also participate in it. To this end each Core is organized upon democratic principles with officers, committees, and organization to enable it to function effectively. Each pupil, therefore, has many opportunities to be a member of a working committee, to assume leadership roles, to develop initiative and responsibility, and, together with the help of the teacher, to plan, organize, and present the materials they select for study. This co-operative planning combined with the problem-solving technique of the "scientific method" helps pupils develop poise and self-reliance. Each Core class has representation in the homeroom student council.

The Core Program at ETHS Includes a Homeroom as Well as a Classroom Program. All pupils taking Core share in common social and educational experiences. Each Core class has a Core mother who helps co-ordinate each class with the total program. Core meetings are held to help teachers and parents understand and improve the program. A *Parent Planning Committee*, a *Newsletter*, and a *PTA Board* help maintain balance and continuity. By working together for the four years of high school, pupils, parents, and teachers know each other very well and co-operate effectively for personal, college, and career planning.

The Core Approach Is Not New. It has been in operation at ETHS since 1937 and much longer elsewhere. The ETHS Core Program is well known throughout the United States.

Parents Say. . . . The Core Program encourages independent thinking, develops leadership qualities, teaches individual responsibility and initiative, and through the double period, fosters favorable teacher and pupil relationships.

Insight into the functioning of the general education class at Evanston can be gained from the following description of a specific unit, provided by the teacher of a ninth-grade class:

CANDIDATES AND CAMPAIGNS

The pressure was on—a national election was in the offing and the air waves and the press were saturated with highly charged political comment. So many questions were being raised, so many new words and historical incidents were being discussed—the whole subject was not only interesting but vital to pupils and voters-to-be.

Having completed its orientation unit, one freshman core was ready to select a topic for study. After considerable discussion it was agreed that "Campaigns and Candidates" met all the requirements of the criteria that had been developed by the class. The core had already studied the "problem-solving" technique as a possible procedure for many types of situations. The new unit presented the problem, we had studied the technique —now to put them together.

After more discussion and preliminary research, the following working outline and assignment of reports was made. It was recognized that in the work leading up to the selection of the topic and the development of the outline that some elements of steps 1 and 2 in the problem-solving technique had been covered. However, a great deal of data still had to be collected by individuals now that some overview of the purpose and scope of the unit had been achieved.

REPORT OUTLINE

I. Political Parties
    A. Historical Beginning: Republican, Democratic, and   { Bill C.
        Third Parties   Dave S.
    B. Founders: First and Great Leaders   Bill S.
    C. Present Status and Strength: Traditions, etc.   { Jay
        Chuck
    D. Party Platforms: Background to Stand   { Phil
        Sandy
    E. Present Organization: State, Local, National Com-   { Helen
        mittees, etc.   Dave C.
II. Election System
    A. Electoral College   { Gerry
        DeWitt
    B. Primary and Voting qualifications, etc.   { Boyce
        Tom B.
    C. Conventions, "Political Machines," etc. and Actual   { Ronnie
        Voting   Carlton
III. Candidates (President and Vice-President)
    A. Qualifications—Constitutional Provisions   { Roland
    B. Record, Previous Experience   Bill M.
    C. Personal Life   Andrea
    D. Campaign Routes—Procedures   Carolee
    E. View of Candidates on Platforms, Other Issues   Ken
    F. Supporters   { Lucille
        Box S.

IV. Current Situation
   A. Radio, Press, and TV   Ginny
   B. Public Opinion: Polls, etc.   Caroline
   C. Developments—State & Local Elections   Andy

This outline was more than a report outline—it was also the basis
for assignments in the Scholastic publication "America Votes" and in
Rienow, *Calling All Citizens*. Each pupil had copies of these books. Many
pamphlets and current magazines were also available.

The following time schedule and chart was drawn up to show relationships between the planned reporting, the developmental steps of the
problem-solving technique and the individual responsibilities of the pupils.

UNIT PROCEDURE FOR "CAMPAIGNS AND CANDIDATES"

Approximate Time Table	Problem-Solving Steps	Steps Applied to Unit
Sept. 22– Sept. 26	1. Statement and analysis of problem—think through purpose and subject matter involved.	Read and study information on all phases of the topic. Pupil-teacher planning to determine purpose, scope, and content of the unit.
Sept. 29– Oct. 10	2. Collect data on unit, general reading for perspective and background. Use many sources.	Develop bibliography on unit—books, pamphlets, magazines, local sources, etc. Take notes on area of report. Class instruction in use of library, how to find information, evaluation of data.
	3. Develop hypothesis —course of action, specific plan.	Prepare data for interesting and informative report to class. Class instruction in organization of materials and practice in techniques of presentation. Committee meetings to plan group reports; work on committee techniques.
Oct. 13– Nov. 5	4. Act on hypothesis—plan.	Present data to class; this to be followed by discussion. Names on unit outline give person in charge of reports.
Nov. 5– Nov. 7	5. Evaluate course of action.	Evaluation of all phases of report—presentation, discussion, test, etc. Develop standards for improving quality of next project undertaken.

Further analysis of the pupils' responsibilities resulted in another
check list. Its major purpose was to relate the unit work to the rest of
the core activities. (Actually, about half of the class time was devoted
to this unit as such. Time was also spent on literature, on how to do research, techniques of oral reporting and discussion procedures, business

meetings, current news, book discussions and reporting, and on writing and note taking.)

Procedure for Homework Related to the Unit Being Studied (*in Order of Importance*)

1. Read material pertinent to the section of the unit outline assigned to you.
2. Take notes on the topic of your presentation to the class.
3. Prepare and practice presentation—panel, debate, skit, etc.
4. Read and study the other sections of the outline. Prepare to answer, or ask questions; participate in discussion on all phases of the unit.

Procedure for Core Work Other than "Unit"

1. Continue writing core journal daily:
   a. What we did in class.
   b. Why we did it—objectives/purposes as you understand them.
   c. Your opinions, suggestions, for improvement.
2. Read regularly in good periodicals, newspapers ⎫ approximately
3. Watch and listen to good TV and radio programs ⎬ one hour
4. Continue work on your individual reading program ⎭ each day.
5. Participate in committee meetings (fine arts, planning, news, social, etc.) and in core activities.
6. (Specific assignments in "Practical English," *Youth Thinks It Through, How to Study*, on your term paper, etc., will be made by the teacher or a core committee.)

The unit reports ended on schedule—November 5, with the next day or two being spent on discussing some of the results, and possible implications of the election and its role in American politics and life. The whole unit demonstrated very well how a citizen could be an intelligent, participating member of society. It followed a plan—the problem-solving technique—adaptable to any situation that might arise. It was a cooperative enterprise capitalizing on the interests of the pupils and utilizing the vast fund of information in current literature. It dealt with the great issue of the day, but brought to that issue historical background and perspective.

3. PENNSBURY JUNIOR HIGH SCHOOL

The focus of the general education program in the Pennsbury, Pennsylvania, junior high schools is an interesting one. In the seventh and eighth grades the class is called core and bears a very close relationship to the other subjects in the school day. A description of the junior high school program reveals the nature of this relationship.[11]

[11] Pennsbury Junior High School, *Core at Pennsbury* (Yardley, Pa., n.d.), pp. 3, 12.

The program in seventh and eighth grade is constant for all students. Comprehensive and exploratory in nature, it includes experience in English, social studies (history, geography, government, and other social problems), mathematics, science, art, music, homemaking, industrial arts, physical education, and health. In addition, a core period provides students with an opportunity to study and solve the many problems of living— at school, at home, and in the community. Starting with their own group and their school program, which is the immediate community, common to all, the students progress to a study of the local community.

After learning what services their own community renders, they compare it with others throughout the United States. In this way they discover the advantages and disadvantages of the different ways in which people live together. The natural result of such activity is the building of a model community and this is exactly what students do in the eighth grade.

Studying one's community and building a model one requires many different skills. For example, students need to know how to read, interpret, and draw maps to scale; they need to know how local and state governments are organized and operated; they need to understand the influence of geographical environment on the ways people live; they need to understand the role science plays in daily living; and they need to know how to read for information, how to organize material, how to write acceptable reports and letters, how to interview, and how to report effectively their findings and recommendations to the rest of the group. Students also explore the fields of art, homemaking, and shop, and from these gain techniques and skills which they use in developing their model community, such as home planning, interior decorating, and model building. These are some of the experiences students gain in regularly organized classes and use in their core activities as they study their own and then build a model community.

Objectives of the Junior High School Program

A. To place the emphasis on the learner rather than the subject.
B. To encourage planning by pupils and teachers around a center of interest: Early communities
   1. At present—the Pennsbury Community; county, state, nation, as communities.
   2. The selection of a "community" in the U.S. in Grade 8.
C. To utilize all types of experiences as avenues of learning.
D. To relax classroom tensions by bringing all children in the co-operative effort.
E. To broaden the interests and expand the horizons of all pupils.
F. To learn to share interests and experiences with others.
G. To learn to share co-operatively in group undertakings.

H. To have an opportunity to feel a sense of accomplishment.
I. To feel adequate in social skills which are needed on the level of the experience and maturity, such as listening, speaking, reading, and writing.
J. To learn to identify group problems, as well as personal problems, and intelligently seek their solution.
K. To learn to search for needed materials of all kinds.
L. To learn the value of constructive criticism.
M. To learn to work co-operatively as leader and follower citizens in a democratic order.
N. To learn to stick to the task in hand until a degree of accomplishment has been reached.
O. To render service to the school and community of which the pupil is a member.
P. *Note:* There are two very important concepts to be kept in mind by all teachers in a core program:
   1. Core should provide experiences needed by all youth.
   2. Core should provide experiences which cut across subject lines.

In a highly creative way the actual happenings in a classroom situation are described and give a more specific picture of what students do in a program with a general education focus.[12]

AN ADVENTURE IN CORE

A few weeks ago I was invited to the Pennsbury area for a visit. My hostess, who was quite respected, very proud of the community, and who had a civic pride unimaginable, proceeded to inform me about the area. Her plans included an itinerary of the historical and current local institutions, which led to the most fascinating and strangest experience in my life.

Early on the second morning of my visit, when most vacationists are in bed, I visited a large red brick building, modern in appearance except for the tower which gave it a tie with the past. Though thoroughly impressed with the physical plant, I remembered that a school is still a school, quite artificial and a place to learn but, nevertheless, one from which most students wish to make a hasty retreat.

My first step was in a class called "Core," my first impression, bedlam! Some students were painting posters depicting the Pacific Coast states as the land of sunshine, leisure, wealth and plenty. In the same group, I saw one boy making slides tracing the history of that area. Two other students were writing a dialogue for a skit which, I learned, was to be used to see their particular section of the country as the best

[12] *Ibid.,* pp. 4–5.

place to settle and live. This was bedlam? Only in that no two students were doing the same thing. Looking around the room, I couldn't help but observe the keen interest and enthusiasm displayed by the different students and groups engaged in too many activities to note here. Through more casual observations, informal questions, and, just plain "busybodying," I learned that each student had a job, that each group was well organized in that they had well-defined objectives and goals. Never before had I seen so many activities going on simultaneously in one classroom. Yes, I was on the verge of being somewhat envious of these students too; I was anxious to join them in their tasks.

But now, I asked myself, with so many activities and with so much interest and enthusiasm, can these students be learning anything? What is Core? Is it English, social studies, mathematics, and science combined? Does one teacher take care of all? If not, who teaches the students to write skits, letters, to make contour maps, slides, and scale drawings?

Gradually the mystery began to unfold. From core class we proceeded to science. Here they were studying about the vast water resources, the extensive mountain ranges, and the climate of the United States, facts about contours and how to read maps. Now I could see where students learned these skills and techniques.

Following the science class we entered mathematics. The teacher was reviewing fractions with the group, a topic which had also been very boring to me. In this classroom not only were the students using fractions in drill, but applying their knowledge to the making of scale drawings. Now I was more than ever anxious to take part.

In English, the same was true. Some students were learning to interview, write letters, and investigate the literature of the different sections of the United States. I was certainly surprised to learn that all letters written were not graded! Instead, the letter when corrected was actually mailed to seek information necessary for the core class.

The social studies class was no different from the others. As in the other classes the students were learning and acquiring facts that were necessary for the selection of a community site somewhere in the United States. At last, I was able to see what was being done. In the various subject areas, the students learned techniques and facts that were later utilized in core.

I learned later that the Pacific Coast states were found to be the most attractive. It seems that the pamphlets and materials acquired through letter writing, the climate studied in science, its varied terrain discovered also in science, its rich history seen through social studies, and the illustrative techniques developed in art and science, convinced the class that the West Coast was the place for an ideal community.

This little tale, which very well could have happened, is written to give you an inside picture of a portion of the core program and its workings. We hope by now that you have a clear picture of the type of experience program that we have been developing in grades seven and eight at Pennsbury for the past five years.

Then, too, we hope you see our aim in trying to overcome the artificialness of most school programs. Here we have developed a program in which the students weigh experiences in accordance with the most generally approved patterns of behavior and the best ideals of the culture in which they live.

To summarize, the needs which are essential to the development of personally adjusted and socially competent citizens can be more effectively organized if they are related to broad problems without reference to any one subject area. Thus, in core, life situations and problems make up the curriculum. Organized bodies of subject matter, which will be taught in varying degrees as they are needed, contribute to the learner's immediate concerns which, in reality, are future problems for a lesser scope and complexity.

4. THE UNIVERSITY SCHOOL, THE OHIO STATE UNIVERSITY

The University School is, like our first example, a laboratory school. It dates from 1931 and was an active participant in the Eight-Year Study of the Progressive Education Association. From the beginning, the school has assumed leadership in developing programs and procedures based upon sound research evidence; it has continued to engage in research and has made several important contributions to our professional literature. One of the more refreshing publications to reach the public eye is "Were We Guinea Pigs?" [13] written by the high school students who were members of the first graduating class at University School to come through a general education program. This first-hand account should be read by everyone who would like a student viewpoint on his own education and an inside view of an embryo general education class.

The experimental nature of the school has led to continuous revision of its curriculum, and the following report is taken directly from *A Description of Curricular Experiences,*[14] which gives an account of the general education program as it has existed in the latter 1950's.

The University School staff feels that there are common problems which all young people who live in a democracy must face. The secondary

[13] University School, Ohio State University, Class of 1938, *Were We Guinea Pigs?* (New York: Henry Holt & Co., Inc., 1938).
[14] Ohio State University, *The University School; A Description of Curricular Experiences. The Upper School* (Columbus, 1952), pp. 10–13.

school is responsible to help all young people define the major problems of our society and arrive at generalizations and conclusions which will make it possible for the democratic way of living to thrive. To this end, a program of general education, consisting of common learnings required of all students, is an integral part of the secondary program. These common learnings and experiences are cared for in the core class.

In the secondary program at the University School the core classes

1. are required of all students.
2. are scheduled for a longer period of time than are other classes. (Approximately three hours—grades seven, eight, and nine. One and one-half hours—grades ten, eleven, and twelve.)
3. are responsible for a major part of the common learnings which are defined as the learning activities that are thought to be basic to the education of all students.
4. provide learning activities which cut across conventional subject-matter lines.
5. provide learning activities and experiences which are in harmony with adolescent interests, needs, and concerns.
6. function in such a way as to care for individual differences in a learning climate conducive to personal and class guidance.

The core classes also carry responsibilities for

1. the continuous experiences as stated in the philosophy and purposes of the University School.
2. activities related to student government and school organizations.
3. immediate problems of group living (planning class dances, class money-making projects, participation in Red Cross drives, etc.).
4. individual reading and writing programs.
5. free choice experiences in other areas (science, arts, physical education, social sciences, and mathematics) to the extent that it is feasible.

The teacher or the core counselor of the core class, assumes the following responsibilities (in addition to the responsibilities implied above):

1. The core counselor will be responsible for the guidance or counseling program for the grade.
2. The core counselor will be the chairman of the grade staff.
3. The core counselor will be responsible for keeping all records on individuals, the group, and the records and materials related to the learning units studied by the group.
4. The core counselor will assume the major responsibility for instruction in the learning unit.

Special area teachers serve the various core classes by assuming the following responsibilities:

1. The special area teachers (e.g., music, related arts, home arts, and others from subject areas who relate themselves to special problems arising from the core activities) serve on the grade staff and help in the planning, carrying out, and evaluation of the learning units.
2. The special area teachers participate directly in the teaching of the core group when the learning situation demands his particular knowledge and ability.
3. The special area teachers also advise, with the core counselor, concerning appropriate learning experiences which the core counselor would guide. It is the joint obligation of the core counselor and the special area teacher to decide which one should assume the teaching responsibility for any classroom situation.

Grade Staff Organization

The grade staff is one of the more important organized faculty units at the University School. Each grade staff is composed of the core teacher, who serves as counselor of the grade and is chairman of the staff, and all teachers who come in contact with the students of the grade. The grade staff is responsible for the educational program of the students in a particular grade. The membership of a typical grade staff would include the following teachers: core, physical education, related arts, music, home arts, English, mathematics, science, and social studies. This group would consider such problems as organizing and enriching the core learning unit, individual pupil counseling and guidance, parent relations, and special projects for the grade group.

Problem Areas in the Core

The staff at University School has designated areas of learning in which fall many problems confronting young people today. These problem areas are selected in terms of student interests and personal-social needs. They are the result of careful study of the school's philosophy, child growth and development, and the social concern impinging on the individual in a democracy. Core groups derive many of their learning units from these problem areas through the process of teacher-pupil planning.

The list of problem areas is not final and all-inclusive. In the process of selecting a learning unit, pupils and teacher will occasionally find their major interest to be in a problem not included in the list. When this occurs the teacher will present the matter at a grade staff meeting for the purpose of obtaining permission for the group to study the topic. Seldom, if ever, is permission denied when the proposed topic appears promising to pupils and teacher who have expressed desire in studying the topic.

Problem Areas for Grades Seven, Eight, and Nine

1. Personal Living (problems related to growing up)
   a. Understanding My Body
   b. Beliefs and Superstitions
   c. Hobbies
   d. Managing My Personal Affairs
2. Personal-Social Living (problems related to living with others)
   a. Sports and Recreation
   b. Living in University School
   c. Living in the Home
   d. Living in the Neighborhood
   e. Personality and Appearance
3. Social-Civic-Economic Living (problems of living in and understanding society)
   a. Earning a Living ⎱
   b. Housing ⎰ in Columbus
   c. Natural Resources ⎰
   d. Community Agencies and Services   in Ohio
       Recreation ⎱
       Protection ⎰
       Government ⎰ in other countries
       Education ⎰
       Welfare ⎰
   e. Communication
   f. Living in Columbus
   g. Living in Ohio
   h. Living in Another Country or Other Countries

   In grades ten, eleven, and twelve the following problem areas are the basis for learning units:

Tenth Grade

Problems of Healthful Living
Problems of Living in an Urban Society
Problems of the Family as a Basic Social Unit
The Development of the American Scene

Eleventh Grade

Problems of Living in the Atomic Age
The Problems of Establishing Beliefs

The Problems of Making a Living (Exploring Vocations)
Current World Problems

Twelfth Grade

Problems of Producer-Consumer Economics
Implications of Scientific Advancement
Major Conflicting Ideologies
The Bases for Determining Values by Which to Live

The following is a description [15] of a twelfth-grade unit:

PRODUCER-CONSUMER ECONOMICS—TWELFTH-GRADE UNIT
Unit Organization Sheet

What are we trying to accomplish in the study of our unit?

1. Each person should gain a better understanding of the existing variety of goods and services available which make for better living.
2. We should develop a guiding set of principles for making wide and wise choices of goods and services.
3. We should gain an understanding and appreciation of the social-economic principles which affect production and distribution of goods and services.
4. There should come an awareness of how democratic group action protects and promotes the interests of the consumer.
5. We should find out how government and private organizations provide for the needs of the consumer.
6. We should learn how the productive capacities of our country are organized and have been organized in order to provide an even higher standard of living for our people.
7. We should investigate the problems of the past and the present which stand in the way of better production, distribution, and consumption of goods and services in our economy.
8. We should develop an understanding of our "free enterprise" economy as compared to other economic theories held by other people in other parts of the world.
9. We should understand the productive capacity of our country as compared with other nations of the world and investigate the meaning of this comparison.
10. We should study the interrelationships of our economic health with the economic health and future of the world.

How are we organizing our study?

It seems advisable to organize the unit around three general areas of problems:

[15] *Ibid.*, pp. 80–85.

1. Problems of the individual consumer.
2. Problems of the producer.
3. Problems of distribution of goods and services.

What shall be the procedure in studying the unit?

1. The unit will be divided into three parts as suggested above.
2. For each part the following things will be done in order:
   a. Preliminary research and the preparation of questions.
   b. Research on the questions.
   c. Presentation of the questions for sharing through discussion, speakers, trips, films, etc.
3. Following the study of the three parts of the unit, there will be a period of approximately one week in which general and controversial questions related to the unit will be elaborated, discussed, debated, and argued.

Problems of the Individual Consumer

I. Sources of Consumer Information

1. What publications are there on which we can rely in order to know whether or not we are making the "best buy"?
2. Are there any regularly published magazines which a consumer can consult on best buys?
3. Are the organizations which claim to function for the consumer financed by consumers?
4. Who has developed standards for consumer goods and how can we obtain and use this information?

II. Consumer Techniques

1. How can the consumer tell when something is really pure silk, 100% wool, Sanforized, etc.?
2. Is it usually better to buy brand names?
3. Does the consumer usually gain by purchasing goods on sale?
4. Is it wise for consumers to buy from door-to-door salesmen?
5. Is it better to buy at a chain store or a privately owned and operated store?
6. Is the yearly change in style of dresses, cars, etc., worth the price and trouble involved?
7. When should one buy for quality and when for appearance, or do these two qualities usually appear in the same product?
8. What are some of the quick, on-the-spot ways the consumer can detect a poor grade of merchandise?
9. What is the best way to handle a "super-salesman?"

III. *Guarantees on Products*

1. What kinds of guarantees and service policies should consumers get on goods bought?
2. How reliable are guarantees on new products?

IV. *Buying Bargains*

1. Is it a good idea to buy things in large quantities and "stock up" in order to get the lower price on the larger quantity?
2. Is it wise to buy soap, toothpaste, and other "specials" on the one-cent and five-cent sales?
3. Is it wise for consumers to buy goods through a company catalogue?
4. Are prices getting so standardized and fair trade so "fair" that a consumer can't pick up a bargain without wondering about its worth?
5. Do you always get good values when you attend sales?

V. *Advertising*

1. What ads can we believe?
2. Should consumers rely on advertising?
3. Who pays for advertising?
4. How does the appearance of a product determine its sale?
5. How can one avoid being prejudiced due to advertising?
6. Are unadvertised products to be trusted?

VI. *Services*

1. Is there any standard repair charge for electrical appliances or does each dealer or service man try to get the most he can for his services?
2. Are there any organizations or associations which assure the consumer of high quality and reasonable services?

VII. *Credit and Instalment Buying*

1. What is gained and what is lost by instalment plan buying?
2. How do loan companies operate? Do they actually help people?
3. How, when, and under what circumstances can the consumer use credit buying to his advantage?
4. How is the seller and consumer protected by credit unions?

VIII. *Government Regulations*

1. What are the "hidden taxes" and how do they affect the price of an article?

2. Do government regulations and restrictions cause black markets?
3. How does the government's plan of lending money in great quantities to other countries affect our economy and consequently the prices the consumer pays for the products?
4. How are producers protected from articles being marked down in price? Is this fair to the consumer?
5. Can the government control prices in such a way as to avoid inflation?
6. Where do the billions of dollars that our government is lending continually come from?

IX. *Miscellaneous Questions*

1. What agencies, if any, hinder the consumer from getting good value for his money?
2. Do consumers, by hoarding, cause prices to rise?
3. How do new inventions and products affect our buying and the prices of new and old products?
4. How would another all-out war affect our economy?
5. How does the consumer benefit from sales competition?
6. Do the "wants" of the consumer have much to do with the type of articles produced?
7. Are public opinion polls a necessary part of buying and selling?
8. Will more of our buying in the future be done at neighborhood shopping centers?
9. Should there be more consumer co-operatives?
10. What percentage of the national income is spent on what different kinds of goods and services?

PRODUCER-CONSUMER ECONOMICS

Suggested Activities

1. Draw a map of one block in a business section of your community. On the map, classify the different types of business enterprises.
2. Visit a local factory and report to class on the following:
   a. Of what industry is this business a part?
   b. What evidences did you find of specialization and division of labor?
   c. Describe the factors of production as used in the factory.
3. Work out a test concerned with various facts of production and distribution (to be given to class and discussed). For example:
   a. A group of related business enterprises is called an industry.
   b. "Capital" means any produced goods used for further production. It includes the tools, machines, buildings, and materials used in the production process.

4. Work out a group of words or terms necessary to know the meaning of in order to understand this unit. For example: business enterprise, capital, entrepreneur, processing industries, etc.
5. Read and report on the history of a large corporation.
6. Collect samples of financial statements in the newspaper or in reports and pamphlets of business firms. Analyze.
7. Discuss the following questions:
   a. Why do costs differ among producers of the same items?
   b. What are the advantages of large-scale production?
   c. What problems are created by large-scale production?
8. "There are too many middlemen." "Middlemen can be eliminated, but not their functions." Explain and discuss these statements.
9. Write a report on how the use of middlemen is lessened by the use of (a) farm co-operatives, (b) consumer co-operatives, (c) mail-order house.
10. Discuss the following questions:
    a. Is big business a threat to the American way of life?
    b. Should all laws restricting big-business growth be repealed?
    c. How can we get the best contributions of large-scale business without suffering from its disadvantages?
11. Consult a history textbook and report on the following topics:
    a. The political influence of big business.
    b. The effect of monopoly on the use of resources.
    c. The attitude of farmers toward big business.
12. Name and discuss at least four business functions involved in bringing goods to the retailer.
13. What American inventions or devices have affected life in your home?
14. Do you think that large-scale production and distribution have helped this country? Give reasons for your answer.

Some Economic Terms to Understand

business enterprise	retailer
capital	wholesaler
capital goods	incorporation
consumer goods	insolvent
cost of production	overhead or fixed costs
division of labor	unit cost
durable goods	direct or variable cost
extractive industries	cutthroat competition
factor of production	diversification of product
labor	fair trade laws
mass production	interstate trade barriers
middleman	monopoly

nondurable goods   copyright
processing industries   franchise
producers' goods   patent

•   In these four examples of general education classes, we have
seen an interesting variety of foci on certain common learnings for
adolescents. There was one that highlighted citizenship responsibility
and understanding in terms of election processes, another that involved students in a realistic way in the development of a community
with all the attendant planning and organization. A third emphasized
understandings of our American heritage of physical expansion and
its reflection in our literature, showing how one can illuminate the
other; and a fourth example focused on a very realistic problem
of adolescent-societal life—producer-consumer understandings. Whatever specific orientation a school faculty decides upon for its general
education program, the program cannot escape its responsibility for
meeting common needs—personal, civic, social, economic—of all adolescents living in today's world.

Part Two

Teaching in the General Education Class

4

Getting Started

The old proverb "Well begun is half done" has a message for us as educators in its emphasis on getting off to a good start. Whether it be revising a curriculum, starting the new school year, beginning a fresh unit, the manner in which we get underway, the amount and kind of preparation we engage in, the attitudes and understandings we bring to our task will determine in large part the effectiveness of our venture. Especially important is how a teacher and a group of students begin their work together; for, in the classroom, as in many other aspects of our life, first impressions are vivid, compelling, and, all too often, lasting. The first few days set the stage for the drama that unfolds as a teacher and his students work together in the intimacy of a classroom, in a variety of activities for two or three hours each day.

What is involved in getting started? How do thirty human beings begin to create a teaching-learning environment in which they can live and work together in reasonable harmony? There is no single answer to questions such as these. Getting started means many things and can involve a variety of approaches.

A. Getting Started Means Becoming Acquainted

In many schools the need for getting acquainted is a strong one. Seventh and eighth grades in large junior high schools are composed of boys and girls from a number of elementary schools, often varied in nature and environment. The description which one seventh-grade class gave of its first day in a large urban junior high school is typical.

One September morning a very frightened group of freshies arrived at Forest Junior High School. We all gathered in a crowd and talked of all the terrible things we thought would happen to us. The bell soon rang and we followed the crowd into the school. The first problem was, "Where is Room 118?" "Well, we might as well look down this corridor." "Oh, my goodness, here it is!" "I do hope Miss Lewis is nice." "Well, in we go."

Miss Lewis proved to be as nice as we hoped she would and many happy hours were spent with her during the morning.

At lunchtime we ate our lunch and went outside. "Oh, my, what fun! A ramp!" That was a mistake! Nobody is supposed to walk up the ramp, as the Ranger lectured to us a few minutes later.

The lunch period was soon over, and we found ourselves wandering around looking for the math room. We proved to be fifteen minutes late for math, but our teacher was very nice about it.

The afternoon was very exciting as we persisted in getting lost again and in breaking rules that we had yet to learn.

When we returned to our homeroom, we were asked how we liked our first day at Forest. We replied like this, "It's a wonderful school, but, oh, so *big!*"

How much more frustrating could this experience be if the members of the class were complete strangers to one another or knew relatively few classmates. Such a situation can exist also at the senior high school level where teen-agers come together in the ninth or tenth grades in high school buildings often some distance from their home communities.

Therefore, in many instances, the first step is that of breaking down barriers of uncertainty and unfamiliarity. The process really starts with the teacher, who may find it rewarding, for example, to give a brief autobiographical sketch of himself to his students. When boys and girls hear that Mr. Shannon is a Dixieland jazz fan or that Miss Jones can cite their favorite National League pitcher as one of her current "idols," the classroom already starts assuming a "we-ness" that will bear rich dividends. The process can be continued with the boys and girls telling informally about themselves, their interests and hobbies, current enthusiasms and pet peeves, recent vacation experiences.

Other ways which teachers have found effective in this getting-acquainted process can be easily cited. One group of ninth graders became interested in discovering where everyone lived, and very shortly there was a large wall map of the city, with pictures of the students, indicating their homes. Such vivid pictorialization showed clearly various residential groupings, and many teen-agers discovered one more thing in common—proximity of residence, with subsequent new friendships easily formed. From this initial interest the class moved on to choosing a person about whom each would like to know more. As a result of further getting acquainted, each class member wrote a biography of one of his classmates.

To facilitate the getting-acquainted process, one teacher asks his students to learn the names of four classmates each day—the four nearest him; in this case, the one in front, in back, and on both sides. Then each day, for several days, the boys and girls change their seats until they have an opportunity to learn everyone's name. Another teacher duplicates a class directory of names and addresses of the students so that each may have a complete list of his classmates.

As another aid to getting to know names, some teachers find it helpful to have a name card for each student that can be placed on his desk for all to see. These name cards may be written in advance or may be made up by the class when the students arrive. The advantage of the latter procedure lies in giving the boys and girls something concrete and worthwhile to do at the outset that contributes to a lively, friendly atmosphere.

One school faces a specific problem in the area of helping students get acquainted. At the ninth-grade level the class is doubled in size by the admission of new students into the school. Much attention is given to helping the boys and girls develop a "we" feeling so that there will be no division into two groups, the former students and the new ones. During the past year a twenty-four-hour camping experience at the County School Camp was decided upon as an effective means of bringing the students together in an informal situation where they could get better acquainted and learn to work and play together.

The whole venture was a co-operative one, since parents had been consulted in planning sessions with the teachers. Students assumed responsibility for planning the day's schedule, menus, transportation, and all the other necessary details. Many resource people accompanied the class, including the two teachers, four parents, the camp director, and two physical-education teachers.

During ensuing evaluation of the trip the consensus was that the whole experience had been a highly successful one. In terms of getting better acquainted progress had been made; for, when class elections were held shortly after the trip, some of the new students were elected to office.

B. Getting Started Means Establishing a Friendly Atmosphere

The climate in which a class gets under way has much to do with ensuing success and effectiveness. Not least important is the physical climate, for increasingly the relationship between successful learning and one's physical surroundings is being recognized as a close one. Some teachers like to have an attractive, appealing classroom awaiting the arrival of the boys and girls. Others prefer to have their students "get started" with a developing interest in decorating the room. In either case the emphasis is on a friendly atmosphere, a room that says "welcome" each time the students enter.

One group of seventh graders, discovering that they would be spending three hours a day in a room that left much to be desired from an aesthetic point of view, very early in the first week gave serious attention to improving the appearance of their surroundings. The usual suggestions were made for pictures, plants, and flowers. Soon, however, imagination was running wild, and some of the students proposed painting the room a brighter color and making draperies for the windows. After much discussion it was agreed that decorating plans would proceed slowly and be a continuing part of their work together. As a first step, the students enlisted the help of the art teacher and made sketches of school life which they placed on the cupboard doors and above the blackboards. They brought plants and flowers, and made a comfortable reading corner by adding a reed armchair and a small table. Plans for painting the walls and making draperies were carried out later in the year. In the meantime, however, much had been done to create an atmosphere conducive to pleasant living and working.

Contributing to the friendliness of the room is the arrangement of the desks or tables and chairs. Many teachers have discovered that it is difficult for students to be friendly when a boy or girl sees little more than the backs of other students' heads. As a result, a variety of seating arrangements can be found in general education classes, ranging from the circle, the square, groupings of tables and chairs, to other ingenious and provocative furniture arrangements which suit the purposes of the class at any given time.

In general it might be said that for purposes of getting started, the more informal the arrangement the better. So, as boys and girls introduce themselves or their neighbors, they can frequently be found seated in a circle or a square, speaking in conversational tones, seeing each and every class member, the teacher one with the group. Such a practice contributes much to the friendliness that is to be desired from the very first day.

Establishing a friendly atmosphere involves interaction of various kinds. From time immemorial, groups have found games a most effective means of "breaking the ice." In their own way guessing games have much to offer as they frequently lead to pleasant humor. One teacher has found that boys and girls often enjoy writing briefly about themselves and, after having their descriptions read aloud, trying to guess who's who. This is one of the less formal ways of getting acquainted and one that begins to concentrate interest on classmates as individuals.

Because names assume a psychological importance to everyone, giving each a unique identity, their recognition becomes a factor in the whole pattern of friendships and friendly working relations. Often, a teacher will say, at the close of the first class session, "Now, how many of you can name everyone in the room?" A few will make an attempt and do a surprisingly good job. The other side of the coin, of course, is for the teacher to name everyone. One teacher of a new eighth-grade group remembers how impressed the boys and girls were when she could name everyone after their first morning together.

Another lively approach to building friendly relations is the use of baby pictures. Here again, a variation of the "guess who" technique is useful, as boys and girls try to match infant and adolescent faces to the accompaniment of mirth and often amazement. One teacher has found singing a good way to develop the kind of psychological climate so desirable for people starting to work together. He has used camp songs effectively, one in particular being "How Do You Do?," in which each youngster's name is included.

C. Getting Started Means Sharing

Many teachers find it helpful in the very beginning to develop with the class, experiences that involve the kind of sharing that is to be such an integral part of general education work. The sooner the young people realize that they have ideas and experiences which interest each other and which they are permitted to discuss informally, the sooner they will develop some of the skills of co-operative action and mutual give-and-take that should be part of the general education class.

Many teachers have found that seventh graders like to exchange elementary school experiences. At the same time this approach offers an opportunity for small groups to start working on a problem of special concern to the class members. The students group according to their former elementary school and plan how and what to tell the rest of the class about their experiences. Some of them talk about the kinds of things they studied in the sixth grade, indicating which they enjoyed and which they disliked. Then, too, there is always the matter of school spirit to be communicated, even if one is only a former student. Pride bubbles over in the enthusiasm to describe various aspects of school life.

Sharing with the whole group can occur when each student introduces himself and tells something about his life; or it can occur between two persons when an interview procedure is used. The interview may be followed by an oral introduction to the class or by a written biographical account. When the latter is the case, a variety of procedures may be used for sharing with the entire class. Small groups may form to hear or read these accounts, so that at least five or six boys and girls are getting to know a good bit about one another. From these group sessions one or two biographies may be selected to be read to the entire class. Sometimes a class requests that all of the biographies be mimeographed so that each may have a set.

If the sharing is to be genuine and meaningful, the teacher must take an active part in the process. He may, as was mentioned earlier, introduce himself with a brief account of his interests and background. When interviews are the order of the day, the teacher joins in as interviewer and interviewee. Regardless of approach or technique, teacher and students together are involved in sharing.

D. Getting Started Means "Getting Down to Work"

Getting started does not limit itself to the operational level of discussion and conversation only, but frequently involves "getting down to work" in the more traditional meaning of the term. Many skills need developing, and attention must be focused on achieving worthwhile objectives.

For example, a class can begin by preparing a bulletin board on some topic under study or of particular interest to the students. In the process much will be learned about skills of working together to attain a specific goal, characteristics of an attractive and informative bulletin board, to say nothing of helpful information acquired about the topic.

Sometimes getting down to work can combine elements of getting acquainted with a focus on some desirable skills and understandings. A description of the way one teacher involved his class in some serious study through a getting-acquainted approach may be helpful.

It was decided that the students in this particular eighth-grade class had much to learn about each other and that the teacher, who was new not only to the class but to the school, needed to learn even more. Together they agreed upon a procedure whereby the students paired off to interview each other, after which they were to write informal biographies.

In preparation for this work, the students spent several sessions in reading biographical articles in magazines in order to get the "feel" of this kind of writing. Analysis was made of style as well as the kinds of information included in the articles. The class then decided what these ideas meant in terms of their own biographical writing. The students then developed the following list of suggested items, which served as a guide for their interview and writing.

1. Work, e.g., chores, paper routes, hobbies
2. Appearance
3. Residence
4. Childhood
5. Interesting experiences
6. Family
7. Interests at different ages
8. Predictions—ambitions
9. School
10. Travels

As part of this initiatory experience the students were immediately involved in reading, interviewing, note-taking, writing, discussing. No time was lost in coming to grips with communication skills. Also, the teacher, in addition to learning much about her students, very early had a set of papers that served in a diagnostic way as she appraised the strengths and weaknesses of her students in communication. The following biography illustrates the kind of work she received.

There was a tense silence in the operating room. A new baby had just been born. That day was February 23, 1944. A few weeks later the baby came to a road block. She could not drink cow's milk. The doctors tried one formula after another. None worked. As a last resort they tried goat's milk. On this the baby thrived. The child that had had all this trouble was Ann S.

A short time later Ann was moved from the hospital to the farm that was to be her home until, when she was five, she and her family moved to the city. During her life Ann had many pleasant and a few unpleasant experiences. A few of the more noteworthy I shall relate.

One day Ann was playing in her play house on the porch, and her brother came up and asked where all her playmates were. Instantly Ann began introducing her imaginary friends around the circle. As she came to the end she said, "And please move, you're standing on Inky."

Once when she was sitting in her swing a big black snake came along and coiled up beneath her. Her yells brought the family running and she was quickly rescued, and I think that there was one less black snake to bother the world.

None the worse for that harrowing experience, Ann lived happily on until one day her mother asked her to get her father who was plowing a field.

Between the house and the field was a pasture through which she must pass. Loose in this field was a billy goat. Quickly Ann hopped through the fence and started to run across the field. That was a grave mistake. The instant the goat saw her he charged and knocked her flat on the ground. Undaunted Ann got up and started to run again only to find herself flat on the ground again. Right then her father saw her and soon the goat was driven off and Ann was safe in the house, mission accomplished. Happy and unhurt, Ann lived on still looking for trouble.

When she was five, Ann moved to town and has been living here ever since. She entered our school in the first grade and likes it but is not too fond of homework.

In Ann's family there were four people until the last war when her brother lost his life. Ann's father likes to pick a banjo but is not too good at it. They own a cottage on the lake. They have a rowboat in the lake and Ann likes to row around in it. She likes it there and sometimes takes a friend.

Ann's jobs at home are to keep her room clean, make the beds, do the dishes and sweep. Her hobby is music; she likes to sing and is pleasant at all times. I think that someday she will be the homecoming queen for our class.

E. Getting Started Means Discovering Abilities, Needs, and Interests

In the first few days of working together in any of the ways already discussed, teachers learn a great deal about the abilities, interests, and needs of their students, information that proves of incalculable value as they help guide these young people in the ensuing year.

Mr. Thomas, for example, found that, as his class divided into small groups according to elementary school attendance to plan their sharing of experience with one another, he learned much about his students' ability to work co-operatively. He considered this a "first probe into group action." He gained evidence about their ability to plan wisely, to organize effectively, to be informative and entertaining. He spotted the potential leaders, the nonparticipants, and noted individual needs in the area of human relations.

When her eighth graders read the biographical articles in the magazine, Miss House noticed which magazine each student selected and the person about whom each article was written. It helped to know who chose articles about Mickey Mantle and Marilyn Monroe and who selected ones about Mamie Eisenhower or Ralph Bunche.

Written work also revealed current hobbies, travel experiences, home life, and a wealth of other information out of which emerged a picture of thirty or thirty-five individuals with distinctive personalities. In addition, weaknesses and strengths in skill areas were noted, such as spelling, language usage, diction, reading, and speaking. Creative potential in the group was not overlooked nor the human relations aspect of their work together.

For much of their experience the first few days revealed evidence of a sociometric nature. In a class where everyone else chose a member of his own sex to interview, what was the significance, if any, of the pairing of Ann and Jim? Why did Gertude and Mary choose one another, unlike as they seemed to be in temperament and behavior? How interesting and revealing that choices were not made strictly according to racial lines but that white and Negro met on common ground.

There is, then, much food for thought for the perceptive teacher as he helps students get started in the general education class.

F. Getting Started Means Learning What General Education Is

In all but a few situations, very early in the first or second session, the class finds itself coming to terms with the basic question, What is general education? This need is especially acute in schools where students can choose between a general education class or a traditional program of separate-subject organization, or else are in a school where general education is being initiated.

Usually there seem to be two approaches to this task. One consists of "explaining," the other of "experiencing." Sometimes the teacher explains what general education is and helps to develop understanding through discussion of questions boys and girls raise. Such a discussion might revolve around students' explanations of why they chose the general education class (where choice was involved) and what *they* think it is.

Through experience the first few days the students have met face to face some of the basic essentials of general education—working together on genuine concerns and problems, establishing good human relationships, utilizing and developing skill areas, participating in individual and group work of a purposeful and meaningful nature.

Such understanding of general education can be tested through communicating with others. A class can have Parent Night a few weeks after the start of school, at which time the boys and girls explain in effective and convincing fashion to their parents the nature of this "new" program of which they are a part. Or classes can write letters to friends or incoming students, describing general education and giving vivid accounts of their activities and learning.

G. Getting Started Means Identifying Problems for Study

One of the important responsibilities to be faced at the beginning of the year is that of identifying and selecting problems for study. There is a wide range of practice with regard to this aspect of the general education class. Some approaches will be discussed in the next chapter. One approach that is particularly relevant to our discussion of getting the general education class underway deserves our attention now.

While a teacher is always cognizant of the general needs and interests of a particular age group, there are many general education classes in which the identification of problem areas rests with the specific class and teacher. Together they set up criteria, explore possibilities, make decisions, and plan their study.

For classes that may not be so familiar with the process of identifying meaningful problems, teachers will find it helpful to use various exploratory devices to promote and provoke interest and thought. Films, interest inventories, personality adjustment instruments, in addition to discussions, can help launch many a planning session. Teachers or students can be permitted to browse leisurely and at will through a variety of materials as a way of discovering promising avenues of interest and need.

Two specific examples will serve to illustrate ways in which different classes have moved into problem study through co-operative planning.

1. AN ELEVENTH GRADE PLANS FOR THE YEAR

During the first week of their junior year the boys and girls decided to plan for the whole year in terms of broad problem areas to be studied. Together the class drew up a set of criteria like the following to serve as a guide in the consideration and selection of problems.

1. Is there sufficiently widespread interest in the problem?
2. Is the problem within our present level of understanding and abilities?
3. Does it present enough new learning to make it worthwhile?
4. Are there adequate and interesting materials and resources?
5. Will it be a valuable learning experience for the entire group?

Then, meeting in small groups, the boys and girls suggested problems, asked one another questions to clarify the suggestions, talked through the reasons for their ideas. The recorder in each group then submitted the list for that group.

Here are the suggestions:

Group 1

1. Electricity
2. Personal relationships with other countries
3. Civil defense
4. Vocations
5. Study of conditions and developments in India
6. Study of Germany in its present state and of vicious borders between communist and capitalist countries
7. Religions of the world
8. Current events discussion on Monday; keep up with the U.N.
9. Try two subjects in one quarter

Group 2

1. Current events and events to come
   a. Iranian oil situation
   b. Korea
2. Future wars
   a. Civil defense
3. Atomic energy
4. Sex education

Group 3

1. Atomic energy—science: What is it? Who discovered? Uses in peace and war
2. Psychology—school, home life
3. Personal problems
4. Sex education
5. World today—Japanese Peace Conference
6. Anatomy—Study of living organism
7. Oil situation

Group 4

1. Sex education
   a. Movies
   b. Speakers

2. How other schools compare with College High
   a. Study of educational methods
   b. Speakers
   c. Observing other schools
3. Personal problems—teen-age problems
   Either a short three-week unit or one hour set aside each Friday for this discussion
4. Civil defense and first aid
   a. How civil defense program for the city is set up—three-week unit
   b. Movies
   c. Speakers
   d. Inquire about bomb shelters and see if there are any at present
   e. What other cities have done and how we compare
   f. Most likely places for bombs to be dropped
   g. Study effects and precautions from atomic bomb

A committee consisting of the recorders from each group met and compiled a "master" list which was then submitted to the entire class for further discussion and consideration. This is the list as it was presented to the class with instructions.

ELEVENTH GRADE GENERAL EDUCATION

Choice of Unit

The following is a list of suggested areas for unit study. Included are your individual written suggestions as well as your group ideas. Read them over carefully.

Meet in your groups again and talk over the whole list. Try to note the merits and disadvantages of each for our study this year.

1. Ancient history—Rome, Egypt, etc.
2. Anatomy—study of living organisms
3. Atomic energy
   a. What it is
   b. How it was "discovered"
   c. Its uses in peace and war
4. Civil defense—first aid
   a. How the civil defense program for our city is set up
   b. What other cities have done
   c. Effects of and precautions against the atomic bomb
5. Electricity
6. How other schools compare with our school
   a. Study of educational methods
   b. Observing other schools

7. Natural resources
8. Personal and teen-age problems—sex education
9. Psychology
   a. People—their reactions, ideals, and actions
   b. School life, home life, etc.
10. Religions of the world
11. Vocations
12. The world today
    a. Relations with other countries
    b. India
    c. Germany
    d. Iranian oil situation
    e. Korea
    f. Russian satellite nations and the iron curtain

It has been suggested by some that we devote a certain amount of time each week to current events and a time for teen-age personal problems rather than take those areas as concentrated units. How do you feel about this possibility?

After further small group consideration the entire class engaged in lively and at times heated discussion of the possibilities. Bob expressed the opinion that you were not an educated person unless you knew ancient history; he was immediately challenged by a classmate, who wanted to know what he meant by "educated." A third joined in and asked who determines what constitutes an educated person.

Ronny felt that a study of people would be an important and fascinating subject and urged serious consideration of "psychology" as a problem. He had difficulty in clarifying for the class how they could go about studying such a broad problem. A few of the girls voiced approval for some attention to sex education and problems of a personal nature, while many of the boys, already eying the draft, argued that they would do well to give some attention to world affairs. All seemed agreed on the need to look at vocations in view of the choices and decisions that were facing them in the coming years.

In addition to discussion the class explored the materials that were available for each of the suggested problems and consulted with the librarian on this question. After considerable thought and careful exchange of opinions the class decided upon the following three problems, with the understanding that after study of the first, they would reconsider their choices to see if they still felt the same way: "The Influence of Early Civilizations on Our World Today," "Problems of Living in the Atomic Age," and "Vocations." They were then ready for specific planning for their first problem.

2. TWELFTH-GRADE GIRLS STATE THEIR PROBLEMS

One high school has a senior problems general education class that meets for seventy minutes, four days each week. There are eight sections, divided into four boys' groups and four girls' groups. The first two or three weeks of the year are spent in exploring areas that students feel have not been discussed sufficiently or at all during their past high school life. One of the teachers, in addition to discussion, asked her girls to write briefly and anonymously the things they would most like to learn during the year. As the teacher put it, "This was my first effort to get some problems to start building what we wanted to do this year. I wanted their most personal reaction before it was colored by much discussion. These were incorporated in our objectives later."

Here are some of the girls' statements:

I would like to know more about myself, to be more friendly, how to act around boys, and to get to know more about boys. To know when you are ready to get married. To know more about sex.

Find out if I'm smart enough to go to college, what kind of job I will be fitted for, how to talk to a young girl about sex, what kind of boy will be better suited for me, what faults I have and correct them.

I would like to be able to understand myself and my friends better when I get out of this class. Also I would like to learn more about the different colleges and the courses they offer. Also I would like to learn about the various jobs and how to go about getting them.

What I would like to get out of this core class: 1. To be able to talk and discuss things in class; 2. To be friends to everyone; 3. To help one when he or she is in trouble; 4. To keep house neat and clean; 5. To learn how to take care of children so that you will be a good mother.

I would like to learn how to overcome certain actions of mine. By listening to the problems of the other girls and how they cope with them I may be able to settle my own. I want to know how to talk to the other girls and also to boys since I'm not very popular with the boys.

From an analysis of statements like these, it was possible to detect specific areas of concern which eventually evolved into working units —problems such as family living and personal relationships, educational and vocational guidance, problems of human relations, among others.

• **And so teachers and students get started on the road to learning in general education. The approach varies with the age of the stu-**

dents, their previous experience together, the status of general education in the school, and the particular make-up of the class, to which each teacher should be immediately and continuously sensitive. What succeeds with one class may fail with another; what is effective one year may have negligible results the next.

However, regardless of procedure or practice, most classes in the process of getting started find themselves actively involved in a number of genuinely worthwhile learning experiences: reading, writing, speaking, discussing, working together, creating. The class is on its way!

5

Using a

Problem-Solving Approach

Since the general education class is designed to focus upon learning experiences common to all youth in today's society, a major consideration for all interested parties is that of problem identification. For it is no simple matter to identify those needs, interests, and concerns that cluster together to form problem areas—the major content of the general education class. Nor is it an easy task to assess the relative value of such problems and the appropriate placement of them in the developmental pattern of adolescence.

Along with our discussion of problem identification some attention ought to be given to what many people consider the core of the general education class—the problem-solving process. It is through this approach to learning that boys and girls acquire the skills needed for mature participation in adult democratic society—self-direction, decision making, co-operative action with individual integrity intact, research skills, value judging.

It is to these two important topics, then, problem identification and the problem-solving process, that we now turn our attention.

A. Problem Identification

As we start our discussion of ways and means of identifying significant general education problems, two cautions need to be clarified and kept in mind. First of all, we must remember that what seems a purely personal problem of a teen-ager upon closer inspection often is revealed to be also a societal problem deserving attention and study.

For example, through the use of the Three Wishes technique a teacher learned that one youngster wished for "enough money to keep my family and me happy so we could have nice clothes and carpets." Another wanted a new home for his parents. Sue wished that her "family could move into a new modern home"; Carol wanted to "live in a beautiful home"; and Evelyn asked for "a pretty house and to be happy."

The number of these comments about a new house or a pretty home should raise some thoughtful questions in the mind of the teacher who is sincerely interested in helping his students. In searching for answers the teacher of the above class discovered that residence in low-cost housing projects was having an effect on the attitudes of these young people that adults all too often overlook. Such sensitivity to their surroundings was deserving of respect and reflection.

However, equally significant was the fact that these wishes reflected an important societal problem. The entire question of public housing—how much and what kind, psychological implications as well as sociological—is a pervading problem in American political, social, and economic life in the twentieth century.

Again, consider Ann, who wished that "she and her girl friend could get along better." Florence would like to have a nice family when she gets married. Mary Louise wished that her "father would work six days instead of four," and Joan "would like to be able to make my own spending and other money so I wouldn't have to bother either of my parents."

Who can deny that the problems of effective human relations, marriage and family living, earning a living and budgeting are societal in nature as well as personal problems in the lives of young people? As such they deserve attention in the general education class.

A second caution relates to the meaning attached to words like *needs* and *interests*. In developing a program evolving out of the needs of adolescents, it is important to realize that these needs are not always overtly expressed. There are existing needs which the youngster cannot verbalize and some of which he is but dimly aware, if at all. Needs also range widely over the whole development of the adolescent—physical, emotional, intellectual, social.

In the same way, the word *interests* requires understanding. Too often, it is thought to refer only to fads that capture the young imagination at any given time. However, many studies have shown us that adolescents at various stages in their development tend to be concerned with certain ideas, hobbies, activities, people, and the like. A recognition of such concerns can be very helpful in guiding young people to mature development. Such recognition, though, has no relationship to the fallacious belief that all learning is guided by young-sters' answers to the question, "What would you like to do today?"

With these cautions in mind, let us look at some ways in which significant problems for study can be identified. One way has already been discussed—that of co-operative problem identification by teacher and class. There are two other approaches that can be cited, though these ways are by no means mutually exclusive: (1) the use of pre-planned problem areas; (2) a projective approach.

1. THE USE OF PRE-PLANNED PROBLEM AREAS

Numerous studies have been made of adolescent needs and inter-ests, studies which often serve as a framework for building a general education program. The faculty of any given school can and should consult these studies and determine problem areas that seem most appropriate for the young people of that school and the community setting. Any teacher preparing to meet a general education class should study the research concerning characteristics of adolescents, their interests, needs, and concerns, and should in this way become familiar with problems that will be meaningful to his students.

In short, one approach to problem identification is that of general agreement in advance on broad problem areas after careful, co-operative study and analysis of the appropriate research. Many schools have done this kind of planning. The account of the curriculum direc-tor in one such school is worth citing at this point.[1]

A TECHNIQUE FOR DETERMINING PROBLEM AREAS FOR GENERAL EDUCATION IN THE SECONDARY SCHOOL

General education in the secondary school is primarily charged with the responsibility to provide all youth with opportunities to develop *common* skills, values, qualities and understandings needed for effective citizenship. It is, therefore, required of all students. Excellent motivation for identifying, developing, and refining common qualities of citizenship occurs in situations as part of the young citizen's emerging responsibilities. The problems which impinge upon the adolescent, the aspects *he* recog-nizes as well as those aspects about which he will need to be informed, thus provide a vital and dynamic structure for general education.

To identify the problems which are of gravest concern to adolescents, those who are most aware of them—adolescents themselves and their parents and teachers—should be questioned. This hypothesis was tested in a problem-area study conducted by the writer in a junior and a senior

---

[1] Marani, Jean Victoria. *A Technique for Determining Problem Areas for Gen-eral Education in the Secondary School.* Unpublished doctoral dissertation. Ohio State University, 1958; pp. 162–163, 312–326.

high school in the city of Sarasota, Florida. A group of social scientists in Florida universities also participated.

Students were given a free-response problem survey and the Science Research Associates Youth Inventory. These instruments yielded problems of immediate concern as well as those long-range aspects youth felt they would need to face and attempt to solve. The adult groups were given a semi-structured problem survey to identify both the immediate and long-range aspects of problems they believed all or most youth face—problems which should become the structure of general education.

As a structure for the adult surveys and as a framework for treating data, the writer formulated a series of basic areas of responsibilities and relationships which characterize adolescent development. The responses of teachers and social scientists supported the validity of these areas; the appearance of many problems in each area further substantiated them. The nine areas, none of which is mutually exclusive, are listed below:

Basic Areas of Responsibilities and Relationships in Adolescent Development

1. Gaining maturity in meeting personal problems
2. Achieving a more independent and responsible status in home and family relationships
3. Developing successful and maturing relationships with other adolescents
4. Developing new and successful relationships with adults
5. Achieving satisfactory and appropriate school experiences
6. Assuming increased participation and responsibility in community activities
7. Developing competent participation and security in economic relationships
8. Gaining understanding in meeting intergroup and intercultural relationships
9. Developing a mature system of values

Analysis of questionnaire data revealed certain common and persistent problems which were grouped into problem areas. A problem area is a broad area of living in which cluster problems common to all or most adolescents. They are appropriate for determining the structure of general education as it has been defined above. The sequence of problem areas and their assignment to grades are part of faculty planning. From each problem area, specific learning units suited to the needs and maturity of a particular class are drawn.

The development of problem areas should be the result of local research. Those listed on the following pages illustrate, however, how this structure is formulated from a problem-area study. The procedures used

in this study are suggested as a valid approach for teachers and adminis-
trators who are undertaking curriculum reorganization in the area of
general education.

SUGGESTED PROBLEM AREAS APPROPRIATE FOR GENERAL EDUCATION IN THE SECONDARY SCHOOL [2]

The common and persistent problems of adolescents cluster in the
problem areas described below.

1. *Self-Understanding.* The focal points of adolescent concerns in this
area are: (a) achieving a sense of responsibility, (b) accepting the obligations and privileges of adulthood, (c) understanding the forces which
mold personality, (d) developing desirable characteristics of maturity,
(e) understanding the relationship of self to peers and adults, (f) developing a wide range of interests, (g) achieving a sense of personal
satisfaction in leisure activities, (h) learning to select worthwhile leisure
interests, (i) learning to make wise decisions, (j) developing personal
value and standards of conduct, (k) achieving self-respect and a sense of
personal worth, (l) gaining a sense of security in meeting new situations.

2. *Healthful Living.* The focal points of adolescent concerns in this
area are: (a) understanding and accepting bodily change, (b) learning to
care for and improve personal appearance, (c) developing appropriate
health and nutritional habits, (d) accepting physical handicaps in self
and others, (e) recognizing the relationships between personal health and
the health of others, (f) understanding the relationship of health to success
in school, employment, and social life, (g) learning to deal with problems
of mental health, (h) accepting a personal share in solving community
health problems, (i) achieving a healthful balance between work and play,
(j) learning to evaluate advertisements pertaining to health and personal
appearance, (k) learning to seek reliable advice in health matters.

3. *Home and Family Living.* The focal points of adolescent concerns
in this area are: (a) recognizing and respecting the rights and privileges
of family members, (b) co-operating in making family decisions, (c)
recognizing the need for family recreation, (d) developing a more mature
understanding of parental standards of conduct, (e) assuming a share in
home responsibilities, (f) adjusting to family's financial resources, (g)
developing a more independent status within the family, (h) respecting
the values of family life, (i) experiencing security in one's family situation, (j) understanding the role of family life in our society, (k) learning
to accept one's family in relation to the families of peers, (l) contributing
actively toward strengthening the family unit, (m) recognizing the responsibilities of marriage and family life, (n) discovering the characteristics of personality which make for a happy marriage.

[2] *Ibid.,* pp. 312–326.

4. *Personal-Social Relations.* The focal points of adolescent concerns in this area are: (a) achieving satisfactory relationships with the opposite sex, (b) gaining understanding of the obligations of marriage, (c) learning to select a marriage partner, (d) choosing friends wisely, (e) understanding the significance of popularity, (f) understanding and respecting adults, (g) maintaining standards in the face of group pressures, (h) recognizing the responsibilities and obligations of friendships, (i) learning the responsibilities of group participation, (j) achieving maturity in meeting interpersonal relationships, (k) maintaining individualism in a group-centered society, (l) understanding and accepting the personal strengths and weaknesses of others, (m) developing socially acceptable behavior, (n) understanding the pattern of relationships between adults and adolescents in our society, (o) meeting intergroup and intercultural situations with tact and tolerance.

5. *Education and School Living.* The focal points of adolescent concerns in this area are: (a) evaluating personal talents and abilities, (b) learning how to study, (c) selecting appropriate subjects, (d) adjusting to interpersonal relations with classmates and teachers, (e) developing a wholesome attitude toward success in school, (f) choosing school activities wisely, (g) recognizing the values of educational attainment, (h) preparing for the financial obligations of education, (i) planning for college, (j) planning for military service, (k) co-operating in community efforts to improve schools, (l) recognizing that education is continuous, (m) understanding the school's obligation to meet individual differences, (n) forming an intelligent opinion of what constitutes good education, (o) recognizing the basic premises separating various educational systems at home and abroad, (p) examining the responsibility of the school to alter its program in response to pressure groups.

6. *Vocational Preparation.* The focal points of adolescent concerns in this area are: (a) learning to evaluate personal talents and abilities, (b) investigating a wide variety of careers, (c) evaluating the advantages and disadvantages of preferred vocations, (d) determining the preparation required for a specific career or vocation, (e) experiencing a feeling of security in a vocational choice, (f) recognizing the responsibilities of employee and employer, (g) recognizing the real satisfactions of employment, (h) planning military service in relation to vocational preparation, (i) recognizing that there are no "soft" jobs, (j) considering the expense required to prepare for a preferred vocation, (k) evaluating parental and social demands for entering a particular vocation.

7. *Living in the Community.* The focal points of adolescent concerns in this area are: (a) finding appropriate teen-age recreation, (b) taking an interested part in community projects, (c) co-operating with adults in civic activities, (d) helping to create a good neighborhood, (e) recogniz-

ing the social forces shaping community life, (f) developing ways of preventing juvenile delinquency, (g) planning to meet the needs of growing communities, (h) understanding the political and financial responsibilities of community life, (i) understanding the obligations of a community to its citizens, (j) developing rapport between adults and adolescents in the community, (k) helping younger children develop their interests (e.g., assisting with Little League projects, etc.), (l) experiencing the satisfactions of being an active participant in the conduct of community life.

8. *Democratic Government.* The focal points of adolescent concerns in this area are: (a) accepting the rights and obligations of a voter, (b) understanding the role of political parties in government, (c) understanding the structure and function of the several levels of government, (d) developing the desire to be well informed about governmental problems, (e) accepting the responsibility to support and at the same time work for the refinement of a democratic way of life, (f) recognizing the expanding role of government in our lives, (g) recognizing the existence of inequalities and injustices in governmental activities, (h) evaluating the propaganda of political parties and pressure groups, (i) discovering the theoretical bases of competing forms of government.

9. *Economic Understanding.* The focal points of adolescent concerns in this area are: (a) finding appropriate ways of earning money now, (b) considering the economic status of a preferred vocation, (c) learning to handle money wisely (e.g., saving, budgeting, and investing money), (d) making wise consumer judgments, (e) learning to live within family economic resources, (f) evaluating the various kinds of advertisements, (g) gaining experience in making economic decisions (e.g., buying and selling, investing, credit buying, evaluating various employment benefits, etc.), (h) accepting one's financial obligations to all levels of government, (i) gaining a sense of the real value of money, (j) understanding the function of supply and demand and the consumer's role in determining price, (k) providing economic security for the future, (l) understanding economic cycles, (m) recognizing and guarding against bad business practices, (n) discovering how labor and management solve their economic problems.

10. *Relationships with Minority Groups.* The focal points of adolescent concerns in this area are: (a) dealing intelligently with problems of integration and segregation, (b) recognizing scientific research about the bases of race and racial characteristics, (c) gaining insight into the origins and functions of prejudices, (d) handling intergroup relationships with tolerance and respect, (e) depending on intelligence rather than force in solving minority problems, (f) discovering the bases for differing beliefs and customs, (g) recognizing the inequalities faced by those of certain races and religions, (h) respecting the contributions of minority groups

to our culture, (i) recognizing that each person has an individual contribution to make toward the solution of tensions in this area.

11. *Intercultural Understanding.* The focal points of adolescent concerns in this area are: (a) recognizing the factors influencing differing cultural patterns, (b) finding ways to gain a personal knowledge of various cultures, (c) analyzing the bases of conflicting ideologies, (d) exploring the ways for settling disputes peacefully, (e) recognizing basic conflicts among nations, (f) finding common ground for building a lasting peace, (g) co-operating in the peaceful exploration of space, (h) utilizing science and technology for the benefit of all men, (i) learning to evaluate propaganda, (j) respecting varying cultural patterns, (k) understanding the beliefs and customs of other lands.

12. *Finding Values by Which to Live.* The focal points of adolescent concerns in this area are: (a) understanding the origins of our beliefs, (b) making wise value decisions, (c) understanding and respecting the beliefs of other people, races, religions, and cultures, (d) recognizing the development of the values of a democratic society, (e) understanding the need for a continuous examination of values, (f) building a consistent and functional pattern of personal values, (g) learning to deal intelligently with value conflicts, (h) understanding the function of values in directing behavior.

2. A PROJECTIVE APPROACH TO PROBLEM IDENTIFICATION

Along with the above procedure, teachers can utilize various techniques of an indirect or projective nature to uncover needs and concerns of young people which might be fruitful sources of general education problems. The story of one teacher's study of student needs furnishes much information concerning this procedure for identifying problems. Let us follow Miss Smith as she works with her general education class.

a. *What techniques did Miss Smith use?* In the course of a couple of months' work with her class, Miss Smith used several procedures to help her gain insight into the nature and characteristics of her students. She was careful to establish first a friendly working relationship between herself and the class so that students would be willing to reveal some of their personal feelings. She was also careful to try to place these techniques in a meaningful framework so that they did not seem like unrelated intrusions among their everyday activities. Three such techniques proved very helpful.

(1) AUTOBIOGRAPHIES. By writing about themselves in an informal, friendly fashion, the eighth graders gave their teacher new insights into their problems and needs.

(2) "THE THREE WISHES" OR "THE WISHING WELL." The desires and wishes of the youngsters were helpful clues to their needs. From an analysis of the wishes of the entire class, Miss Smith detected certain problems common to the entire group.

(3) WHAT ARE YOUR DIFFICULTIES? OR WHAT DO YOU OFTEN THINK ABOUT? After a great deal of rapport had been established with her class, Miss Smith found that the responses to these questions gave invaluable leads to some important areas of study. Other questions that were asked included, "When do you feel out of place, not knowing what to do or how to act?" and "What are you afraid to discuss with parents and friends?"

b. *What did Miss Smith find out?* After a careful study and analysis of all the data she had collected in this fashion, Miss Smith made some generalizations concerning these boys and girls.

(1) *Familial Relations and Economic Background*

(a) Family life was in many instances unstable with many broken homes.

My mother and father are always arguing. I'd like to have a mother and father that don't argue.

I would like to go to Atlantic City to live with my mother.

I would love to be able to live with both parents instead of just my mother.

Fighting between everyone in my household, I seem to get all upset.

At home my parents are thinking of separating, and they both want me. (I don't know which side to take.)

My father always arguing and coming home drunk.

I worry about how my dad is and sometimes where he is.

(b) Several students seemed to be dissatisfied with their present living conditions, they expressed a desire to live some place else or to have a new home. One third of the youngsters expressed a wish for a nice new home.

I wish we had a good home.

I want a new home.

To have a pretty house.

A beautiful home to live in.

I would want a new home for my parents.

That our family could move into a new modern home.

(c) Health was a matter of great concern to these children; they not only had many health deficiencies themselves, but were also worried concerning their parents' health.

I wish that I could be cured of heart trouble because I have it.

I wish that my mother would not be sick and get better.

My wish is for my mother to get better. She is in the hospital; she has had two operations.

Let my sister walk and run soon because she's been in bed five months.

I would first wish for my mother's sight and my father's health.

I should like my mother to be out of the hospital.

(2) *Social Growth and Inclinations*

(a) After-school play took place "on the lot," "in the alley," "out front," "in the woods," "in the street," with only an occasional playground, park, or ball field mentioned.

I wish that my friends and I would have better places to play.

I'd like to have some place to go in spare time.

(b) The children's chief interest in the evening was watching television or listening to the radio.

(c) One of the greatest desires on the part of many students was to travel and see other places. Whether this was just a normal, healthy adolescent desire or whether their opportunities for travel had been limited or nonexistent needed more investigation.

(d) Enough boys and girls expressed a desire to have more friends and be popular to make Miss Smith wonder concerning their social development.

I wish I could make more friends.

I like everyone to be friends with me, and I like to be friends with them.

I would like to be more liked in school.

Why can't I be as popular as the other fellow?

(e) Some of them were beginning to verbalize their interest in the opposite sex.

[I wish for] a nice boy friend who is true, good-looking, etc.

[I wish for] an intelligent girl, not beautiful, but attractive.

For my boy friend and I to get married and live happily ever after when I get older.

I worry about how to act when you go out with a boy, what to talk to a boy about.

(f) Clothes assumed some importance to many of the girls, a natural development, although the following wish on the part of one might lead the teacher to wonder how prevalent was the practice she mentioned.

I get all my sister's old clothes. I wish I could get new clothes of my own.

I have wished for pretty clothes.

Have some nice things and a lot of clothes and my mother have a lot of clothes.

To have nice clothes and plenty of them.

(g) Many of the girls were thinking a great deal about their appearance and personality.

To be pretty and have a good shape.

I would like to be thinner.

I don't exactly worry, but I think about: Is my personality the way I want it to be. Do I get along with the people in my community and class and school the way I want to?

(h) When asked, "When do you feel out of place, not knowing what to do or how to act?," the largest number replied, "Among strangers," again a natural adolescent trait. However, there was other evidence that these youngsters were less mature socially than most of their age.

When I am with a strange group I feel like I'm not wanted so then I don't know how to act. I don't mean that I should get all the attention but I don't think I'd like to get ignored either.

When I am at a party and talk with people I have just gotten introduced with. When I am around my friends I talk freely, but when I am with a new group of people I have trouble getting acquainted.

I feel out of place when I go to parties and don't know anyone.

(i) When asked, "What are you afraid to discuss with parents and friends?" most of those who answered, replied, "Nothing." This might have indicated a healthy, well-balanced relationship between parent and child. A few youngsters indicated that sex matters, problems of growing up, marriage proved difficult to discuss. The fact that a large number of children did not answer the above question might or might not indicate reticence on their part concerning the above subjects.

I'm afraid to discuss my growing up.

I am afraid to discuss the facts of life. I have two men neighbors I can talk to—both are single and around thirty.

[I am afraid to discuss] intimate facts.

[I am afraid to discuss] what makes the body tick.

Well, I like to know about life, the boys and girls if you know what I mean. I hear about it but I want the truth.

c. *What did Miss Smith do about her findings?* The chief question then facing Miss Smith was, How can I translate these findings into meaningful learning experiences for these boys and girls in our classroom? From her own analysis she decided that the following problem areas would be fruitful ones for general education study:

(1) How well do we know ourselves? What kind of person am I?

(2) How can we learn to get along with others?

(3) How can we use our money wisely?

(4) How can we make the best use of our spare time?

(5) How can our homes and our home life be improved?

(6) How can we prepare ourselves to earn an adequate and satisfying living?

(7) What can we do to improve and maintain good health?

She shared her findings and conclusions with the class, and together they considered the possibilities, eventually making choices that seemed especially pertinent to them.

B. Studying the Problem

One of the challenging and stimulating characteristics of general education learning is the variety of approaches to problem study. Each problem or unit lends itself to its own peculiar methods of attack and exploration, and rarely if ever does a class need to study two units in exactly the same way. Though specifics will vary, certain common threads weave through all unit study and provide a continuity of process that makes for effective learning.

Studying the general education problem, then, involves the following threads: organizing for study, working co-operatively, engaging in a variety of learning experiences, studying individually, sharing the findings.

1. ORGANIZING FOR STUDY

Planning ways of studying a unit provides students with valuable experience in critical thinking, the exercise of good judgment, and discriminating decision-making.

One eleventh grade began its planning of the unit, *Problems of Living in the Atomic Age* in the following way:

PHILIP (leader for the day) : I'm going to ask what you want to get out of our study, why did you choose it? I'll start with Evelyn.

EVELYN I'm interested in the everyday uses of atomic energy.

YVETTE Is the unit just on the atomic bomb or on the atomic age? More people will appreciate it if it's about the atomic age.

ANNE I'm interested in the international relations and the relation of each person in the class to atomic power.

PHILIP Yvette, back to what you said; some of the boys want to study scientific details.

YVETTE Well, I think the girls would be more interested in the religious feelings and the effect of atomic energy in that way. What is the out-look for our life?

PHILIP What do you think, Betty?

BETTY I agree with Yvette, not about religion; but I'm not interested in the atom bomb, maybe to hear about it, but I'd rather study about the changes in our living brought about as a result of atomic energy.

JOHNNY What are cities and states doing about civil defense?

PHILIP How about other interests besides these?

The students, having decided upon the broad area of "Problems of Living in the Atomic Age," were attempting to define and delimit the area preparatory to more specific organizational planning. After much exploration that involved serious probing and critical thinking, the class was ready to give a small planning committee the responsibility of formulating their thinking into a specific program of study. This committee met two or three times, sometimes with and sometimes without the teacher.

The following recommendations were the outcome of the deliberations of this committee and were duplicated and given to each member of the class. After careful examination and questioning the students accepted the recommendations without change.

LIVING IN THE ATOMIC AGE

The Planning Committee on the unit, "Living in the Atomic Age," has met and decided on the following recommendations:

1. Each person will select and study *three* of the four following topics:
   A. Understanding Atomic Energy
   B. Peacetime Uses of Atomic Energy
   C. Civil Defense
   D. National and International Problems of the Atomic Age
2. Of the three topics selected by each person *one* will be a *major, two* will be *minors.*
3. The time for the study of the major will be half of the time allotted for the unit; the minors will consume one-fourth of the time each.
4. The people with the same major will compose a panel. The class will ask them questions concerning their topic. The questions will be compiled to make a work sheet to be used by everyone studying that topic either as a major or as a minor.
5. To complete the study of your major topic you will have a choice of a term paper or a project. To complete your study for your two minors you will hand in notes taken on the work sheet.
6. Miss Hasson will plan general class meetings to discuss the different phases of the unit.
7. A committee has been set to *secure* and *preview* movies.

The "work sheet" mentioned in item 4 is included here as an illustration of the breadth of content that the students desired in this unit.

LIVING IN THE ATOMIC AGE

The following work sheets are sketchy and suggestive and are meant to serve merely as guides to your research. We shall devote six weeks to this unit; all work must be completed by Friday, April 4th. All plans for term papers or projects should be presented in written form and discussed with me before you become too deeply involved with them.

Understanding Atomic Energy

I. The Atomic Bomb
   A. How does it work?
   B. What is used in making the bomb?
   C. Where are bomb parts made?
   D. Who are the important people connected with bomb construction?
II. The Hydrogen Bomb
   A. How does it work?
   B. How does it compare with the atomic bomb?
III. Atomic Energy
   A. What is it?
      1. What are atoms? Isotopes?

2. What is atomic fusion and fission?
3. What is radioactivity?
B. Machines connected with atomic development
   1. Cyclotron
   2. Atomic piles
      a. What are they?
      b. What are chain reactions?

Peacetime Uses of Atomic Energy

I. Uses of Atomic Energy in Peacetime
   A. Lighting and heating
   B. Motors
   C. Atomic appliances now in use
   D. Possible appliances to be made and used in the future
   E. Medicine
II. Effects of Atomic Energy Used in Peacetime
   A. What are some of the dangers of atomic energy?
   B. How will atomic energy affect travel?
   C. What changes would atomic energy make on our life?
      1. Social customs
      2. Morals
      3. Dress
      4. Size of cities, etc.
III. Who Is Working on the Development of Atomic Energy for Peacetime?

Civil Defense

I. What are the Possibilities of an A-bomb attack on the U.S.?
   A. What are the vulnerable spots in the U.S.? in our city? in our state?
   B. What are the preparations for warning and defense?
   C. What preparations can and should the schools make?
II. What are the Chief Problems Connected with Civil Defense?
III. What Can and Should We Do as Individuals?
IV. What Are the Chances for Survival?

National and International Problems of Atomic Age

I. How Do the Different Countries of the World Feel about Atomic Energy?
   A. France
   B. Great Britain
   C. Germany
   D. Russia
   E. United States

F. Nationalist China
II. What Are the Views of High Political Figures in the U.S.?
  A. Nominees for President
  B. Truman
  C. Ridgeway
III. What Is the Position of the United Nations?
  A. Can the U.N. control atomic energy?
  B. What countries can make atomic bombs?
  C. How do other countries feel towards the U.S., knowing that we have, and have dropped, the atomic bomb?
  D. What are the chances of another atomic attack on any country? on the U.S.?

An interesting feature of the planning of this class was its provision for a panel of students to hear questions from the class and then formulate a work sheet. A variation on this use of a panel as a means of formulating and organizing questions is the practice used by several teachers of having each table group or proximity grouping in the class formulate questions for the unit. A planning committee then organizes all of the questions and evolves an outline for class consideration.

Another kind of organizational structure was evolved by the same eleventh grade mentioned above when the students began work on "Exploring Vocations." Again a planning committee developed the specifics after total class discussion.

RECOMMENDATIONS FOR UNIT ON VOCATIONS

Our suggestions result from a belief that we should not only explore our own personal interest choice of vocation but should also become somewhat familiar with various vocations, so that we will have an understanding of the "other fellow's" job. We are therefore making the following recommendations:

1. We have considered the following broad vocational categories; we would welcome your suggestions for additions or changes.
  I. The Arts
    A. Music
    B. Dance
    C. Theater
      1. Stage
      2. Screen
    D. Fine Arts
      1. Commercial art
      2. Photography
      3. Ceramics
      4. Interior decoration

      5. Painting and sculpture

      6. Architecture

   E. Writing

   F. Radio and television

      1. Technical aspects

      2. Production

II. Social Administration

   A. Religious work

   B. Child welfare

   C. Social agencies

      1. Case work

      2. Guidance clinics

III. Business and Commerce

   A. Accounting

   B. Secretarial work

   C. Selling

   D. Advertising

   E. Self-employment

   F. Hotel management

IV. The Professions

   A. Law

   B. Medicine

      1. Doctors

      2. Dentists

      3. Nursing

      4. Psychiatry

   C. Education

      1. Nursery school

      2. Elementary

      3. Secondary

   D. The sciences

V. Professional Sports

VI. Journalism

VII. Government Service

   A. Politics

   B. Diplomatic service

   C. Armed services

   D. Civil service

VIII. Engineering

   A. Civil

   B. Chemical

   C. Industrial

IX. Skilled and Unskilled Occupations

2. Each person will choose a career or vocation in which he is most interested and make a detailed personal study. This is to include not only reading and research, but also exploring vocational possibilities in and around the city contacting people who can give advice and suggestions. Your own interest and enthusiasm will be the chief determinants of the quality as well as quantity of your study. The only written requirement will be the attached form which each of you will fill out.

3. We are suggesting that we try to have a series of "Career Conferences," perhaps once a week, centering around each of several of the vocational categories listed above. A small rotating committee will be responsible for planning these conferences which might be two or three days in length. Each conference should include the most effective means possible of familiarizing us with each career—speakers, films, trips, panel discussions, etc., or a combination of these.

4. In addition, we recommend that we explore different colleges and their characteristics and requirements.

5. In order that we may have practical experience with work we include in this unit the opportunity of locating summer jobs. Such a project would give us a chance to learn about such things as how to dress for an interview and for the job, how to be interviewed, how to write letters of application, etc. Class time could be devoted to job-hunting, if we share with each other our experiences, that is, where we went, what happened, etc.

2. WORKING CO-OPERATIVELY

It is evident from much that has already been described that a great deal of general education work revolves around co-operative action. Perhaps the first thing that impresses a visitor in the general education class is the quantity and quality of total class discussion. In fact, along with the more traditional skills, effective working relationships have added another "R" to the classroom lexicon.

These relationships are achieved through a multitude of ways as groups and committees are formed and re-formed, complete their work and disband. The *planning committee* has already been cited as an effective means of moving a class toward its goals. In addition, various other kinds of committees operate in classroom practice.

For example, there is the *buzz group*, which can be a helpful time saver. These sessions are quick, spontaneous, brief meetings for the purpose of bringing forth as many student opinions as possible in the shortest time. Teachers find buzz sessions effective for several reasons. They often release the tension that occasionally prevails in a total class situation. Usually, too, there is less reluctance to express opinions to a few than to many. At least one teacher believes that a large part of the success of buzz sessions derives from a natural inclination to *converse* with a few others; the feeling of conversation is somewhat dissipated in a large group.

The *working committees* probably furnish the real substance of unit study, as students divide into groups for purposes of attacking specific aspects of a problem area. The use of these groups is subject to much variation in practice, but there seem to be two general procedures for the utilization of groups. In some classes each group assumes responsibility for detailed study of one particular aspect of the unit; in others, each group concerns itself with all aspects of the problem, probably differing in the order in which these aspects are studied.

Membership in a group is determined in a variety of ways. In many instances choice is based upon interest in the topic; in other cases choice grows out of social relationships, with friends choosing friends. Occasionally teachers find it helpful to assign students to groups, for a variety of reasons. It may be more productive for certain students to work together; or the boys and girls may be so consistently limiting their selection of friends that a wider acquaintance is desirable.

Learning how to work with others is an integral part of general education practice, and much time and attention are devoted to analyzing and acquiring skills of co-operative action. Usually students are helped to recognize the need for a leader, whether he be called chairman or not, and some kind of recorder, usually referred to as a secretary. In addition, the students discuss the characteristics of a good group meeting. Here is a list drawn up by an unsophisticated seventh-grade group that was inexperienced in co-operative learning.

1. Be courteous
2. Co-operate; use teamwork
3. Everybody participate
4. Listen to others
5. Let one person speak at a time

Sometimes it is helpful to have a "rehearsed" group meeting in front of the class, with analysis and discussion preparatory to class committee work. Since the skills of group work need continuous attention and constitute developmental learning experience, it is sometimes necessary, even if some group work has been used, to stop for such "demonstrations" of effective group techniques.

The whole question of individual participation in class discussions and group sessions is one that concerns both teacher and students. In one class there was such a strong feeling about the responsibility of each member to contribute to the general welfare that the students, while discussing the question of evaluation, indicated that they thought a nonparticipant should not receive a higher mark than a C for general education. What is even more important, however, is that they discussed ways of helping everyone feel at home and free to speak out under all circumstances. It was suggested that a "little brother or sister" approach might do much toward meeting the problem. Then, too, they felt that group leaders should make a greater effort to help members acquire skills in co-operative action.

Because individuals and groups often need several weeks for their research and investigation, attempts must be made to keep the teacher and class informed about their work. These "progress reports" may take several forms. Perhaps a short time each week can be devoted to telling the class of the planning that has been done, the activities in which the students have engaged, the problems they are facing. As questions arise concerning the location of suitable materials or the advisability of a particular field trip, the entire class can offer suggestions. These reports need not be regularly scheduled but can occur when teacher and students want to be brought up to date on everyone's progress or when they need help.

Sometimes progress reports should be made in written form and given to the teacher so that he knows what everyone is doing and where there are problems needing specific guidance from him. Such written reports may come from each group when committee work is under way or from individuals when the problem under study has a great deal of individual work involved.

Because co-operative planning and learning play such a large part in the general education class, gradual induction into the procedures is often considered desirable. For classes unfamiliar with ways of working together it is often desirable to start with a one-to-one relationship, rather than groups of five, six, or seven. The interview between two students as part of orientation is an example of this kind of face-to-face relationship. It has the advantage of giving students an opportunity to work together without having too many personalities involved and without having to make weighty plans or decisions.

At other times it is helpful, when small group work gets under way, to center it around immediate concerns and interests of the students. For example, planning a party offers an excellent opportunity for working groups to operate, with real needs to be met regarding food, decoration, entertainment, and many other things. Another class may find a stimulating project in decorating the classroom to make it a more appealing and attractive place in which to live and work. Both of these activities have an immediate and tangible goal to commend them and will give students valuable experience in working together in areas where they have some interest, understanding, and experience.

Before moving into work groups for attack on the unit of study, it might be well to give students a chance to meet in small groups for the purpose of sharing *opinions* rather than head-on attack upon *factual information.* This approach can be used in connection with student writing, for example. In one class situation, after a story or composition had been written, the question arose concerning the most effective way of sharing the work. Since the reading aloud of all thirty or forty would be a deadening process, the teacher asked the class if they would like to share in small groups and then select one or two for reading aloud to the entire class. In that way each boy and girl had the pleasure and profit of having his work heard or read by several others. Each group decided for itself whether the papers would be read aloud or passed to each member for silent reading. When this technique is used often, with guidance, the youngsters soon learn to vary their selections for class sharing so that a few will not monopolize the choices.

3. ENGAGING IN A VARIETY OF ACTIVITIES

Any general education class in the course of a year will find itself involved in numerous and varied activities, all important learning experiences in the process of achieving their goals. Some of them take place within the confines of the classrooms; others occur in various parts of the school; while many move outside the walls of the schoolhouse into the neighborhood and community setting.

One twelfth-grade teacher reports the following activities:

We believe strongly in making the general education work as practicable as possible. Last year our Family Living Unit was one which the students felt was quite successful. The boys decided they should have a short course in actual homemaking skills as they would involve the masculine side of the family. This involved a great deal of pre-planning with the administration and with one of the home economics instructors. It involved a matter of scheduling. The girls had the same procedure in arranging shop classes during general education time so that they could learn simple skills with electricity, etc., around the home.

In connection with this same unit the class ran a kindergarten for a day in order to observe individual differences. A great deal of planning had to be done, such as arranging with the cafeteria staff for lunch, bus drivers for transportation, parents for permission to bring children, etc. It also meant setting up objectives and then evaluating results.

Many seventh-grade classes, during their orientation to the new school, can be seen "touring" the building, peering into every nook and cranny, locating various parts of the school, meeting teachers, interviewing school staff members. Occasionally a class will visit other schools nearby as their interest broadens to include some of the wider aspects of education. One seventh-grade class gained some valuable understandings through a visit to a nearby school for handicapped children, developing insight into the needs and problems of those less fortunate than themselves. Shortly afterward, these same students visited a neighboring high school to which many of them would go a couple of years hence.

An eleventh grade, involved in a study of comparisons and contrasts among schools in their county, did an extensive piece of traveling.

Altogether ten or twelve schools were visited after letters had been written to arrange dates and explain purposes, parents had been told of the project and had given permission for students to drive cars, and final arrangements had been made by telephone. Some schools requested that only about ten students come; others allowed the whole class. Their visits included public and parochial high schools.

The students looked at and asked about cafeterias, libraries, the curriculum, general facilities, like the gym, auditorium, etc. They collected bulletins and were careful to ask the school if it could be quoted. (One school brought up the problem of smoking: "We don't want you to name us, but we do have a smoking zone.")

Upon their return to their own school the students each did one piece of experience writing. A symposium was held, consisting of a chairman and one representative from each committee. Someone from every department in the school was invited to attend, and recommendations were made for their high school. After the presentation there were questions from the class and guests.

Some classes find interesting ways of relating their work to other aspects of the school life and program. In one school, during a nature unit in the tenth grade, some of the students made sewing cards of flowers to be embroidered and gave them to the kindergarteners, along with some models of birds which a few had constructed. Occasionally general education activities can be shared with other classes, as was the case when a class gave an assembly presentation of their revised version of *The Taming of the Shrew.*

It is not unusual to find a class holding a party or dance as a culminating activity that is really evaluative in nature, as they attempt to put into practice some of the skills and understandings they have acquired in the course of a study of teen-age problems or getting along with one another or understanding themselves. Camping experiences, too, are valuable and interesting projects for some classes, either in direct relation to a specific unit or as an unrelated experience that has meaningful learnings of its own.

4. STUDYING INDIVIDUALLY

Along with much class planning and small group work, there should be a wealth of opportunity for individual study and attention in general education classes. Often the small group planning provides for individual pursuit of specific assignments as the group decides upon the best approach to its particular areas of study. In addition, the planning for many units can include provisions for each student to engage in individual study or to develop projects in line with his own needs, interests, and abilities.

Sometimes the teacher might suggest these individual assignments; at other times the student and teacher together might determine them. The following is an individual assignment schedule given by one teacher to an eleventh-grade general education class that was studying the influence of early civilizations on our world today. Although the teacher decided the specific nature of these assignments, there was total class discussion of them, and, as is evident, ample opportunity for choice within a wide range.

GENERAL EDUCATION ASSIGNMENT SCHEDULE

1. *Friday, November 30*

   Unit paper—"The Contributions Made to Civilization" by the _____
   Select any of the following:

   Prehistoric man
   Egyptians
   Peoples of the Fertile Crescent
   Greeks
   Romans

   This should be more than just a list. Rather, it should be a presentation of important contributions with some description of each. It is highly possible that you might wish to illustrate it.

2. *Monday, December 10*

   Two book reports—Write a brief account of two books taken from the unit reading lists. Tell something about the story, characters, style, etc., but stress especially your personal reaction.

3. *Wednesday, December 19*

Project report—This project will relate to our general education unit and will involve some kind of art, music, science, literary activity. We shall discuss it in more detail later.

The *Vocations* unit referred to above was developed as much on an individual basis as on a group study approach. As each student pursued his individual study of a career of interest to him, he kept the following Personal Interest Study record.

PERSONAL INTEREST STUDY

Name _____ Choice of Vocation _____

What are your reasons for being interested in this vocation?
How much and what kind of education preparation is needed?
How much, if any, experience is required?
What kind of personal characteristics seem desirable for this kind of job?
What are the possibilities for advancement?
In what parts of the country or world are job possibilities in this field most available?
What is the salary potential?
What activities did you engage in as you studied this vocation? (Trips, interviews, reading, etc.) Give a detailed account of them.

As the students pursued their study of specific careers in which they were interested, interviews with appropriate persons became a helpful practice. Arrangements for such interviews were made by the individual student, and each planned for the visit by formulating questions to be asked of the expert. Usually such firsthand contacts brought new insights into potential professional choices and clarified the nature of the work so that students could tell more definitely if this was the job for them.

Such was the case with Joan, who was considering becoming a veterinarian. The following firsthand report of her interview with a local veterinarian is interesting.

MY INTERVIEW WITH DR. WYNN

1. How much and what kind of educational preparation is needed?

The education for a veterinary doctor is much the same as that for an M.D. It is very difficult for men, let alone women, to get into veterinary medicine at State. The country is in need of veterinarians who will doctor food-producing animals rather than cats and dogs, etc. Usually men going into veterinary medicine have a degree in arts or a master's degree first or have worked in agriculture. Even then some people are not sure of getting into the college. The education takes at last six years and usually more. At State there are 300 applicants each year. Out of those only 60 applicants are admitted.

2. How much, if any, experience is required?

No experience is required, but usually people take one or two years of apprenticeship.

3. Do you have to serve an internship?

No.

4. In what part of the country or world are job possibilities in this field most available?

In any large cities or well-populated vicinity the practice of this medicine is very lucrative.

5. What kind of training ought you have to run a kennel to board dogs or to breed them?

No training is required but you would have to take a course in genetics and do a lot of reading and studying yourself if you wanted to have a successful kennel. Among other qualifications you would have to learn about infectious diseases. You would, perhaps, have to see that the sick animals were doctored by a veterinarian. However, if anything happened to an animal you could not be held responsible because you are not required to have a license and are not stated as being qualified for being a vet.

6. Do you need a license to board or breed dogs?

As I said above, no license is required but you must watch the zoning laws and the place you locate your kennels if it is to be a thriving business.

7. Once you are settled in a place of your own, how does your kennel become known to the public as an excellent one?

You are known by your reputation. Perhaps some of the veterinarians in the city would recommend you to their customers when they asked for a good place to board their dog while on vacation and you in turn would give them your business if a dog or cat became ill.

8. Do you have a difficult time getting assistants? What training do you require that they have?

Dr. Wynn has two to four assistants and has no difficulty getting them. There are no requirements for the assistants except being interested in their work and working hard. Some of the assistants are students at the university. His receptionist also has had no special training except having had enough experience in other fields to be able to cope with the rush of people they have all the time and to be able to handle calls efficiently.

9. Is veterinary medicine a good vocation for a girl?

It definitely is not a good vocation. It's almost impossible for a girl to get into.

I asked Dr. Wynn how it happened he chose this vocation. "I like animals," he said.

The job of veterinarian is a hard one. Just like a doctor you are expected to answer calls at any time and any place. As I observed Dr. Wynn, he had to be able to do many things at one time and not get nervous or upset. I am quite sure I could not do that, nor would I want to do it. However, as a hobby I would enjoy owning a small kennel and breeding dogs.

5. SHARING THE FINDINGS

Sharing occurs at two major points in student study; first, within the group, when group work has been in effect; and second, with the total class. As a committee of students engages in study and research on its particular aspect of the problem area, there should be continuous reporting to one another about the findings. Sometimes plans need to be modified as the boys and girls discover that their original ideas are not producing results or there is a shortage of materials and resources in a particular area.

When it is time to report to the class the results of several weeks' study, plans must be made for the most effective means of presenting material in terms of purposes and goals. These reports can take many forms and involve a great deal of learning in their preparation and presentation. Often reporting can be done in drama form, either with a prepared script or in more spontaneous fashion, after ideas have been carefully considered and a general plan agreed upon. It is not unusual to find student committees adapting favorite radio and television formats to their own purposes. A panel-discussion style is a frequent choice, and students become adept at the art of conversing in an easy manner, yet convincingly, with the ring of truth and accuracy in their expression. The tape recorder is a very helpful instrument when boys and girls want to present material in ways that would be a little difficult under ordinary classroom circumstances. Sometimes a recording of an interview with a resource person can bring to the entire class the benefit of one student's visit or that of a committee. Often boys and girls can duplicate materials to be distributed to the class, as one means of reporting.

Many times the sharing becomes more extensive as other classes and occasionally an entire school are included. Assembly programs often develop as an outgrowth of problem study and offer a class an opportunity to present to their schoolmates the interesting and informative ideas they have been learning over the weeks. In some schools a public-address system is used for this kind of sharing when the presentation lends itself to emphasis on hearing. In other instances the written results of problem study are placed in the school library for everyone's use. For example, after a study of orientation to their new junior high school, a class of seventh graders presented to the library a large and attractive book they had prepared as a guide to the incoming students.

Whatever the means used, emphasis should always be upon helping others understand as effectively as possible what the students have learned as they have engaged in specific study over a period of time. In this sense, sharing their findings becomes a teaching process in itself as well as a continuation of the committees' own learning. For many skills are involved in preparing to communicate to others what individual students or committees have been studying. Skill in organizing material is necessary along with ability to speak and write accurately and well. Learning, then, is truly a continuous process as a class works together.

C. A Problem-Solving Approach—A Case Study

A detailed account of the work of two senior general education classes as they pursued some problems of interest and concern to them will illustrate the total process involved in problem study. The following description was written by the teacher of these classes.

I have two distinct groups. The one is mainly an academic section. Right at the first of the year their attention focused about getting ready for college or other further education. For this reason, they decided to make a study of problems relating to the field of education. They felt that this study would be a good background for other units such as making a living, family living, the effect of science on living, etc. Since there are a number of vocational students combined with the academic students in general education, the class set up the outline of the unit to cover the needs of all. This necessitated a beginning group activity of determining what an education is. In forming our conclusions here the class had to launch on a broad reading and discussion activity. We had numerous debates and panels on various questions which arose.

From conclusions drawn from our reading and discussion we saw that it was best to divide into committees to work on specific questions which had arisen—adult education, the effect of radio and television, the cost of educating a child, the educational status of the United States, the educational system of the United States as compared to that in other countries, and how to prepare for college, etc. Each committee shared its finding with the rest of the class. One committee was concerned about withdrawals and went to the administration to see about making a study of the holding power of the school. They were granted permission to make a survey which the school administration had been contemplating making itself. The group worked with the vice-principal and the guidance counselor in forming a questionnaire. The school bore the expense involved in mailing letters to withdrawals and in sending follow-up cards. I would like to list a few of the learning skills which this committee acquired.

1. Learning the importance of knowing what you want to do (exactly) before asking permission to do it.
2. Making contacts with adults in the best manner.
3. Recognizing that what is being undertaken is important and must be done well.
4. Learning the way to draw up questionnaires and the importance of the wording of questions.
5. Learning to compile statistics and to interpret them.
6. Understanding the value of acting upon the results obtained.
7. Learning such skills as interviewing, letter writing, grammatical construction, outlining, expressing ideas in written form, etc.
8. Knowing the satisfaction that comes from contributing something worthwhile to the school and the community.

Here are the recommendations made by this committee after an analysis of the questionnaires which were returned.

Recommendations

According to the questionnaire there is a tendency for interest in school to decrease in the ninth grade. This lack of interest has led to an increase of withdrawals in tenth and eleventh grades. Since the majority of the withdrawals are from the General Course, with the Vocational Course a close second, one might assume that the world of work is their main interest. Many of these students do not feel they need any further education for the type of work which they are interested in. This might indicate that these students withdrew as soon as they were sixteen. The questionnaire definitely shows that a large number of students have withdrawn to go to work.

Over half of the students who answered the questionnaire stated that they withdrew because of dislike of school subjects and dislike of teachers. This might point out a lack of interest in school in general.

The committee would like to recommend a larger activity program.

The statement was made in a Vocational class this year that there is not enough variety in classes. For example, many of them this year have one study hall every day. Many of them have chores after school that prevent them from taking part in school activities, but we feel that the program should be set up to allow more participation at the present. Most of the participation comes from the Academic group. This creates a feeling of antagonism between the Academic and other sections. We suggest that a broader program of Physical Education, assembly programs, and social activities be provided.

The classrooms should have a pleasant, friendly, interesting atmosphere. Perhaps if students were divided into sections, not by courses, but heterogeneously, specially in General Education, more interest would be developed in school. This would prevent the same sections being together each year and break down barriers between groups. There has been in the past a feeling of dissension over the fact that some sections are made up of boys while others are almost all girls. We believe that if the boys and girls would be more evenly divided, there would be a better atmosphere in the classrooms.

As students we would like to see more actual doing things in the classroom. This definitely should be started in junior high and continued through senior high. We feel that this should definitely be true in Science classes where there could be an expanded program of field trips, experiments, and the like. Math classes should be made more practical for everyday living. These same things should apply to General Education and all the rest of the subjects. Visual aids should be used to the best advantage in promoting interest in all classes.

The primary need of high school students is good guidance, an area in which our school is doing good work. However, emphasis should still be placed on the fact that every member of the school staff should be vitally interested in his or her students. The understanding of the students' personal problems can sometimes keep them in school.

My other senior group is a section which is taking the General Course. For a number of years they have been antischool and have given difficulty. The I.Q. of the class is average, ranging from quite low to quite high. They have been nonparticipators and yet extremely jealous of those who participate in activities. A few of them will continue a formal education but most of them will go to work. Therefore at the first of the school year they wanted to find out what jobs they were best suited for and the like. They just didn't know what they wanted to do after school was out. This is an agricultural and resort area with few work opportunities for the around one hundred boys and girls who graduate each year.

We read, discussed, and had speakers in on such questions as "How to Choose a Job," "Interest and Ability," etc. We used visual aids quite extensively. Then each student decided to explore a specific area in which he thought he had interest and ability. They did this in the form of a research paper, complete with footnotes, bibliography, etc. It was surprising how well they did. There was quite a bit of pride in those papers! As a consequence of this study we worked ourselves into a unit of study which they entitled "Live and Learn." This was a study of the progress man has made in the field of work, especially in science and industry. This involved a great amount of committee work in such areas as transportation, inventions, atomic energy (peacetime and wartime uses), advances in medicine, etc. As an example of a project, one committee working on a study of the advances in radio and television became interested in the effects of T.V. on school life and family living. They found some interesting facts from a survey they made. They, in turn, presented their findings to the school and community through the school paper. We drew the committee work together in this whole unit by arranging our tables and chairs in conference style and presenting our findings in reporting and discussing.

In the meantime some of the pride in research papers was forgotten, and in talking in this round-table way we found that the number one question still was "What shall I do when I graduate?" They began to realize that they had little or no commercial training, no academic training; in fact, it dawned on them that they had been wasting a lot of time. Somebody said, "I wish I could try out a job to see if that's what I wanted." I held my breath. These students weren't ones you would particularly want to see representing the school in public relations—their attitude was poor! But the remark made an impression. The ball rolled fast and gained momentum. They played around with the idea for a number of sessions. Then the question came point blank, "Can't we actually observe and work on a job somewhere for a few weeks?" I realized that here was a big learning experience for them in many ways. At the same time these students were wishing their math classes were more practical, as was their math teacher. So the ball got rolling there.

The math teacher and I decided to work together on the idea. I had the class for the fourth and fifth period in general education, and he had all the girls of the class in math the sixth period and the boys the first period. The boys had physical education the sixth period. In these math classes they had been working in committees to see how they could find out what particular math they would need on the job in which they were interested. In general education we began to explore the possibilities of a work project. They learned that it was necessary to have the thing carefully organized if it was to gain the approval of the administration. They were wholeheartedly in favor of doing this.

When the procedure was determined and approved by both the math teacher and me, a committee went to the principal and presented the idea. I believe it was one of the first times that members of the group had gone before the administration with a constructive idea! They realized this when their motives and objectives and intentions were thoroughly examined and questioned. This was an eye-opener. And they began to wonder if they were being looked down upon by other senior sections because of their behavior, and they began to wonder if they were justified in calling the other seniors snobbish. But the administration approved their plan and praised their organization of the work. They had drawn up a questionnaire for themselves and one for the employer. They had mimeographed their objectives and procedures. They then appointed a contact committee to contact the employers. This work scared them a little and we did some practice interviews in class. Because this was a new experience for them we split the committee into groups. The math teacher went with one group and I went with the other. After the first interview or two they gained confidence and wanted us along merely as a stamp of approval. We had 100 per cent cooperation from all contacts. Then those going on jobs began to be a little perturbed. So it was necessary for the class to draw up some suggestions. These were discussed. Neither the math teacher nor I (nor the principal) let them forget the importance of their success not only for themselves but for the public.

Jobs started two weeks ago and ended Friday for most (from 12:00 to 3:00). But the Forestry Department and the lumber company want their boys back for more learning experiences! And several students said, "That's the job for me," and got themselves jobs and work on Saturday and promise of work this summer. I'm anxious to have the whole group back together now. We'll just talk tomorrow about the things they learned and what they would suggest if other students want to do it in another year. And, believe me, room 120 is the center of attention. One boy came in the other morning and said, "Boy, are those other seniors jealous of us." I said, "Why?" "Because we got to do things." I asked him why we got to do them.

And that's been our follow-up and will continue to be. They are getting recognition because they did something worthwhile, because they saw an opportunity, planned, and carried it through. They are proud of what they've done and they know we are proud of what they've learned. And in the next few weeks, as the employers' blanks come in (the students furnished self-addressed and stamped return envelopes), both the math teacher and I will have new impetus for their study of math and basic English grammar. And their confidence in themselves has grown. And there is a committee of nine (who already had work experience and are sure of what they are going to do after school closes) who are ready with a new project on a study of work opportunities in the community and why almost all graduates leave the county to live and work. They have already made a survey of senior high school students with some pertinent results to whet the interest of the class and with plans and procedures for a public survey, a businessman's survey, a study of the work last year's graduates are engaged in, and plans to work out some suggestions as to possible industries and work opportunities which could benefit the county. They anticipate a session with the Chamber of Commerce as a spring activity. So we've got a spring's work laid out.

• In such experiences as these is a problem-centered general education class engaged—experiences that involve the students actively in their own learning. And there is scarcely any aspect of the learning process that students cannot help plan. As has been seen, they often initiate a particular problem or topic for study and set their own goals; together with the teacher they do careful planning of ways and means to achieve these goals, ways that involve them in individual study, small group work, total class sessions, as the case may be. Finally of course, they participate in the important task of assessing their progress and growth, utilizing various means like those discussed in Chapter Eight.

6

Meeting the Challenge of Individual Differences

An obviously important task of the general education teacher is to enhance and develop individual potential, at the same time promoting understanding and appreciation for those common elements in our life and culture deemed essential for all people. The wide range of differences existing among members of any group poses a constant challenge to the thoughtful teacher; while the vast knowledge we have of such differences and of the teaching-learning process provides helpful resources for coping with them.

However, recognition of differences among our students is of little value unless we know how to deal with them and are willing to utilize whatever techniques and procedures seem best. It should be readily evident to the most casual observer that a stereotyped assign-recite-test procedure is woefully inappropriate to meeting the needs of differing individuals, depending as it does so frequently upon the students' reading the same material, teacher-led "discussion" in class the next day, use of a common textbook, and routine testing of limited knowledge. Such an approach to teaching is a travesty upon all we know about learning, perception, psychology, communication, materials, and the like. In addition, it results in such a narrow grasp of a limited amount of information that one wonders at the wisdom eventually displayed by students who have emerged from such a system of schooling.

Certainly, the general education class has no place for such stereotyped approaches, such narrowness of focus, such enforcement of conformity. The general education teacher has many advantages in his struggle to meet the challenge of individual differences. He has time at his disposal; he has a content that resists narrow boundaries of subject-matter divisions; he has a goal that necessitates the use of democratic practices and problem-solving procedures.

Broadly speaking, the general education teacher has two chief means at his command whereby he can focus attention on individual differences. He needs to be constantly on the alert to use teaching procedures that recognize and respect the differences that exist among his students. And he must use his responsibility for guidance and counseling to help him develop each individual to the highest potential. Let us look at some specific ways in which the teacher can use these means effectively.

A. Through Teaching Procedures

The very nature of the work in a general education class provides many opportunities to adapt teaching procedures to individual differences. The focus on a unit of study through a problem-solving approach permits students to engage in learning experiences appropriate to their ability level, skill performance, and interest area. The need to work with others in planning and pooling and reporting brings out the best and the unique in each student. Research activities permit a wide latitude in individual pursuit of knowledge through varied materials and resources.

In fact, the focus in the general education class on varied learning experiences—some individual, some small group, some total class— is an important asset in dealing with individual differences. Through individual work a student can devote time to needed skill development—in reading and writing, for example. Through occasional individual reporting, students can be helped with learning the ways of effective oral communication. Through individualized reading and writing programs each student can be helped toward greater literary appreciation and excellence in creative writing.

In small group work, students have many opportunities to make individual contributions of merit to group planning and discussion. Also, they can be helped to overcome weaknesses, such as tendencies toward monopolizing discussion or undue reserve or argumentativeness. Because students are involved in such varied learning situations, the teacher has ample opportunity to see them as individuals, to note their strengths and weaknesses, to guide and modify and direct them toward maturity.

Because a general education class is committed to a process that requires student search for knowledge, a wealth of materials and resources must be at the disposal of students. Greater attention will be given in the next chapter to the endless variety of such sources for knowledge. At this point, though, it would be well to mention the relation between the use of materials and the recognition of individual differences.

With youngsters of any given age, reading at such different levels, printed materials must be provided that will make it possible for slower learners to gain understandings and information from the printed page while retaining their interest level of maturity, and for more rapid learners to be challenged by the printed word to provocative thinking and thoughtful probing. It goes without saying that one set of books cannot achieve this kind of success. Rather, a great variety of books of differing reading levels and maturity levels must be provided, along with pamphlets, magazines, leaflets, and the like.

Care must be taken, also, to provide other means for learning, since the printed word is not the sole source of knowledge. Pictures, maps, models, charts, graphs, records, films, tapes—all have a place in the classroom and should be used by the students in their pursuit of ideas. The youngster who has difficulty reading can learn much from pictures and records while he is endeavoring to improve his reading skills. For too long have we relied almost exclusively on the printed page. Recognition of individual differences may, at long last, be forcing us to give due credit to the contribution that other instructional materials can make to effective learning.

B. Through Guiding and Counseling

It should be evident from preceding accounts of a multitude of activities that teaching in a general education class involves guiding and counseling young people in all phases of their growth and development. And it is through such guidance that much can be done by the teacher to meet the challenge of individual differences observable in his classroom. A teacher cannot do his best job, however, unless he devotes much time and thought to genuine study of his own—study of young people and their needs.

1. STUDYING YOUNG PEOPLE AND THEIR NEEDS

Once the students are in the classroom there are many ways in which teachers endeavor to discover as much as possible about their individual and group needs, problems, concerns, strengths, and weaknesses. Through on-going class activities, through projective techniques, through tests, questionnaires, and inventories, through conferences and interviews with students and parents, the teacher day by day adds to his fund of knowledge about the adolescents with whom he is working.

His concern is with all aspects of their development—educational, emotional, social, and physical.

In some schools it is customary for general education teachers to have conferences with the nurse at the beginning of each year. Such discussions help the teacher to become familiar with and keep up to date with the physical well-being of their students. The following notes were taken by an eleventh-grade teacher.

Elizabeth—eye problem, almost no vision in left eye, glasses when she reads
Henry—rheumatic heart
Thomas—broken home; mother feels he has eye trouble
Mildred—myopia, mild eye problem, glasses most of time
Sue—severe eye problem, myopia, glasses at all times; epilepsy
Juanita—myopia, glasses at all times
Dick—myopia, glasses for close work; extremely tense
Lillian—athlete's foot; some impertinence
Jim—myopia, glasses at all times; ill from psychological reasons
Mary—myopia, muscular imbalance; emotional adjustment
Harry—mild myopia, glasses at all times; leg problem, bones at joint tend to separate
Sally—mild eye problem; doesn't see well from a distance; parents told but have done nothing about it
Francis—almost hypochondriac
Larry—slight hearing loss

Information such as this proved of invaluable help to the teacher as she worked with these boys and girls. It is interesting to note, too, that the nurse was aware of other characteristics of these young people besides the physical. Her references to a broken home, impertinence, tenseness indicate a concern with the total development of the students.

Studying young people extends beyond the four walls of the school building, for it is evident that the out-of-school life of boys and girls has much to do with their success in school. For wise and effective guidance teachers need to know as much about the outside activities and interests of their students as possible. For this reason the students in one tenth-grade class were asked to complete the following questionnaire.

EXTRACURRICULAR ACTIVITIES AND RESPONSIBILITIES

NAME	GRADE	DATE

Every student in the upper school has made out a schedule of his class appointments from which his counselors can get a rough idea of the amount of homework which he will be expected to do. However, there are a great many other demands on the student's time which the schedule does not show, and it is in an attempt to get the whole picture that we are asking you to fill out this blank. Of course, the pattern will change from time to time, and it would be very difficult for you to try to keep this up to date, but it will help us if you will give us the picture as of this time.

1. *School activities which take a substantial amount of time beyond the school day, or within the school day, but beyond the regularly scheduled periods.*

Athletics (name the sport)   Days of practice

Estimate of time in hours per week

Offices and responsibilities   Estimate of time
                                                        in hours per week

2. *Lessons outside of school and practicing or preparing for them.*

| Music (mention kind) | Number of lessons per week | Amount of practice time in hours per week |

| Dancing (ballet, social, modern) | Number of lessons per week |

Amount of practice time in hours per week

| Other lessons (name them) | Number of lessons per week | Amount of preparation in hours per week |

3. *Clubs and activities not connected with school, such as church groups, scouts, orchestras in which you play, etc.*

| Name of group | Nature of your participation (organizer, officer, member) | Approximate time in hours per week |

4. *Work.* If you work regularly or frequently at some job, whether paid or not, please give the information requested below. Do not include hobbies here, no matter how hard you work on them.

Regular work   Kind of job   Hours per week ( ) For pay
                                               ( ) Volunteer

Irregular work   Kind of job   Estimate of the average hours
                                 per week, or the minimum and
                                 maximum

---

5. Other activities which consume fairly large amounts of time. These might include home responsibilities for some people, hobbies for others, trips back and forth to school for those who live far away, etc.

Activity   Approximate amount of time spent
(describe it)   per week

---

6. Do you have a regular time for reading the newspaper?   ( ) Yes
( ) No
If so, when and for how long?
Do you have a regular time for listening to the radio or watching television? ( ) Yes ( ) No
Do you read or study with the radio turned on?   ( ) Yes   ( ) No
Do you have a regular time for study and reading?
( ) Yes   ( ) No
Where do you study at home?

From these replies the teachers gained deep insight into the total load carried by their students. At the same time they discovered the specific interests that consumed part of their time and their habits with regard to study, reading, radio, and television.

Wherever possible, teachers should try to understand the status of students in relation to their fellows. Sometimes it is not enough to operate on the basis of teachers' perceptions only; efforts can also be made to discover what young people think of one another. While such attitudes are occasionally self-evident, in some instances they are difficult to detect. As a means of obtaining a clear picture of status relationships in an eleventh grade, one teacher used the following opinionaire, asking for an anonymous reaction with just an indication as to whether a boy or girl was responding.

Male ( )   Female ( )   (*Please check*)

Students frequently have more insight into the characteristics of their fellow students than do faculty members. Therefore, we are inquiring as to who in your opinion are the outstanding people in your class in the characteristics listed below. Name as many people under each heading as you wish to name. However, take care not to list someone who is not outstanding in your opinion; include boys and girls.

(1) Sense of humor rather than humorlessness.

(2) Conspicuous leadership rather than almost always being a co-operative or perhaps rebellious follower.

(3) People I would like to have with me on a committee which intends to get things done for a dance rather than to waste time and interfere with progress.

(4) People I would like to have with me on a committee which intends to get a community activity underway and keep it moving rather than let it stall.

(5) People who are socially conscious, who try to give the underdog a break in class or out; who help the weaker to defend their rights rather than to lord it over the less able or seem indifferent to social problems which do not directly affect themselves.

(6) People who have a broad range of friends rather than a select few.

(7) People who throw ideas into many kinds of discussions but aren't windbags, talking to glorify themselves.

(8) Good thinkers rather than loose generalizers or illogical people.

(9) People who would definitely help the crowd have a good time at a party, dance, group meeting, rather than be a wet blanket or simply another one of the bunch.

(10) Good team player rather than would-be star performer.

(11) Friendly and helpful rather than disagreeable and self-centered.

(12) Democratic with others rather than snobbish.

(13) People who, on the whole, are the kind of people I like best and would prefer to be with.

The names mentioned on these opinionaires reflected in many instances the impressions the teacher had already received. In some cases, however, some helpful clues appeared regarding the esteem or lack of esteem for certain individuals. This kind of information provided another avenue for effective guidance.

Two other approaches to studying adolescents are the individual case study and the class profile. Gathering data, keeping anecdotal records, assembling all available information about a student, is not a new idea. Nor is it effective only in the case of so-called problem youngsters. Rather, it has been found that the insights gained through the study of any one boy or girl prove very helpful to teachers as they examine their working relationships with all their students. Also, the more intensively a teacher studies one student, the more readily he will grasp understandings about others, being able to draw upon the fund of knowledge already accumulated.

The following is a series of excerpts from notations made by a teacher about a student in an eleventh grade in a Southern city.

Dave W.—Eleventh Grade
Florida High School
Cumulative Guidance Record

White, Male
Place of Birth—New York, N.Y.
Date—1939   *Mo.* 2   *Day* 2
Economic Status—Good
Lives with—both parents
Only Child

Father—Publisher
Mother—Housewife
Health of both—Good

Grades in 9th and 10th grades
9th—5 B's, 1 C
10th—4 A's, 1 B (Phys. Ed.)

Extra Activities—Grade 10
Spanish Club
Letter Club
Dramatic Club
Swimming Team (Varsity)

Tests
Grade 10
Aptitude Test—Language   —92 percentile
                Quantitative (math)—80
                Total   —92
Grade 11
Intelligence Test—I.Q.—108
Diagnostic Reading Test
Reads 261 words per minute
High School percentile—90–99
National Norms for Southern Schools—80–89

Special Interests and Hobbies—Swim, read, speech, jobs.

Counselor's Comments in Record—Grade 10
"Self-confident, easy-going, can be overbearing, talks excessively but just a

'talker'—good swimmer—individualistic . . . great breadth of knowledge; mature humor . . . lives with parents; Spanish club and letterman; loafed last summer; reads a lot."

Teacher's Reactions

Dave is 16 years old and in the upper 50 percent of the junior class. Most of his fellow classmates are 16. Physical Education seems to be his most difficult subject as evidenced by his grades. He appears to be a good swimmer as it appears on his interest list and he is a member of the swimming team. In addition to varsity swimming he is a member of Spanish club, dramatics club and the Letter Club. Although this does not appear on his cumulative record, he is business editor of the school newspaper. Thus he appears to have a variety of interests.

His economic status is good and his parents are well educated and well traveled. Dave, himself, has traveled a good deal as will be indicated later in this study.

Dave is somewhat of an extrovert as indicated by the counselor's comments and his participation in speech and drama. He is ranked high in personal and social assets.

Glimpses from His Personal Folder

What I Expect to Get out of School

"What does anyone expect to get out of school? An education. But just what is an education? To me an education is more than just readin', 'ritin' and 'rithmetic.

"To me an education is knowing how to meet and get along with people.

"Well, that's the kind of education that I want but how do I intend to get it? Well, I could stay home and study all the time, or I could stay out at shows and parties all the time, but neither of these fulfill what I expect an education to be, one leaves out the other, so I will try to divide them equally—fun and work."

Habits and Interests

Attends church regularly—Catholic . . . likes to read and watch TV . . . attends three movies a week . . . collects semiprecious stones . . . enjoys soccer and swimming . . . has a job on Saturday stamping envelopes.

Kuder Preference Form C

1. Literary
2. Persuasive
3. Artistic
4. Musical

5. Clerical
6. Social Science
7. Outdoor
8. Computational
9. Mechanical
10. Scientific

Philosophy of Life

Dave doesn't believe in making below a B. So, he is "going to have fun and still make A's and B's." The church is very important to life. He doesn't believe that one religion is better than any other religion. "Anyone who follows the Ten Commandments is O.K. in my book, Jew, Moslem, Catholic." He doesn't believe in the "principle of segregation." "What you are, you are primarily because you make yourself that way. . . . You're generous and kind because you like people with the same qualities, not because your mother read Shakespeare. . . . Environment may make a person more learned but I don't think it can change you on the inside." Enjoys dancing . . . thinks teen-agers shouldn't drink but sees nothing wrong with adult social drinking . . . as for smoking, thinks it's silly to draw dirty tobacco smoke into lungs. . . . Believes that one should not take the Lord's name in vain . . . hell or damn is O.K. but worse than that "not my speed" . . . sleeps and eats well . . . likes classical music, dislikes jazz . . . doesn't like modern art; does like Grandma Moses . . . wants to get on student council, edit annual in senior year . . . in college wants to major in drama; has no great desire to be an actor (not dedicated) but likes what acting offers . . . "I believe in taking what you want, not just what life offers you; I believe in having fun."

Autobiography

He spent the winter of 1944 in Florida. At that time Dave was too young for school. He learned to swim. ". . . most important thing in my life." In his second winter in Florida, he entered school. ". . . wasn't very smart." One year he went to camp . . . "I liked camp O.K. because I had my own way and drove my counselors nuts." His mother went to Europe that summer. "Dad worked to pay for the luxuries." In the fall of 1949 he won his first swimming medal. One of the happiest winters he spent was in Mexico with his mother. In 1950 he won a medal and a trophy for swimming. He swam on the junior high team. ". . . always had a great love for gems." Dave spent one summer in New York. In the spring of 1954 Dave moved to present city . . . "In this book of my short life I have tried to tell something about myself and my past. I have often mentioned swimming and why not? I am a lousy athlete and it is all I can do to make a C in gym, so I am proud that at swimming I am better (just slightly) than the average. I hope that no one will think proud means conceited."

Teacher's Reactions

Dave's mature humor and academic ability are evidenced in his style of writing. Obviously, he had advantages of travel, swimming lessons, working with the theater, dancing lessons, and has been exposed to fine music and art. I think that this type of background contributes to his present maturity. Dave is an individualist. He believes in getting what he wants. I believe that he could try to use people to a certain extent to obtain his goals without trying to hurt them. His writing reflects honesty. He states his opinions in no uncertain terms. He works at swimming because he is good at it. He worked with his dramatic interest last fall when he appeared with the County Players in *Life With Father.*

I would say that he is quite fair-minded but he doesn't hesitate to go as far as he can go to gain some end. He mentions his interests, work, and travel, but I find a lack of mention of friends his own age. I assume that he did not have too much opportunity to make or play with friends his own age.

Conference With the Boys' Counselor

"In the ninth grade Dave was the best all around swimmer. He is not a good team worker as he is too individualistic. He is interested in himself before others. He is not greedy but will help others if it will help or not harm himself. . . . He admits that he likes to hear himself talk. Dave wants to be a leader very much. But he goes about it in the wrong way. He is dictatorial. He likes to 'lord it over people.' He really thinks that this is the way of leadership. He can also be too sarcastic. He is not accepted as a leader by his classmates . . . Dave wants to excel. He will try things he knows he will excel in—not things he won't. . . . If he finds that he is not going to win a race, he gives up. He won't strive. Because of this he has taken fourth place many times when he could have taken second place.

"He is a ham actor but has nerve and bravado. He admits this. He doesn't want scholarships for financial reasons but would like the prestige of being awarded an academic scholarship. His parents evidently get along fine. His father is away often. He lives with his mother and aunt. . . . His father is an individualist, critical, and extremely outspoken. He has held a variety of jobs in journalism or publicity field. He has lived and worked in many places. When he can't get along with policies of his job, he picks up and gets another job. He is good in his field. The boy is very much like his father in personality respects. . . . At the present time the father is working in Chicago. The mother and aunt stayed here so he can finish school here.

"He is a good son but disagrees with his parents at times—he is quite adult in his arguments. Very seldom is he childish. . . . The family has a good financial status. Stocks and bonds plus a small inheritance make this possible. At the present time they are living in an apartment. . . . He is extremely unco-ordinated at all sports except swimming. A good instructor got him started very young. He likes swimming because he excels in it. . . . One summer here he spent practically without any young companions. He read, swam, listened to the news, etc. He enjoyed this."

Teacher's Observations and Anecdotal Record

1. He told me personally that he did not want an athletic scholarship as his dad could send him to school and he wouldn't want to take it away from someone who needed it.

2. One afternoon after school, he called me over to his car.

"Miss W., I want you to meet my mother." She was sitting in the automobile. She was a small, attractive, charming person.

3. Today he gave out some spelling words. He appeared to be quite pleased to do so. He made a point to have everyone quiet down so that he could give the words. He used sentences with the words in them. Made quips often. At times they weren't too amusing to the class. He referred to one girl's *fashion* as stylish twenty years ago. This did not go over as a funny joke.

4. At times he does not pronounce words distinctly. He seems to have a slight lisp at times.

5. Dave was one of the four juniors who rode on the chartered bus to State University Homecoming Celebration. The bus was sponsored by the sophomores. He sat with a junior girl throughout the trip. He and some other passengers spent a good deal of time quizzing each other out of a pocket history book.

6. His oral book review was on *Uncle Tom's Cabin*. His background information and summary were garnished with comments. He compared a building in the book to an actual building in town. The report was lengthy but interesting.

7. He keeps busy during journalism class. He is business manager and he does a good job with the books. He also works on the annual. He is the only junior on the annual staff.

8. He usually pays attention in class. He likes to contribute often.

9. Dave's mother died rather unexpectedly in the hospital on Saturday, December 10. He returned to school the following Thursday. He was talking to some students when I entered the room. He turned to me and said with a big smile, "Well, well, how is the accident girl?" (I was in an automobile accident the week previous.) Throughout the day he remained in good humor. At lunch he bought

me some potato chips because he owed me a nickel. He started telling me about his mother's lovely jewelry. Then he noticed my plaid scarf. He said that it was pretty and that his mother had a dress made out of the same material. He asked me if I wore size 10. When I answered in the negative, he said that was too bad because he would have given me the dress. He then went on to say that he took some Army test for fun and he found out that he was just this side of being a sniveling coward.

10. Today he announced to me that his dad has ordered him a new car. He carries on his work as usual.

Summary of Teacher's Impressions

Dave has a good sense of humor. It has served him well and in a time of great need. It is common knowledge that he and his mother were very close. I understand that he was quite broken up about her death and had an emotional breakdown that weekend. When he returned to school he appeared tired and strained but his attitude was jovial. True to form, he will not let this great loss hinder his "goal seeking" because "life must go on." He has taken a quite mature attitude for a sixteen-year-old.

Obviously Dave is a smart boy. He is also smart in that "he uses what he has got." Dave wants to get ahead and to be successful and he isn't going to let sentiment get in the way. He will try to be a success in those fields in which he can excel. He will not try a field where he can't.

He is an individualist. Perhaps this comes from his father's influence. It is evidenced on the swimming team. His idea of leadership is somewhat overbearing; thus his classmates do not accept him as a leader. He is ambitious and a hard worker as evidenced by his scholastic and journalism work. He is an extrovert and entertaining and interesting but sometimes can get on one's nerves.

If someone "calls him down" he takes it seriously and does not pout about it. At times it is necessary to tone him down with a few words. Usually that is all it takes. I am with Dave a large part of the school day.

He has much to contribute to a classroom, as he has had some interesting experiences and he can tell them in an interesting manner. The problem often arises, however, that his comments are not welcomed by the class, as he is inclined to be sarcastic and loud at times.

I try to tone him down so that he will not offend the class. I attempt to be subtle. However, I find that if I am honest with him in any criticism I get better results. He respects honesty. Perhaps this is because his father is so outspoken.

In his records he stated that he wanted to be on the annual staff during his senior year. Now he is the only junior working on the staff so there is an excellent chance that he will be editor. As far as his wish to be on Student Council, I don't know. Dave will have to mend his ways, so to speak, with his classmates before he will be elected. The counselors have talked to him many times about his attitude on leadership but he firmly believes that his theory is correct.

My teaching of Dave is not too much of a great problem. At times I have defended Dave's opinions or contributions when the class has deliberately "shut him up." Of course I do this for anyone as I believe that any student has a right to be heard if there is a thread of reasonableness in his statement. So far this has worked rather well as some students have said, "Why, sure, I see now."

I have done a lot of work with him individually and have been satisfied with the results. I often drop hints to him which more than likely he picks up. However, the big problem with Dave consists of improving his relationship with his peers. Another thing which helps in this respect is to praise him casually in front of others sometimes for some particularly good contribution or suggestion which he has made.

Although information like the foregoing guidance record of one student is extremely worthwhile, even more insight can be gained by gathering valuable data regarding an entire class and assembling it in a form that will give an immediately clear-cut view of the range of differences within the group. We are all too familiar with the dangerous fallacy of the "average," whether it refers to age, I.Q., reading score, or grades. Knowing that the average I.Q. of a class is 106 is meaningless; but knowing the number of students in various I.Q. ranges is of great value as we see the span of ability and the concentration of ability at any given level. In the same way, knowing that the average age of students in a tenth grade is 16 tells us very little; but to know, for example, that three students are only 14 and two are 18, gives a distinct picture of a class that helps us in determining ways of working with it most effectively.

To help prospective teachers develop understandings regarding individual differences, some college instructors are requiring class profile studies. We are including one such study to show the kind of analysis that would help every teacher faced with the problem of teaching common learnings to uncommonly different individuals. Few of us would have time to do the extensive and creative job that follows at the end of this chapter; it would be easier to keep simple lists or graphs showing range of differences among students in various categories.

2. PROVIDING INDIVIDUAL AND GROUP HELP

Individual conferences are an important part of general education practice, as the teacher attempts to know Johnny better through face-to-face interview. Conferences can be teacher-initiated and may even be regularly scheduled. For example, at the beginning of a year some teachers prefer individual conferences with each boy and girl as part of the getting acquainted process. Later conferences can be scheduled for purposes of evaluating and assessing progress toward goals. Frequently conferences are student-initiated, as a boy or girl finds a need to discuss a specific problem or concern with his teacher.

Conferences should be held during general education time as often as possible or at other convenient times during the day. The lunch period can serve as a time when both student and teacher are free. In some situations conference sessions must be held before or after school.

The story of two interview situations with Sam will serve to illustrate the way one teacher tried to meet the needs of an eleventh grader.

Here are the reactions of Sam to some unfinished stories [1] which the general education teacher was using as a projective technique to discover adolescent needs in the area of boy-girl relations.

"There is no problem in this story. What is so horrible about letting her friends know that she had a date with any one person?"

"The girl should show the boys that she didn't care even though she did feel very bad."

"This story is absolutely senseless. I would be very happy if you could show me any educational value in these stories."

It was apparent that Sam was not so ready for a class discussion of these matters as were many other members of the class. A few days after the last reaction had been written, Miss Sims had a conference with Sam. She mentioned his feelings about the stories and told him in some detail the purposes of them. Sam said little or nothing, but listened attentively and unperturbed. After the conference was over, Miss Sims felt sure that she had made no impression whatever and that Sam was no more accepting of the purposes of their class discussion than before.

Several weeks later, however, Sam asked her for a conference. When they were comfortably settled, he said, "Miss Sims, what do you talk to a girl about, on a date?" She evidenced no surprise at the question, although

[1] An unfinished story is one in which a situation is described, but with the ending or solution unstated. The students then complete the story or react to the situation.

it was unexpected and even a little startling, coming from Sam. She guided the boy to talk about the reasons for his question. It seemed that an important dance was coming up, and Sam wanted to ask a girl. He had had a few dates but they were not too successful, and Sam was beginning to realize that he was not exactly Prince Charming. He and Miss Sims discussed the problem, and he left in a somewhat satisfied frame of mind.

Apparently the earlier indication of interest on the part of the teacher, coupled with a careful effort to avoid pushing him before he was ready, had paid dividends in Sam's trust in her.

Effective guidance often calls upon the ingenuity of the teacher in utilizing appropriate techniques at appropriate times. It also depends upon his recognition of needs and his willingness to try to meet them. One teacher describes an approach he used to a perennial problem.

I have had a rather gratifying experience during the past two months. As you know, at the ninth-grade level, among boys, being an athlete is one of the most important things in life. In fact, for those who are nonathletes, this particular period of life is sometimes quite unhappy because of the sharp delineation between athletes and nonathletes and the brutal frankness of youth. Such was the case with my groups of boys. In an effort to find something that would serve as common ground where all the boys could get together and also to demonstrate that there is something more to life than physical prowess, I introduced the Oriental game of "Go" during the noon-hour recreation period and after school. Initially, only "bright" boys participated but gradually I was able to interest one or two of the football and basketball players as well as several of the girls in trying to play the game. Happily, nearly everyone enjoyed the experience and, at the present time, twenty out of thirty members of the class are regular devotees of the game. Coincidentally, there is a noticeably greater unity of spirit and action in the class, particularly among the boys. Boys who were obviously moving farther and farther apart just two months ago can now be seen head to head over a "Go" board and, after the game, chatting and talking quite amicably.

3. KEEPING RECORDS

To facilitate the guiding process, various forms of record keeping should prove helpful to both teachers and students. A common practice is that of keeping a manila folder for each student. These folders serve many purposes. They provide a convenient and safe repository for all student materials, including writing, unit work, notes, tests, and a variety of papers that are part of the on-going work of the general education class. Students can refer to them when the need arises.

In addition, these materials are available for the teacher's use whenever he wants to refer to a particular piece of work. The cumulative nature of the folder also provides opportunities for teachers to see at one glance growth and development in the student over a period of time.

One teacher has found folders a great help when assignments are individualized or long-term. Students can place papers in their folders as they are finished, and the teacher is not bothered with the responsibility of collecting and assorting them. So that she might know immediately whether any new material has been added to the folder, the teacher one semester distributed the following sheet to be placed in front of each folder. When the student placed an assignment in his folder, he indicated the nature and title of it and the date. After the teacher read it and made comments on it, she placed a check mark next to the title so that the student knew it had been seen.

GENERAL EDUCATION ASSIGNMENTS

Long-term Writing Program *Date*

    Group 1 _____

    Group 2 _____

    Group 3 _____

    Group 4 _____

    Group 5 _____

Other Writing Assignments *Date*

    1. Picture Story

    2.

    3.

    4.

Unit Assignments *Date*

    1.

    2.

    3.

    4.

    5.

    6.

So that the experiences of boys and girls, as they move from grade to grade in a problem-centered general education class, may be meaningful and not repetitive, teachers should keep accurate records of the work of the general education class each year. In some schools at the end of the year the teacher writes up an account of the problem areas dealt with that year, suggests "shortage" areas in which additional experiences are needed, and comments specifically on weaknesses of individual students. Teachers also make a practice of "forwarding" examples of student writing and sometimes their free reading records, so that guidance in these areas can be continuous. In addition, each teacher keeps individual records, including anecdotal records, logs, test results, etc.

C. Through Effective Use of Materials and Resources

There is apparently no limit to the variety and kinds of materials and resources that can be utilized by general education classes. In a very real sense it might be said that the whole world is their province, and teachers and students have become ingenious and creative in their approach to the location and utilization of a wide assortment of materials and resources. The least promising object, in the hands of an imaginative group, can become an interesting and constructive adjunct in the pursuit of learning. There should be an energetic effort on the part of teacher and students to gather books, maps, magazines, and a wealth of other necessary materials for the well-dressed general education room.

1. MATERIALS

One of the outstanding characteristics of general education materials is their variety. While textbooks are often distributed, they are but one of many kinds of references upon which boys and girls draw for their research. All kinds of books, pamphlets, and magazines are standard fare.

Because of the increasing attention given to personal-social problems of teen-agers, various guidance pamphlets, like the Life Adjustment series, are invaluable sources of help. Books devoted to helping young people understand their problems and do something about them should be used, along with leaflets put out by various teen-age magazines as well as by magazines of more general appeal.

Magazines especially can be utilized as helpful sources of information for a variety of problems, and the use of current periodicals should be encouraged. Newspapers, too, have an important place in classroom experiences. The list is endless, as room after room reveals maps, models, pictures, and a host of other attractive and useful sources of information.

Materials such as these are obtained in many ways. Students themselves supply much of the material needed. They can write for free and inexpensive materials or bring magazines and books from home. One class, after a paper drive, culled the most helpful magazines and kept them for their own use. A classroom library should be built up, with the assistance of the school librarian, who will sometimes gather materials related to a problem under study and check them out to the general education class for an extended period of time. Occasionally a local public library will perform the same service.

An important feature of all these materials is the range of reading level for which they are intended. Every classroom will contain materials needed by boys and girls of widely differing reading abilities. Also, materials of varying interest appeal are sought.

An imaginative use of materials is illustrated by this account by a ninth-grade teacher of the way in which he has utilized a variety of approaches to unit study.

I would like to mention several little things that have stimulated interest in our present unit, "Countries of the World."

One of the items that I used was a crossword puzzle pertaining to the unit; another was a list of forty of the more famous people in the news; still another was a list of common words and phrases that are heard on television and radio and read in the newspapers and magazines; again, a daily newscast by one of the students helped to stimulate interest in world affairs; finally, a game called "Who Am I?" created a surprising stir. I collected pictures of well-known public figures from current periodicals and mounted them (eight at a time) on manila folders after removing all identifying explanations. Then, I added one clue for each picture. These clues were not necessarily common knowledge about the person. For example, under Winston Churchill's picture, I might say, "I served as an officer in the Boer War." Next, I posted the folders, one at a time every other day. As soon as five students identified all the pictures on a folder, the folder was taken down. Amazingly, it was a tremendously popular game and resulted in intensive use of "The Reader's Guide."

With the emphasis on guidance in the general education class and the frequent focus on personal-social problems of adolescents, a need has arisen for materials that will help teacher and students deal with such content in a significant way. Sometimes these materials take the form of questionnaires, the results of which help a teacher better understand his students. In other instances they may be unfinished stories or picture series that help students look at problems of human relations and personal development. In the hands of trained counselors and psychologists some of these techniques are used in a projective way, as students reveal hidden fears, wishes, hopes, and the like. Although the average classroom teacher is unprepared to use such procedures in the projective sense, he can learn much about his students from them and can obtain clues that might lead him to further study and understanding.

2. RESOURCES

As with materials, there is no limit to the kinds and variety of resources utilized by a general education class. They should include people and places and should range from the school itself to the widening community and even further, with trips far afield.

a. *Students as a resource.* Teachers should make increasing use of the students' own experiences and backgrounds as a valuable resource for learning. Personal experiences shared with one another provide helpful sources of information and understandings. Such sharing is not limited to the class membership but can include students from other grades and classes or even other schools. One teacher describes an instance of students learning from students.

Twenty-four members of the junior class clustered around an attractive and provocative display of models, posters, and charts on atomic energy. As they stood or sat on the graduated floor of the music room, they were completely engrossed in the words of the speakers, who were giving a learned and informative exposition on the power of the atom. The speakers were not, as might have been expected, leading scientists from the university campus or research workers at the nearby institute, but were two members of the senior class in the same school.

Bill and Lisa had been making an intensive study of atomic energy for three years now, and each year had entered a state-wide scientific competition. In addition to their display they had printed a little pamphlet, entitled *The Power of the Atom,* copies of which had been given to the eleventh graders.

When the juniors were planning their study of "Problems of Living in the Atomic Age," an early suggestion was made to extend an invitation to Bill and Lisa to talk to them someday about their project. As the discussion moved from alpha and beta rays to by-products, Roentgen, the distinction between fusion and fission, examination of a cloud chamber, explanations of cyclotrons, piles, and the meaning of ionized, it was evident that here were two young people who had much to teach their schoolmates about an area in which they had become more or less expert.

In many other ways students serve as resources for certain areas of competence or experience. Because they can communicate on equal terms with their peers, the learning is often more effective than when adults make an effort to teach similar understandings and concepts. A frequent use of students can be made during orientation periods when Student Council and club officers might speak to incoming classes. They can offer a warm welcome to the new students and help to familiarize them with the activities and organizations of the school.

b. *The professional staff as a resource.* Because general education learnings cut across traditional subject lines, there is often need for more specific guidance in some areas than the general education teacher is equipped to give. It is then that other members of the faculty have a distinct contribution to make. Sometimes they come to the general education room; at other times the general education students come to them.

An indispensable resource is the librarian, who has at her finger tips suggestions about needed materials, ideas for interesting reading, assistance with research skills. In some situations frequent visits by the librarian to the general education room is a usual procedure. Often these visits take the form of book talks, or the librarian may familiarize the class with the quantity and quality of materials available on various problems, as they plan their units of study. Either in the classroom or in the library he helps them acquire library skills.

Other resource people of special importance are the music, art, and science teachers, who should be consulted frequently about various general education projects which are drawing upon their areas for understanding or expression. In one school the arts suite is available during general education time so that students can work there with necessary materials, guided by a member of the art staff. In some instances a general education class schedules an art or music period one or two periods a week, and the teachers work with them not only on general education projects, but also on unrelated worthwhile activities. A science or art teacher may be given a specific responsibility for working with certain general education classes, and this assignment becomes part of his total schedule load. In every instance the general education teacher, the various resource teachers, and the students cooperatively plan experiences that have meaning for them and together arrive at understandings and agreements.

Members of the central office staff of a school system can also serve as good resource persons. The seventh-grade class, which became interested in education during an orientation unit, found the assistant superintendent of schools a first-rate source of information on the subject.

Before his visit to the class he received the following list of questions from the students:

1. How many children attend our public schools in this city?
2. How many schools are there in the city?
3. How many teachers are there?
4. What is the smallest enrollment in any school? The largest?
5. What are the other junior high schools in the city? Where are they located?
6. What is the oldest school? The newest?
7. What are the various special schools, such as vocational, occupational, etc.?
8. What are the conditions of the other schools?
9. What are the qualifications for teachers in various schools—elementary, junior high, senior high?
10. Can pupils attend any school in the city, regardless of residence?
11. What are the plans for new schools?
12. What is the cost of education in our city?
13. What is the work of the school board?
14. What are the duties of the administrative staff—Superintendent, Assistant Superintendents, Supervisors, etc.?

The assistant superintendent spoke easily and informally with the boys and girls, helping them realize that here was a person vitally interested in their educational welfare, and withal a warmly human individual. He responded to additional questions from the class with a candor that indicated respect for their seriousness of purpose and interest.

Before leaving the question of the use of professional staff as resource people, let us look at one of the problems involved in the practical application of this suggestion. Providing time in a school day for teachers to work together, contributing to and participating in the learning of the general education class, is almost as difficult as it is desirable. However, some possible solutions come to mind, and we pass them along for your consideration.

One of the most desirable solutions is to provide teachers with the necessary time by lightening the class load they normally carry. For example, if a teacher is accustomed to teaching six classes per day, the load could be reduced to five, and the teacher could use the "free" period by being a resource person for the general education groups. In many schools, teachers now have what is called a "free period" and they would not object to general education classes asking them to come in from time to time as a resource person, as a way of improving the school program.

Many schools, however, feel that teachers must teach each period in order that the school program may be properly financed, and it is to these situations that the following suggestions are directed. First, in practically all school situations where teachers are required to "work" every period of the day, the school schedule includes at least one study hall each hour of the day. It is not the purpose of this book to condone arbitrarily assigned study halls, but rather to suggest that almost any member of the school staff can "keep" a study hall as it is normally operated. If a teacher assigned to a study hall is competent in some special area which is being examined by a general education class, the general education teacher may change places with the study-hall teacher for a period or two so that the general education class can benefit from contributions the former may make.

Since a great deal of program improvement can be brought about by teachers sharing their resources and competencies, it would be well for a school to consider making similar arrangements among all its teachers. Thus it would be necessary for all teachers to be well informed about each other's qualifications, as well as to know what is going on throughout the school at all times. This knowledge alone can greatly improve the school program. A card on each teacher could be kept in a central file. This card might indicate the area or areas in which a given teacher has special interest, information, resources, or personal experiences. The card might also indicate times at which the teacher would be available as a resource person. Example:

Name: John Smith   *Available:* 9:30–10:30 daily

Interest or competency:

1. Spent two years in Germany as student at the University of Berlin.
2. Was first lieutenant in Air Force participating in the Berlin Air Lift.
3. Widely read in the literature of the Civil War period.
4. Have large collection of model planes.
5. Have wide experience in camping.
6. Am Red Cross instructor in swimming.
7. Have been to Alaska and Arctic Circle.

A general education bulletin board in a central location can serve to inform all teachers as to what is going on in a given class. Each class could keep an up-to-date card on the board showing the unit being studied, objective of the unit, some of the activities in the unit, and resources to be used. A space might be provided at the bottom of the card for suggestions by other teachers.

GENERAL EDUCATION BULLETIN BOARD

9A	9B	10A	10B	11A	11B	12A	12B
__	__	__	__	__	__	__	__
__	__	__	__	__	__	__	__

Sample Card from the General Education Bulletin Board

Grade _____ Room _____ Teacher _____

Date of Unit: From _____ To _____

Title of Unit: _____

Objectives of Unit: 1. _____
2. _____
3. _____

Sample Activities: 1. _____
2. _____
3. _____

Resources:
Materials: 1. _____
2. _____
3. _____

People: 1. _____
2. _____
3. _____

Whatever the arrangements made, teachers should be encouraged to share their strengths and competencies for the improvement of learning in their schools. All too often we neglect our readily available supply of human resources.

c. *Parents as resources.* Just as students and various teachers are serving as effective resources for learning, so also can parents be called upon to assist in many of the experiences and activities of the general education class. Their contributions can be many and varied, and their use can result in a close and desirable three-way relationship among teacher, students, and family.

One of the most frequent ways in which parents can contribute is as speakers. For a variety of reasons—special competencies, hobbies, travels, professional or occupational background—they have much to offer as they bring some of the breadth of community and adult living into the confines of the schoolroom. With camera and slides, with collections and demonstrations, with special skills and talents they come bearing gifts that receive warm attention and thanks.

When students make field trips it is not unusual to find two or three or four parents with the group, not only for chaperone purposes but also as genuinely interested adults who can share with students their interests and enthusiasms. While their services as chauffeurs are gratefully welcomed and even requested, they should also be encouraged to join a variety of activities, regardless of specific contribution.

Parents can also serve as resources in planning for numerous experiences. When the eighth-grade class planned its work experience in order to earn enough for a trip, they immediately enlisted the support of their parents for the whole project. In addition, there had been a meeting of the general education teacher and several representative parents to discuss the whole project, especially the problem of the length of the trip. Although the suggestion of an overnight trip had arisen among the students, the parents felt that such a trip would be undesirable for this group at this time. Through co-operative discussion of ideas and plans the entire experience proved to be a fruitful one for all. (See Chapter Seven, pages 149–151.)

d. *The community as a resource laboratory.* In many ways the community comes to the school when various lay persons, not necessarily parents of the youngsters, bring some of their rich background to the general education class. In one instance the school policeman talked with some classes about a recent trip to Mexico. As a result of his visit one class settled upon a study of Mexico and South America. Another good result was the establishment of a friendly relationship between the students and the policeman. In a ninth-grade class that was learning about personality and good grooming, a personal shopper from a local department store discussed the proper clothes for every occasion. In addition, the store offered a prize—a graduation coat for a boy, a dress for a girl—for the best essay on good grooming.

More and more classes are moving out into the community for special study, sometimes as a total group, sometimes in small groups, and occasionally as individuals. One teacher tells of such an experience.

While studying a unit on our city community my seventh-grade students planned field trips as a learning activity. One committee selected the topic of local education. The chairman made an appointment with the Superintendent of Public Instruction in our county to discuss the problem. The group prepared questions to ask, made arrangements for transportation, and conducted their trip unchaperoned. They returned with detailed information, such as how the educational system was organized in the county, number of teachers employed, number of students, cost per student for education, number of buses in use, salary of teachers, number of bus drivers, etc. With this information the committee prepared a chart on the blackboard and presented the report to the class.

The values gained by this experience were:

1. Working together
2. Working independently of the teacher
3. Assuming responsibility and arranging for transportation of a field trip, also assuming responsibility for proper conduct
4. Learning to use the telephone to arrange interviews and talks
5. Learning how to meet people
6. Learning how to summarize and evaluate their work
7. Appreciation of the educational system and the vast amount of effort and expense that goes into their education

One general education class utilized the files of the local newspaper for research purposes; two students at a time were permitted to work there. Another class visited the local school for crippled children, and were so impressed that many of the less tractable boys took it upon themselves to do some repair work for the handicapped youngsters. During a class study of civil defense one committee made a survey of how many people would know what to do in case of attack. Another class, studying driver education and safety, made a survey of pedestrian and driver habits at the busiest downtown intersection.

Some trips become annual affairs for certain grades, as is the case in a Midwestern high school.

One trip that has become an annual event for our senior general education groups is the church tour. In connection with our study of the major religious faiths in our community and as part of our observance of Brotherhood Week, a field trip is planned to representative churches of the Catholic, Protestant, and Jewish faiths. A student committee, composed of representatives from each general education group, makes the arrangements for these visits.

The committee usually divides into subcommittees which make arrangements with the individual churches, secure from the general education classes questions which the students would like to have answered, and arrange for transportation by school buses to the churches. Usually four churches are visited, and the schedule is arranged so that the students may spend approximately an hour at each church.

Some classes do considerable research into the beliefs and practices of the churches *before* making the tour, while others prefer to do most of their study *after* the tour has been made. In either case there is much discussion after the tour and evaluation of the experience. Since our students are predominantly Protestant, we find this tour and the study they make in connection with it contribute greatly to their understanding of people of other religious faiths and to their realization of the many things which all of these faiths have in common. Making the arrangements for the trip, meeting the representatives of the churches, and listening respectfully to explanations of religious views that may differ from their own have proved to be valuable experiences in human relations. Perhaps the best evidence of the success of this project is the fact that it is requested year after year by each new senior class.

• Thus, through teaching procedures, through individual and group guidance, through effective use of a variety of materials and resources, teachers can go far toward recognizing, respecting, and dealing with the wealth of differences exhibited by adolescents—physical, emotional, intellectual, social. By these means much progress will be made toward individualized development of young people, avoiding the dangers of stereotyped mass instruction.

CLASS PROFILE OF A TENTH GRADE

Seating Plan—According to Name, Age, and I.Q.

ALTON 14 107	BILL 15 106		NADINE ☆ 16 86	TED 15 103	MARY ☆ 16 81	GENE 15 128
	NAOMI ☆ 15 88	JETTY ☆ 15 ?	TERRY 18 ?	SHEILA ☆ 15 93	LOUIS 15 89	LINDA ☆ 15 101
FRANK 15 120	JOHNNY 16 101	NANCY ☆ 16 ?	CAROL ☆ 15 103	DAVID 15 110	RONNIE 15 110	TONY 15 95
ELLIE ☆ 15 ?	LOLA ☆ 15 111	BOBBY 15 ?	JUDY L. ☆ 15 ?	JIMMY 15 93	JEANNE ☆ 14 ?	JUDY K. ☆ 16 ?
		WAYNE 17 ?	VIRGINIA ☆ 15 104	JEAN ☆ 15 97		
FRED 15 106	DONNY 16 79	CARL 15 117	LOY ☆ 15 108	SANDY ☆ 14 118	CAMILLA ☆ 14 112	SONIA ☆ 15 102

☆ = GIRLS

? = Unknown I.Q.
102 = Average I.Q.

Three Wishes—According to Seating Plan

1. To have a million dollars. 2. An automobile. 3. Be twenty-one years of age.	1. For my mother to be well; she has cancer. 2. My father to be here for Christmas. 3. Good health.	
1. Good health. 2. Good mind. 3. One hundred more wishes.	1. A new car. 2. A lot of money.	1. A radio and TV network. 2. A shop in my back yard. 3. A hi-fi system and lots of records.
1. An "A" average. 2. To be willed a million $ by an old, rich uncle. 3. To marry someone who loves and protects me.	1. A first-class construction company. 2. A college education. 3. Some fast sports cars.	1. To be a success. 2. A healthy life. 3. To never let my mother down in any way.
1. Enough money to buy clothes and other things. 2. My own car. 3. Long, beautiful, curly hair.	1. To help bring Christ and His teaching to all. 2. Contentment and satisfaction. 3. Final exams to be abolished.	1. Good grades with little work. 2. Never be sad or worried. 3. To live on a horse farm in Kentucky.
	1. To live on a huge plantation. 2. A scholarship to college. 3. A gold "P" of a boy on the football team.	1. Good health. 2. My family to be normal and healthy. 3. Success.
	1. World peace. 2. Large sum of money. 3. To go to college.	1. To be a ballet dancer. 2. To see a certain boy. 3. To go to New York.

1. Success. 2. Happiness. 3. Successful marriage.	1. I would like to play for the New York Yankees. 2. A million dollars. 3. Make straight A's.	1. A healthy family. 2. A swimming pool. 3. All wishes to come true.	1. To be a model. 2. Enough money to be comfortable. 3. To live in Palatka.	1. A new Cadillac. 2. A 24-room home with a swimming pool. 3. A good business.	1. To have my father back. 2. To be at the completion of the world's great wonders. 3. To never worry about anything.	1. Be a millionaire. 2. The best football player in the world. 3. My parents to be millionaires.
1. To move from Tampa. 2. My brother was near. 3. My mother to learn how to drive.	1. A typewriter. 2. I wish our house was paid for. 3. My mother would marry Monroe.	1. To hurry and get out of school. 2. For my grades to be higher. 3. To get rich soon.	1. A little sister. 2. To marry my steady. 3. World peace.	1. To be a nurse. 2. A car. 3. No freckles.	1. To be beautiful. 2. To make good marks for my nursing career. 3. To make every wish come true.	1. Good health. 2. Average grades because of a thyroid condition. 3. To be a secretary.
1. A ranch-type home. 2. A million dollars. 3. Perfect health.	1. Be a good salesman. 2. A good football player in college. 3. A trip around the world.	1. A long life and good health. 2. Teachers not believing in homework. 3. A 1960 Ford.	1. To live next to someone important. 2. Lots of money. 3. To go to college.	1. To be older than my brother. 2. A 1960 Mercury convertible. 3. To be out of school.	1. To go back home. 2. My parents didn't have to work hard. 3. A healthy family.	1. No more wars and nations to be friends. 2. All people to have enough to eat and wear. 3. A lot of money.

Future Plans—According to Seating

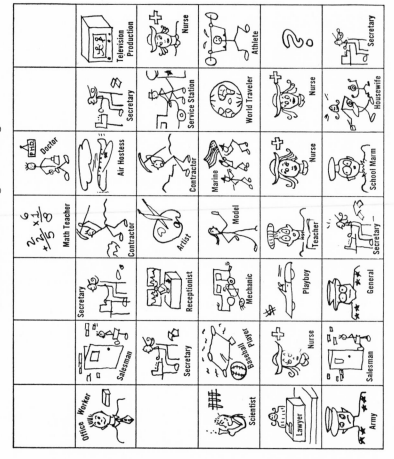

Office Worker	Salesman	Secretary	Math Teacher		Doctor	Television Production
		Secretary	Contractor	Secretary	Air Hostess	Nurse
Scientist	Baseball Player	Receptionist	Artist	Contractor	Service Station	Athlete
Lawyer	Nurse	Mechanic	Model	Marine	World Traveler	
Army	Salesman	General	Teacher	Nurse	Nurse	Secretary
			Secretary	School Marm	Housewife	

Talents Found in Class Members

Piano—6

Art—1

Dancing—3

Guitar—1

Trumpet—2

Singing—2

Clarinet—1

Baton—1

Knife-thrower—1

Employment	No.
Boys employed	2
Boys unemployed	15
Girls employed (baby-sit)	9
Girls unemployed	10

College Pursuit	No.
Yes	23
No	7
Not sure	6

The Sports Participation Wheel

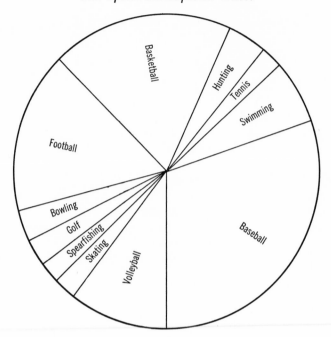

Favorite Pastimes

Number of students

	1	2	3	4	5	6
Art	■					
Baseball	■					
Boys	■	■				
Chemistry	■					
Dancing	■	■				
Football	■	■	■			
Girls	■	■				
Hunting	■					
Fishing	■	■				
Indian lore	■					
Mechanics	■					
Music	■	■	■			
Reading	■	■	■	■	■	■
Skating	■					
Swimming	■	■	■	■	■	
Social activities	■	■	■	■	■	■
Television	■	■				
Writing	■	■				

Favorite Magazines

Number of students

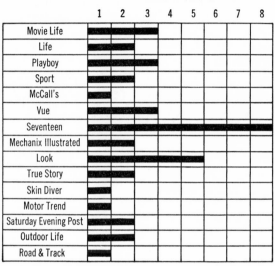

Magazine	1	2	3	4	5	6	7	8
Movie Life								
Life								
Playboy								
Sport								
McCall's								
Vue								
Seventeen								
Mechanix Illustrated								
Look								
True Story								
Skin Diver								
Motor Trend								
Saturday Evening Post								
Outdoor Life								
Road & Track								

Preferred Type of Book

Number of students

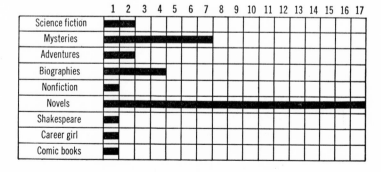

Type	1	2	3	4	5	6	7	8	9	10	11	12	13	14	15	16	17
Science fiction																	
Mysteries																	
Adventures																	
Biographies																	
Nonfiction																	
Novels																	
Shakespeare																	
Career girl																	
Comic books																	

Physical Growth and Development

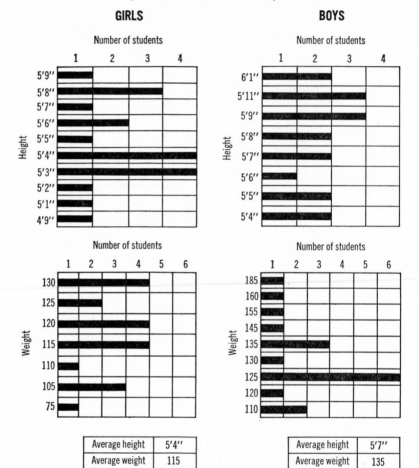

GIRLS

Number of students

	1	2	3	4
5'9"				
5'8"				
5'7"				
5'6"				
5'5"				
5'4"				
5'3"				
5'2"				
5'1"				
4'9"				

Number of students

	1	2	3	4	5	6
130						
125						
120						
115						
110						
105						
75						

Average height	5'4"
Average weight	115

BOYS

Number of students

	1	2	3	4
6'1"				
5'11"				
5'9"				
5'8"				
5'7"				
5'6"				
5'5"				
5'4"				

Number of students

	1	2	3	4	5	6
185						
160						
155						
145						
135						
130						
125						
120						
110						

Average height	5'7"
Average weight	135

General Physical Condition

	1	2	3	4	5	6	7	8	9	10	11	12	13	14	15	16
Fair																
Good																
Excellent																
Sinus																
Hayfever																
Eyesight																

7

Developing Skills,
Values, and Attitudes

The variety and extent of learnings that take place in a general education class can scarcely be catalogued, but, as has already been indicated, general education does have a major responsibility for effective learning of communication skills—reading, writing, and speaking. Along with these fundamentals are the skills which are an integral part of general education study—skills in critical thinking, self-direction, and self-discipline. Because of the nature of the general education class and the way in which teacher and students work together, there is also an inevitable and desirable emphasis upon the acquisition of a set of values and the development of sound attitudes and understandings.

A. The "Basic" Skills

The communication skills of reading, writing, and speaking constitute a necessary part of everyone's education. The general education class offers many varied opportunities for frequent and continuous experiences in these skill areas. Sometimes the experiences represent a direct "attack" on fundamental needs in these areas, or the skills are used as a means toward other goals, as students pursue their study of various problems. In no way are they neglected.

1. READING

The story of one teacher's work with an eighth-grade class will serve to illustrate the kind of attention that can and should be given to the development of reading skills in the general education class.

139

Miss Talbot was concerned with the whole question of guiding her eighth graders' reading diet in such a way that not only would their reading skills improve but their taste and discrimination also. She had given the class a standardized reading test and so had one kind of evidence concerning the present ability level of each student. It was then possible to take remedial steps to help those few youngsters who were far below grade and needed attention in developing increased speed and improved comprehension. An equally serious problem, though, lay in the encouragement of wide reading and the broadening of horizons, so to speak.

One aspect of their general education work was the library period scheduled once a week. During this time the boys and girls could read freely, making their own selections and moving whither their fancy led them. It was evident after the first few sessions, however, that a few students were having persistent difficulty in locating books of interest to them. Some of them spent the major part of the hour in browsing that was often aimless and fruitless. While she and the librarian both attempted to advise and guide, Miss Talbot wondered if there might not be another more helpful approach to this whole question of guiding reading interests.

She decided to ask each student to write briefly about his likes and dislikes in reading and to try to give some indication of how much reading he did and where and under what circumstances. For most of the students she followed this writing with a brief individual conference in order to clarify and extend her understanding of their needs in this area. She was not surprised to discover the more or less usual tastes for this age group— sports, animals, and science-fiction books for the boys, and teen-age fiction for the girls. However, there were some individual reactions that proved very helpful, not only for the ensuing guided reading program that evolved but for new insights which she gained into the thinking and actions of her eighth graders.

There are only about one or two types I really like. I like books with people in them. In other words, I like to read about people. Books dated from about the time of the Revolutionary War to the Civil War interest me most. I also like a mystery if it is not too simple, but not too involved to follow. I like the mysteries best when they are written in our own times. Stories of spies also interest me, provided they take place in another country and that they too take place in our time. Books about young people I also like. Books about animals I do not like. Also science or research. Books written in English yet with funny words stuck in I do not like.

In the first place I do not like to read. The first books I read this quarter was because I thought it would be like last year. We had to read six books a quarter, and I was always behind in my reading. So this year I decided to start reading early. It happened that the first book I read was very interesting and I liked it very much. I read

Some Experiences That Provide Continuity Throughout the General Education Curriculum

Developing Intellectual Power

Expressing Oneself Creatively

Developing Person-to-Person Relationships

Working Together in Groups

Exploring Natural Phenomena

Learning about a Technological Age

Understanding Our Economy
Courtesy of Mamaroneck (N.Y.) Junior High School

Understanding the Democratic Process
Courtesy of the Lakewood, Ohio, Public Schools

the book in six days; that is the fastest I've read any book. If I think I won't like a book I won't read it. I don't have any time to read anyway except on the bus and at school. I have to practice my violin and do the dishes and homework, and by that time I'm all tired out.

Until a couple of years ago about the only kind of book I would read was an animal story. Then I decided that I'd better start reading something different. The big classics in the library had always interested me, so I tried one. I liked it. Since then I have been reading quite a few of them. There is a large variety in the classics. Some have not interested me and others have been fascinating. Especially the historical ones. Probably I have enjoyed Dickens' *A Tale of Two Cities* better than any. Stories about girls in high school, college or looking for jobs are to me dull and uninteresting. I have not read one yet that I liked well enough to finish.

In addition, through interviews Miss Talbot gained further insight into the reading backgrounds of her students. She discovered that Dennis had read two books a second time because he could not find others to interest him. He also commented, "My mom doesn't understand that the books she's bought me and thinks I would like, don't interest me." Ed liked horse and adventure stories so much that his father put a ratio of only two such books to every one of another kind. Linda read *Mama's Bank Account* because she had seen the television program, *Mama,* and thought she would enjoy the book.

Miss Talbot wondered what might be done to stimulate and guide reading on an individual basis. She took the material she had gathered along with the reading scores to the librarian, who enthusiastically and graciously agreed to draw up individual reading lists for each boy and girl. The results were excellent; for Miss Harris, the librarian, had skillfully started with suggestions of books within their own expressed field of interest, then included some on their reading level which might move them from their exclusive interests to a broader scope without ranging too far afield at first.

In this attention to reading it is important to note that both the general education teacher and the librarian were interested not only in encouraging reading but in various other aspects of the reading situation. They were concerned with locating books on appropriate reading levels, with subtly guiding some youngsters from a single interest in sports or animals or science-fiction stories to other kinds of books equally enjoyable, with suggesting a variety of reading fare for those boys and girls who revealed a readiness for broader horizons.

When the lists were given to the students, the librarian discussed them with the boys and girls and answered questions that arose. They were not required to read these books but were strongly encouraged to select from these lists.

Here, then, is one example of the kind of approach that can be used to stimulate and encourage wide reading. In the school where Miss Talbot teaches, a "free reading program" with varying degrees of guidance is a standard part of general education procedure. The students keep a brief record of all their reading so that it is possible to see at a glance both the quantity and the quality of their reading.

Sometimes it is desirable for the general education class to schedule one or two library periods a week, periods which can serve various purposes. Occasionally the reading can be free and unrestricted; at other times the students might read in connection with their unit study. In still other instances, the library periods could serve as opportunities for research for their various unit activities. In addition to the regularly scheduled library sessions, classes should be free to go to the library as the need arises for reading or research. When this flexibility exists, the most functional use of the library occurs, as individuals or small groups of students utilize library facilities as part of their on-going activities.

Often reading suggestions and assignments can be made in connection with the general education unit, and boys and girls are encouraged to read a wide variety of books—biography, fiction, travel, etc., to further their understanding of the problem under study. In addition, so-called "literature" study can be made a functional part of unit study. For example, one class read *Our Town* in connection with a study of "Problems of Democracy"; another read *Rip Van Winkle* as an aid to their understanding of a historical unit.

2. WRITING

Writing can take many forms in a general education class and can receive much attention in all aspects of class study. In general, two kinds of writing can prevail, that which is associated with the unit of study and grows out of the needs of the problem under study; and an independent, more or less creative kind of writing.

a. *Unit writing.* The unit of study offers many and varied opportunities for all kinds of writing. One of the first writing skills for which boys and girls feel a distinct need is that of note taking. In general education perhaps more than elsewhere there is a need to take notes on individual research reading for later sharing with a small study group or for the development of a talk or report. Note taking on group reports and presentations to the class is often a common practice as groups study different aspects of a problem and share their findings with the class. Outlining also assumes great importance for the organization of material, not only for the individual's understanding but also for his effective communication with others, either a small committee or the entire class.

The amount and kind of written work connected with unit study can vary considerably. There might be one paper required for every unit, with the kind varying from unit to unit. For example, the paper might take the form of a "term" paper, with stress on the essential requirements of sound research, selection of relevant data, interesting and appropriate organization of material, and correct usage in its presentation. In this regard bibliographic data can assume great importance, and, along with library skills, students can acquire facility in handling source material.

Other kinds of writing get proper attention as students wrestle with the problem of sharing the fruits of their individual or group labor with the class. Such reporting can take the form of a skit or play, for which a script is necessary. These "dramas" may vary from adaptations of television programs to original plays. Or newspaper reporting can be simulated, whereby students learn about journalistic style.

While there is a laudable trend away from the formalized routine of book reports, it is possible to lead students to write interestingly and refreshingly about books. Originality should be encouraged, and the sharing of these book "reviews" with others can do much to stimulate wider reading by the entire class.

Another kind of writing that assumes a functional purpose in almost all general education classes is letter writing. The nature of general education study requires correspondence of many kinds, inquiries about proposed field trips, requests for materials, thank-you notes, and others. The writing of these can be handled in a variety of ways. The class can co-operatively compose a letter; at other times, each student might write one, and the "best" be selected, or ideas from several may be combined. In many instances, students write letters for their own specific needs and purposes or to further the work of a group or committee.

There may even be occasions for students to write letters to their parents to acquaint them with general education activities, for example, or to ask permission for some undertaking. Nancy wrote such a letter.

Dear Mother and Daddy,

Our committee is planning several trips this winter to places of interest in the city. I am a member of this committee and I need permission to go. The school is in no way responsible in case of accident. Our committee is composed of five members and we make the trip independently.

Your daughter,
Nancy

b. *Creative writing.* Besides the more "functional" kinds of writing that have a specific purpose either in relation to the general education unit or other activities, it is desirable to encourage students to do original story writing of a more creative nature. In many schools a "creative" writing program has long been in effect. The purpose of this program is to encourage frequent and original writing, deriving as much as possible from the interests and imagination of the students.

In actual practice in any given school the program varies from teacher to teacher, not only in the amount of writing but also in the degree of guidance. In some classes the students write a "story" a week. (The word *story* is an all-embracing term used to describe all the creative pieces of writing by the students, regardless of its nature.) Other classes may write three or four or five stories a semester or perhaps one every two weeks.

Some teachers prefer completely "free choice" with regard to the style and theme of the stories, letting the students write at will, drawing upon their own creative resources. Others offer varying degrees of guidance, sometimes requesting a piece of writing of a specific kind, such as a humorous story, or giving opening sentences or paragraphs to serve as "leads" for stories.

In an effort to provide guidance and also to help students with individual kinds of problems and interests, one teacher has used two approaches to the creative-writing aspect of general education. With an eleventh-grade class that had had long experience with creative writing and some of whose members indicated that they had run out of original ideas, she tried to give specific guidance and at the same time choices. Here are the directions that she gave for the writing program about the middle of the fall quarter.

The following writing assignment has three purposes—to aid you in varying the content and style of your stories, to give you suggestions and ideas that may not have occurred to you, and to give you an opportunity to plan your time wisely for the rest of the year. In addition to this assignment there will also be shorter writing assignments from time to time, which will be done chiefly in class.

The suggestions are listed in various groups; I have indicated the number of stories from each group which you are to do. You are to turn in the stories whenever you wish. However, at least three should be completed by the end of this quarter. You may do them in any order you please.

One of the important objectives of this writing program is to improve the quality of your writing. Many of you have been too easily satisfied with less than your best. While I shall not set a minimum number of words or pages, I would like to see you develop your ideas as intensively as they deserve. You may be asked to do a rewrite job if I feel you have not done your best.

Talk over with me any questions or problems which you may have.

There followed five general groupings of suggestions, each directed toward experience with a specific kind of writing. The first group aimed at descriptive writing and suggested written accounts of people or places or art works, even the possibility of a descriptive reaction to a musical selection. The second group was directed at developing the imagination, suggesting the writing of a myth or a "tall tale" or a description of human beings as seen by an insect or other small creature. The third group focused on writing from observation, suggesting descriptions of elementary school children at work or at play or of the students' own classmates. In the fourth group the teacher suggested activities directed toward reportorial writing, growing out of interviews with people about topics of interest to teen-agers. In the fifth group she encouraged the boys and girls to try their hands at poetic, dramatic, and dialogue forms.

For each student she wrote a brief paragraph giving her opinion of his writing up to that time and suggesting areas that needed attention. Here is what she wrote to Philip.

Your writing shows the same care and thought which you give to all your work. You pay great attention to correct usage, and your choice of words is good. Your ideas are varied and original; you handle conversation very well. Your informational writing shows excellent organization. Continue to be original in your ideas and style. I liked very much your letter to Ivan.

With an eighth-grade class Miss Maney tried to give even more specific guidance as she worked out an individual assignment for each youngster. The following is an example.

INDIVIDUAL WRITING ASSIGNMENT

You write well and show good imagination along with rather satisfactory usage skills. Possibly you could devote more thought to correct punctuation.

You might enjoy reading parts or all of the following two books:

Ernst, M. S. *In a Word*
Very interesting accounts of the origin of words, such as "bunk," "flotsam," "ink," etc. Some amusing cartoons by James Thurber.

Barnes, Franklin. *Man and His Records*
Enjoyable account of writing through the ages, the invention of the alphabet and printing press. Good illustrations.

Read parts or all of the following two books, and then write an original story of your own:

Colver, A. R. *If You Should Want to Write*
Excellent suggestions for story writing, with many ideas.

Gould and Coyne, editors. *Young Voices*
Prose and poetry written by high school students.

Read two or three myths or legends from Greek or Roman times or from Scandinavian or American literature. Try to write a myth or fable yourself. You might want to take a look at some of James Thurber's "Fables" of our own time.

Listen to a musical number and describe imaginatively your reactions and feelings about it. Use vivid descriptive words and phrases.

Try to find or write a story that you think would make a good ballet.

Although some of the same suggestions were made to several students, it was rare that two or more students had exactly the same list of suggestions. Wherever possible, suggestions focused on the student's hobbies or talents. Miss Maney included the idea about ballet because of Elizabeth's special interest in it.

c. *Language usage.* Throughout all the work with writing in a general education class there should be a concern with helping boys and girls acquire the skills and understandings of correct usage that will assist them in developing facility in interesting and accurate expression. Such help should be individualized as much as possible. Sometimes students with certain weaknesses in common can constitute a group which devotes time and energy to improving these areas.

On other occasions total class attention can be given to learning skills of spelling, punctuation, correct usage. As one teacher has said, "When I sense a common need, I stop group activity and we work on it." Some classes in their weekly planning provide time for direct attack on grammatical usage and other details of correct English. Drill can occur in general education classes but should be made as meaningful as possible. Grammatical errors and language weaknesses should be drawn from the students' written and oral work, and there should be a direct relationship between their study of specific skills and their need for them at that time.

Spelling can be handled in a variety of ways. The emphasis might be placed on words which the students need and use in their unit and other general education study. In addition, spelling words can be drawn from standardized lists. As with other skills, there will be more effective results when spelling is approached from the individual student's needs.

B. The "New" Skills

One of the major arguments advanced in favor of general education programs is the attention they give to the development of new skills besides reading and writing. The fourth "R," relationships, has already been seen to play an important part in on-going class activity. Attention is also focused on the development of critical thinking, of self-direction, of self-discipline, and of a sense of responsibility.

One of the most meaningful tests of a group's achievement toward some of these skills occurs when the general education teacher needs to be absent for any reason. To what extent can the students pursue their plans in a satisfying and effective way?

In some classes students have made such rapid strides toward self-discipline that they can be left "on their own" when the teacher must be absent for a period or two or a day or two. Because leadership has been shared with them, they do not find it a handicap to continue with their work without the teacher's presence. They have leaders of their own to whom they look with respect and understanding when situations occur that require firm guidance or emergency decision. Usually co-operative planning has been so thorough and so meaningful that there is no doubt in the students' minds concerning the nature of their work on these occasions.

Not all classes may be ready for such complete self-reliance but may need the guidance of another adult. Even here there can be wide variation in the extent to which students have really acquired skills of self-direction and self-discipline. One teacher, who was on a leave of absence for two months, returned to her class to find a discouraging situation. All their gains of a few months earlier seemed to have been dissipated; clearly they had not yet achieved the necessary degree of self-direction to be trusted very far out of her sight. The teacher used this situation as an evaluative one, asking them to analyze it and to arrive at some plans for remedying the state of affairs. She indicated that if they did not come up with some workable solutions she would have to take matters into her own hands, implying a kind of direction from which they had been attempting to emancipate themselves. Fortunately, in this instance the students did work out some remedial approaches to their problems and started anew in their struggle toward self-discipline.

It is gratifying to discover that students can be surprisingly honest in their accounts of what goes on when teacher is away. An eighth-grade class that had the benefit of two substitute teachers (both regular teachers in the school) wrote about what happened while their general education teacher was away for four days. Although perceptions varied, here is a more or less typical reaction.

On the whole I think we did a good job. The classes were for the most part orderly and we got quite a bit of work done. I think we did very well in settling down at the beginning of each hour.

The unit project went very smoothly. Most of the class were finished before the schedule time and I think everyone was done by the end of Wednesday.

I think our worst fault was not keeping quiet during the hour. In the discussions at two o'clock we did quite a bit of talking out of turn. Had this not happened we would have finished our work a lot sooner.

The attitude of the class toward the talent show was good. We decided on the type of show and chose our moderator.

Dance class did not go so well and not many people danced. It would have been much better if Miss R. (the regular dance teacher) had been there.

I think we could have done a better job this week, but I think we are improving steadily.

Occasionally the youngsters are refreshingly honest. "Our business meeting on Thursday was short and sweet and the class cooperated very nicely even better than when you are here. But I'm sure it was just an accident." The teacher had to smile at Jimmy's tactful candor.

Another indication of success in the development of self-direction is the extent to which students can pursue independent study or take the initiative with various activities without the prodding of a teacher. In connection with their general education problem two seventh graders made an interesting field trip on their own initiative and after school hours. A report was made to the teacher; here are the students' own words.

REPORT ON THE TESTING LABORATORY

Stan and I went to the Testing Laboratory for a visit. In the Laboratory we saw all kinds of acids, Ammonium, Nitrate, Hydroxide, Bromides, Merck, and millions of other chemicals; different work instruments, weighing machinery, etc. We saw a gigantic bottle filled with water with a tube coming from it. They use it to watch it evaporate. We saw a gold weigher and also, many bottles marked "Poison."

In the Physical Laboratory we saw experimenting rocks, heating machines, a machine that shows how strong Concrete Blocks are by Compression. We saw a Oven that is used to heat plastic on to cement cylinders and molding cement cylinders.

SAMPLE: Piece of Concrete which was tested for strength

SAMPLE: Piece of Block which was tested for strength

SAMPLE: Piece of Iron which was tested to determine strength and whether it would break or not

SAMPLE: Piece of Roofing Tile tested for strength and water

This report also indicates that it is not only the brightest and most successful students who have the curiosity and initiative to follow through ideas on their own, but that other students also are willing to direct their own activities. While their spelling and grammar skills still leave much to be desired, they seem to have the genuine concern of real scholars.

C. Values and Attitudes

Throughout their entire educational program young people are acquiring a set of values and attitudes whether we acknowledge them or not. Often they are the wrong kinds; often students verbalize one kind and act on the basis of another. The development of a consistent and fine set of values and attitudes looms large among the goals of every general education class. The development can take two forms: acquiring values through "living" them or acquiring them through direct study of problem areas, such as "Bases for Acquiring the Values by Which We Live."

Sometimes the values and attitudes are difficult to detect and measure, as they often constitute "a vast invisible world." In other cases it is very evident that students are making visible and noteworthy efforts to build a sound sense of principles to serve as a firm basis for their life.

Perhaps four specific examples will serve to illustrate ways in which some classes are meeting this area of learning.

1. AN EIGHTH GRADE WORKS FOR ITS TRIP

Thirty-three families received the following letter one day in April:

Dear Parents:

The eighth grade is planning to set aside the next three weeks of this quarter for the members of the class to work toward a goal of some kind of trip. During that time we plan to earn enough money by doing various kinds of odd jobs so that we can pay our own expenses.

We know that the class would appreciate any odd jobs that you or your friends and neighbors might want done. The work would be done on our own time, after school and on Saturdays. The following is a list of suggested jobs; in addition, we would welcome any others that might be available.

1. Private paper drives
2. Baby-sitting
3. Household chores
4. Painting garages, etc.
5. Car and window washing
6. Caddying
7. Mowing lawns
8. Running errands
9. Cleaning out basements, yards, lawns
10. Gardening
11. Working in stores
12. Farm jobs
13. Making and selling cookies and candies, etc.
14. Typing and clerical work

We will appreciate your co-operation in letting your boy or girl work for you and other people. We would like to stress the point that the money is to be *earned;* we do not wish it to be given to us. During this work period our homework assignments will be decreased somewhat in order to permit us to take time for the work.

In addition to the above project we also hope to increase our class treasury by widespread collection of tax stamps. It would be a great help to us if you would save any and all tax stamps that you and your friends receive.

If you have any further questions concerning our projects, your own boy or girl can help give you additional details. Also, Miss Hunt would be glad to supply any information that you might wish.

Sincerely yours,

John Smith
President of the Class

Jane Doe
Secretary of the Class

When the question of a possible trip came up in the eighth grade general education class, the teacher saw an opportunity for guiding the boys and girls into some experiences which would not only give them added respect for the value of money but would also give them an appreciation of the worth of some meaningful work. Although several of the youngsters were already earning their allowances, for the most part expenses for school trips and activities came from father's wallet. After much discussion of the advantages and values of earning their own way for their proposed trip, the class agreed on the idea. The president and secretary were commissioned to write a letter to be sent to all the parents, and everyone began exploring any and all possibilities to earn a few pennies.

It was agreed also that each student would keep a record of the work he did and the amount he earned. Some of the boys evolved a form card and printed enough copies for the entire class.

INDIVIDUAL WORK REPORT
8th Grade

Name _____ Date, from _____ to _____

Date	Kind of Work	Number of Hours	Amount of Money
_____	_____	_____	_____
_____	_____	_____	_____

Etc.,

Total _____,   _____

The girls had more difficulty than the boys in finding kinds of work they could do. Baby-sitting was the most common of their jobs, although a few of them could be found weeding, painting, and mowing lawns. Boys' jobs included mowing lawns, washing cars, and caddying. In a few instances parents had to supplement the earnings as the day of the trip drew near and not everyone had made enough for his expected expenditures. However, some earnings reached as much as $11.50.

The trip itself took on added meaning for the students as they realized how hard they had worked to make it possible. Money was spent with a little more deliberation as the boys and girls made every effort to receive value for value.

2. AN ELEVENTH GRADE LOOKS AT ITS HABITS

When the eleventh grade began to examine the area of teen-age problems, it was not possible to overlook the question of juvenile de-

linquency. In the course of their exploration of this societal phenom-
enon two of the boys came upon the idea of surveying their classmates
with regard to smoking and drinking. They evolved the following
questionnaire.

SMOKING AND DRINKING

Please answer the questions honestly. Do not put your name on the
paper.

1. *Drinking*
    1. Do you have liquor in your home?
    2. Do your parents allow you to drink in the home?
    3. Do you make a habit of drinking (once a week or so)?
    4. If you don't make a habit of drinking, do you take a drink or sip of
       somebody else's once in a while?
    5. If you aren't allowed to drink in the home, do you try it behind your
       parents' back?
    6. Do you believe drinking to be harmful to your body?
    7. If so, would you or do you still drink?
    8. Do you buy liquor or beer yourself?
    9. Do you drink with teen-age friends?
    10. Do you drink because your friends drink?
    11. Do you drink to impress people?
    12. If you don't drink, state some reasons why.
2. *Smoking*
    1. Do you have cigarettes, pipes, or cigars in your home?
    2. Do your parents allow you to smoke?
    3. Do you smoke?
    4. Have you ever smoked?
    5. If your parents don't allow you to smoke, do you do it behind their
       backs?
    6. Do you think smoking is harmful?
    7. If so, do you still smoke?
    8. Do you smoke with friends?
    9. Do you smoke because your friends do?
    10. Do you smoke to impress people?
    11. Do you smoke for enjoyment?
    12. Do you buy cigarettes yourself?

There was much food for thought when the class discovered that
almost half of them were permitted to drink at home and more than
half of them smoked. In fact, there was genuine concern over the results of the questionnaire, and serious discussion followed.

3. A SOUTHERN GENERAL EDUCATION CLASS STUDIES THE SEGREGATION
PROBLEM

An eleventh-grade class in the deep South faced a real-life problem when it began to look at the whole question of race relations and
the significance of segregation. The teacher described vividly how this
particular group met the issue. A paraphrase of her comments follows.

The attitude toward Negroes was very harsh. In our first session or
two on this problem we began by raising questions, such as, Is the Negro
mistreated? Is he as good as others? Why is he downtrodden? We had a
free and open discussion, and I let the students say what they felt in an
effort to get their attitudes out in the open. Only four of the students had
slightly favorable attitudes and attempted to give some positive points of
view concerning the Negro. After class these four said to me, "Miss Sim-
mons, have you ever heard such things in your life, the way the others are
talking?" I reassured them a little and said that for the time being it might
be best to let them talk.

After all of their feelings had been expressed and attitudes revealed,
I said, "Is it about time now to get some facts, to do some research, to be
able to cite some evidence for your beliefs?" Some intensive study followed, with some surprising (to them) information turning up. The only
material they could find supporting their prejudices came from some newspaper editorials and some literature which had been put out by a political
group a few years before.

Before long the students asked to visit the Negro High School. I was
frank with them and said that I was not sure they were ready for such a
visit, that I feared their attitudes were such that they would be rude. They
reassured me, however, and agreed to the usual courtesies, to marks of
respect, such as the use of the titles, Mr., Miss, and Mrs., to shake hands
when introduced, and so forth.

Their visit was an enjoyable and successful one, unmarred by any
untoward incident. In the ensuing discussion they indicated that they had
not had opportunity to talk to enough of the Negro students. Would it be
possible, they asked, for Mr. B. to come and bring some juniors and seniors
with him to our school? Such a visit was arranged, and further mutual
understanding was achieved.

When the students discussed and wrote their evaluation of these experiences, it was evident that their opinions had changed considerably from
those expressed the first day. They felt that they had a greater understanding of the Negro people and of their problems. In general, they concluded
that segregation is bad for the Negroes and about half of them thought it
bad for the whites. However, they were not ready to advocate doing away

with it immediately because of the stress and strain of sudden change. There were still a few who felt that equal privileges would be the best solution.

Here, then, is an example of a perceptible change in attitude, thanks to the wisdom of a teacher who recognized that change had to come about slowly and in a way that was meaningful to that class. She attributes much of the success in this study to the approach used the first day or two, when the students were permitted to air their prejudices and misconceptions without any expression of shock or disapproval from her. By maintaining a judicious, open attitude and guiding the students into real study and investigation she feels that more lasting good was accomplished than if she had tried in the very beginning to quiet and submerge their attitudes. She believes that such a procedure would have blocked all later attempts to develop more wholesome and fair-minded attitudes.

In addition, the teacher was familiar with and sensitive to community attitudes and knew that such a visit as this one was possible and feasible. It would be a mistake to indulge in class planning in certain controversial areas without taking into account community mores.

4. A SENIOR GENERAL EDUCATION CLASS SHARES ITS CHRISTMAS

The class that was engaged in a study of the holding power of its high school found an opportunity to make a real contribution to the whole problem of the drop-out. The students themselves describe what happened.

It was just a few weeks before Christmas when the committee received an answer to one particular questionnaire. With this questionnaire a letter was received giving information on why the children of this family had dropped out of school. One reason was lack of suitable clothing to wear. Since there is still one child in school, the entire class decided it would like to help this family if it could.

After talking with the group about the letter, the class decided to gather clothing and other things which it was thought the family could use. After the garments were assembled it was decided to wrap them in Christmas paper. This was done during the general education class. Names of persons were put on individual cards showing which packages were to be received by individual persons in the family.

With the help of Mr. E., who excused three 12-A boys from his physics class, the packages were delivered the afternoon before the class had its Christmas party.

This project took the place of an exchange of gifts among members of the 12-A class.

How are values and attitudes developed? It seems that patience and understanding play a large part in promoting desirable values, along with a sensitivity to the appropriate moment for action and discussion. General education teachers can develop a sense of responsibility in students by giving them responsibility, through permitting, even insisting on, their taking the initiative in getting speakers and films, through making them accountable for some materials, even to the extent of replacing these if lost. A sense of honesty and integrity can be developed in a variety of ways, as by self-correction of tests and drills. If cheating occurs, it can be used as a teaching situation. Consideration for others and a desire to help those less fortunate can be developed not only in connection with many local situations, such as Christmas baskets for the needy, or in national ones, as contributing to the Red Cross, but also on an international scale. One seventh-grade class arranged a benefit baseball game, the proceeds of which were to go to CARE. The project grew out of an article in Senior Scholastic concerning the many needs of European children. Students planned the game, arranged with a local park for a baseball diamond, sold the tickets, advertised the game, including newspaper publicity, and had the satisfaction of sending a money order to CARE for $56.53.

• **Wherever possible, skills, values, and attitudes are developed in a functional relationship with the problem orientation of the general education class. Need very often determines the timing of specific study, and purpose determines the emphasis. However, there are many times when direct and even unrelated attack is made upon skill areas. In the same way values and attitudes are sometimes examined and analyzed directly and in concentrated fashion, along with efforts to make their development a continuing aspect of the students' life.**

8

Evaluating

Growth and Progress

An on-going process in the general education class is that of evaluation, which can take many forms and serve many purposes. Individually and co-operatively, continuously and critically, students learn to appraise the values that they are deriving from their work together, examine and re-examine their goals and procedures, revise their plans, and determine the effectiveness of their work. Nothing is free from scrutiny as the general education class uses evaluation not as an end in itself but as a tool, a means toward the goal of effective learning.

A. Evaluation Serves Many Purposes

Evaluation is a multipurpose practice, no longer restricted to testing information for purposes of marking and reporting to parents. Rather, it has many uses for both teacher and students that will make their work together more effective and meaningful.

1. IT GIVES A MORE COMPREHENSIVE UNDERSTANDING OF THE INDIVIDUAL PUPIL

In one eighth-grade class, the teacher had for some time been especially interested in Dick, an outstanding member of the general education class, respected by his classmates and often placed in leadership roles. With all his fine characteristics, however, there was a baffling quality about him. It sometimes seemed that he had developed an unmistakable yet invisible shell around himself which prevented anyone from getting close to him.

156

When, at the end of the fall quarter, the eighth-grade students wrote an evaluation of themselves, Dick's statement was especially interesting to the teacher.

I believe that my main weaknesses are story writing and sometimes spelling. I have a terrible memory of names, places, and sometimes math. I am always forgetting to do things that are important.

I do not get along too well with others because I have different ideas about what's what. Therefore some people do not agree. I sometimes forget to think before I speak and often say things I don't really want to say.

As for my personality it is very hard for me to explain, but I will attempt.

I believe I try to help other people get over their troubles and habits. I am not too interested in baseball and basketball; I like football and wrestling and badminton. I enjoy being class treasurer though I would rather be president. I believe I work best in a small group. I like to listen to all kinds of music and I like to see good movies. I sometimes get in moods talkative and not talkative. I often jump to conclusions.

And when I am trying to write evaluations my writing is not very neat.

Dick thus revealed some self-concepts that did much toward promoting more sensitive understanding of him. "I have a terrible memory of names, places, and sometimes math." Such a trait had not been clearly recognizable during these first few months. "I do not get along too well with others because I have different ideas about what's what." If anything, Dick was one youngster who seemed to get along well with all members of the class. Why did he feel otherwise? "I sometimes forget to think before I speak and often I say things I don't really want to say." The teacher's impression was that he was a very deliberative speaker, thoughtful and considerate in his comments.

Here, then, were clues to a deeper understanding of Dick. Perhaps the teacher had not been so observant as she might have been; or maybe some of these traits showed only in out-of-class situations. Again, the boy may have been too critical of himself. At any rate, in such pupil self-analysis lay the direction for further understanding on the part of the teacher.

Self-evaluation such as this can occur at any time during the ongoing work of the class. Some teachers find it effective to request such statements periodically, perhaps at the end of each semester or at the close of each unit of work; or the procedure can be used only when it seems clearly called for in the work of the class. For example, students might be having an especially frustrating time in their group or committee work on a particular problem. To clear the air, so to speak, to take stock, it might be decided that some self-analysis is in order. Another approach that some teachers like is to obtain some self-evaluating statements at the beginning of a school year in order to become early familiar with the students' self-concepts and in order to recognize change and growth over a period of time.

2. IT PROVIDES INFORMATION FOR EFFECTIVE GUIDANCE

With the great emphasis given to individual and group guidance in the general education class, teachers use a variety of ways to uncover as much information as possible about their students. One evaluative technique gave some concrete evidence for an opinion that one teacher had about Nancy, a belief that the girl lacked confidence in her abilities.

EIGHTH GRADE INVENTORY

Do you think that you have a special weakness or need for help in any of the following areas? If so, check them.
Spelling
Reading
    Difficulty in reading rapidly enough
    Difficulty in finding interesting books
    Difficulty in understanding what you read
Writing
    Difficulty in thinking about things to write about
    Difficulty in writing well and accurately
    Difficulty in writing interestingly
Oral Expression
    Difficulty in feeling at ease before a group
    Difficulty in speaking clearly and loudly
    Difficulty in expressing yourself in an interesting way
Any other particular weaknesses

Nancy checked every item in the above inventory, but her opinion of herself did not square with the facts. Though she had difficulty with fundamental skills she could write creatively. She seemed at ease in front of a group and was a natural and spontaneous speaker with a charming manner. The inventory then pointed the way to some needed guidance for Nancy, to help her arrive at a more realistic view of her strengths and weaknesses.

Thomas, on the other hand, was underestimating his difficulties. He indicated that he felt weak in spelling, that he "sometimes" had difficulty in finding interesting books, and in thinking of things to write about. He apparently failed to recognize very real weaknesses in the accuracy of his writing and in his understanding of what he read.

3. IT PROVIDES OPPORTUNITIES FOR PUPILS TO APPRAISE THEIR OWN PROGRESS

Self-appraisal, when based on honest objectivity and a desire to face the realities of a situation, is worth far more than a teacher's estimate of the same strengths and weaknesses. Some eighth-grade boys and girls showed an awareness of their growth that augured well for future progress.

When I first came to school I used to throw my books on the table all the time but I don't do it as much now. During business meetings I used to chew gum, play with pencils, but I've cured the habit of playing with the pencils, putting things on the western window seat cabinet, but I still chew gum.

At the first of the year I didn't like working in groups but now I don't mind it. I think I still am hesitant though to work in new groups.

I have a weakness in reading but I think I have improved since last year. I think I was awful in spelling last year, but this year I have gotten down to work and studied and now it is one of my strong points.

In addition to individual appraisal, the class as a whole can find it helpful to assess its gains. After each unit the group should do some evaluating of its total progress, responding through discussion or writing, to questions like, "What do you feel you have learned from this unit? What do you think you have contributed to this unit? What do you think we can do to improve?"

B. All Aspects of the Learning Process Are Evaluated

In a general education class nothing is safe from examination; goals, activities, procedures, achievement—all should come under the searching eye of the class, as together the teacher and students use evaluation as a means of improving their learning. At the same time, evaluation procedures themselves should be critically re-examined in order that the class may arrive at more and more effective ways of appraising success and failure.

1. A TENTH-GRADE CLASS EXAMINES ITS CAMPING EXPERIENCE

One of the outstanding events in a college campus school in the Midwest is the three-day camping experience which the ninth- and tenth-grade general education classes have each year. Such a learning experience would not be complete without a critical analysis of the entire activity, its planning and execution. The following are some excerpts from the tenth grade's comments concerning the trip.

Faculty Planning and Supervision

1. The tenth grade believed that the large group of ninth and tenth grades was a definite advantage. We made better use of camp facilities because of the large group than in previous years and both grades learned to know each other better. The grade groups mixed well largely because food committees were made up of members of both grades and games included students regardless of grade or sex.
2. Students and faculty agreed that student pre-planning was *much* better than faculty planning. It was recommended that (1) counselors be chosen definitely for the trip well in advance of the actual trip; (2) faculty members co-ordinate their efforts to insure discussion of plans among themselves; and (3) counselors continue to make clear to the students exactly what they expect of them on the trip. The list of agreements which was used proved very useful both to faculty and students.
3. The trip should have been longer by one day so that educational projects could be completed and so that the schedule could allow free time for rest and recreation chosen by the students.

Student Planning and Behavior

1. Student behavior, attitudes, and co-operation were excellent. Breakage of dishes and equipment amounted to only fifty-five cents, which everyone considered exceptional in view of the number of people involved in food preparation and the number living in the camp. The total food bill was $227.58.
2. Students definitely recommend the trip to another group. Several of the tenth graders hope that they may be allowed to consider the possibilities of taking the trip in 1959–1960. The matter was not discussed in the group and no guarantee was given to those who raised the question.
3. The following suggestions were made:
   a. *Nothing* should be left in the lodge overnight.
   b. Take paper sack to camp so that each person will have a place to put waste paper and other debris until it can be properly disposed of.
   c. Keep equipment and personal belongings in your own cabin and know which articles are yours.
   d. Take candy bars if you wish but no one can sell anything on the grounds by state law. The caretakers have a state-owned concession in the lodge.

Educational Projects and Resources

1. Resource people like those from the State Conservation Department and the University should be asked to work with group during entire stay. Men in forestry, entomology, botany, geology, aquatic life and other areas can best work with students over an extended period of time and are often willing to do so. Such resource people should be listed and kept in trip folder for future reference.
2. A group might well undertake a project of drawing a map of the camping area, marking the trails and location of cabins, lodge, lake, fire tower, etc. At present such a map does not exist but would be quite valuable to the campers.

Recreation

1. Free time of 2½ or 3 hours should be blocked into the schedule. Too little time was allowed for playing games, taking individual hikes, relaxing, showering, and recreational activities on this year's trip.
2. Evening program needs to be varied and problems involved foreseen as far as possible. The talent show was not produced because of insufficient time for organization and the lush opportunity for students to "needle" each other. Objections were raised to films on the basis that they can be seen any time under better conditions than those in camp. Some students believed that group singing, dancing—round and square—were the best parts of the programs, but were not done often enough or for a long enough time.

Living and Eating at Camp

1. Clean-up and food preparation were very well done. Washing dishes was easy since each table accepted the responsibility for washing the dishes for that group. Pans of water (one for washing; one for rinsing) were brought from the kitchen and all dishes washed, area cleaned, and dishes returned to kitchen. Since dishes were washed at each table in the dining hall, no dishwashing detail was needed.
2. Cabin inspection in the morning and bed check at night worked as well as expected. Since those situations are common in camp experiences, they were accepted as part of the total experience.
3. The grounds were in good condition on the day we left even before they were policed for stray papers and debris. After policing, the grounds looked even better than they had when we arrived.

2. EIGHTH GRADERS SCRUTINIZE THEIR GROUP REPORTS

Committee reports and presentations come in for their share of attention, as boys and girls constantly strive to improve their ways of sharing their learnings with the rest of the class. One class used the following questions to help each group see its work through the eyes of the rest of the class.

EVALUATION OF GROUP PROJECTS AND REPORTS

1. Was there evidence of careful planning?
2. Was the presentation interesting in form and manner?
3. How well was the project presented?
   a. Did the members speak clearly and loudly?
   b. Were the members sure of themselves and their material?
   c. Did they seem at ease in front of the class?
4. What are your impressions concerning the information presented?
   a. Was there enough presented for you to understand the topic?
   b. Was there a logical arrangement of information?
   c. Was the information clear to you?
   d. List some specific points of information about which you are puzzled.
5. How well did the methods and projects fit the material and information?
   a. Was the form used suited to the type of information?
   b. Can you suggest a form of presentation that would be better suited to this particular topic?
6. Did the results, as you saw and heard them, justify the amount of time spent?
7. List some specific suggestions for ways of presenting information to the class.
8. List some specific problems growing out of this group's work that you think the class ought to discuss as a whole (either problems of information or presentation or ways of working together).

3. CLASSES EVALUATE ACHIEVEMENT TOWARD GOALS AND OBJECTIVES

In addition to procedures and activities, general education classes are also interested in ways of evaluating achievement toward their goals and objectives. A seventh-grade class had just completed a unit of orientation to their new junior high school. As a means of discovering the effectiveness of their study they engaged in the following quiz.

HOW WELL DO I KNOW MY SCHOOL?

I. Have I learned my way around Forest?

1. Can I find rooms, offices and special facilities without difficulty?
2. Do I understand the bell schedule?
3. On which floor is the library?
4. Where do I keep my bicycle?
5. Where is the hospital suite?

6. How many corridors are on the third floor?
7. Where is Ranger paper headquarters?
8. Where is the Lost and Found?
9. How many people does the auditorium hold?
10. Where are the boys' shops located?
11. Where are the home economics rooms?
12. On what floor are the science rooms located?
13. Where is the projection room?
14. At what times may I go to my locker?
15. What is the correct procedure for indoor recess?

II. Have I become acquainted with the faculty and other school personnel?

1. How many faculty members do I know by name?
2. Do I know one teacher from each department?
3. Who sponsors the Glee Club?
4. Who is in charge of the Stage Crew?
5. What is the nurse's name?
6. Who is the school doctor?
7. Who sponsors the Student Council?
8. Who teaches instrumental music?
9. Who is the head janitor?

III. Have I become proud of my school?

1. Is Forest the kind of school in its building and facilities that I would most like to attend?
2. What activities give me the most satisfaction personally?
3. Do I take care of school property?
4. Do I sing the school song with respect and enthusiasm?
5. Did I take an intelligent and active part in the recent Student Council election?
6. Have I done my best in my studies, conduct, and citizenship to make Forest proud of me?

IV. Have I learned about the clubs at Forest?

1. To how many clubs do I belong?
2. Have I inquired about clubs from others?
3. Have I passed on information about clubs to others?
4. Is there a club we do not have, that I think would be a good club for Forest?
5. What can I do to try to start such a club?
6. What musical organizations are there?
7. What are some of the duties of the Stage Crew?
8. In what after-school athletic activities may I participate?

9. Who are the officers of the Student Council?
10. What is the purpose of the Student Council?
11. What awards are given?
12. How may I earn an award?
13. What is the A.A. organization?
14. Who are the faculty advisers of the Ranger paper?
15. Who is editor of the Ranger?
16. What are the duties of the Rangers?

V. Do I co-operate with the rest of the school by doing the right thing?
1. Do I follow the school's regulations carefully?
2. Do I take care of school property?
3. Have I done my best through conduct, courtesy, and sportsman-ship to be a good citizen of Forest?
4. Has it been necessary for any teacher or Ranger to correct or punish me?
5. Do I take part in class sports at lunch time?
6. Have I done any extra work outside the classroom or after school to help make class projects more successful?
7. Have I completed every project I have started?
8. When going on trips, have I conducted myself in such a way that I created a good impression for Forest?

Acquisition of knowledge is not overlooked as boys and girls try to determine the extent of their learning, and tests take their rightful place in the evaluative process. In addition to standardized and teacher-made tests, the students often prepare their own. Occasionally comittees can give tests after reporting; often they can take the form of true-false items. Or a committee can be responsible for formulating questions to be incorporated in tests of one kind or another.

C. Evaluation Takes Many Forms

1. THE STUDENT LOOKS AT HIMSELF

Some teachers believe that the general education class has unique opportunities for helping young people to learn to understand and ac-cept themselves. More and more, education is assuming responsibility for the development of self-understanding. What more suitable setting for such growth than in the intimacy of the general education class situation.

An illustration can be given from an eighth-grade class, whose stu-dents became very much interested in learning to understand them-selves better and decided to do a self-analysis rating. An individual inventory form was used in which each student rated himself with regard to specific items dealing with appearance, voice, good manners, temper, co-operation, and the like.

Individual Evaluation

1. Is very attractive in appearance ⎯⎯⎯⎯⎯
2. Has good manners ⎯⎯⎯⎯⎯
3. Is friendly ⎯⎯⎯⎯⎯
4. Has a pleasant voice ⎯⎯⎯⎯⎯
5. Gets along well with different kinds of persons ⎯⎯⎯⎯⎯
6. Controls temper well ⎯⎯⎯⎯⎯
7. Co-operates cheerfully with others ⎯⎯⎯⎯⎯
8. Is well liked, etc. ⎯⎯⎯⎯⎯

In the ensuing discussion some of the students asked if it wouldn't be possible to find out how their classmates felt about them. One girl said that it would help to know whether others felt that she was friendly or got along well with different kinds of persons. It was agreed that each student would rate and be rated by two others, a boy and a girl, anonymously. Each pupil was then given his sheet with these ratings on it. There was much food for thought for Larry who found that two classmates indicated that they thought him rather vain and boastful, and for Tim who learned that his lack of self control was as evident to others as to himself.

This kind of approach should be utilized only where the learning environment and relationships are of such a nature that everyone recognizes the positive value of helping one another toward self-understanding. If a class is not ready for an objective, unemotional examination of personal qualities, more harm than good can result. A teacher has need for great sensitivity and understanding before embarking in directions such as these.

Another approach to self-evaluation is the relatively unstructured one in which students can do a little soul-searching and try to identify strengths and weaknesses. The writing of one eleventh-grade girl illustrates how perceptive students can be.

At the moment I am on the verge of making a decision which will color and direct the rest of my life—namely, choosing a career. I have a talent in art which may be developed, or I am equipped to go into religious education. I am rather mixed up, so take what I may write (not only this paper, but all that I create) with "a grain of salt."

My main weakness is an absolute fear of making a fool of myself. If

I am to become a leader, I must overcome this. On the other hand, if I believe something strongly enough, I will defend my ideal "come hell or high water." I am far too stubborn for my own good or any one else's. I am lazy, and would much rather read or draw than work. I am rather easily hurt, and this, too, I must correct. To come to smaller things, you will soon find that I cannot spell. My almost constant companion is an eraser.

This may or may not be important . . . I seem to fail miserably in athletics. I love to swim, and can swim fairly far, but not fast at all. I enjoy badminton and I am learning tennis, but I don't know much about them yet. I dislike basketball and as for hockey, I can thus far take it or leave it. So much for sports except that I *love* to walk.

Now for strengths. I have inherited from my father a slight ability to bluff, and I can sell things, but not myself. (Before I forget it, please excuse the pen, it seems to be running terribly—blurry, I mean.) I hate to study, but usually have my lessons and almost always on time. If I happen to forget and turn them in late, please forgive me. If I do not have them entirely, I usually can bluff it out. I can report before the class better if I thoroughly know my subject, but it doesn't really matter. I can take notes O.K., but would rather just listen.

I have often boasted (yes, I admit it, *boast* is the word) that I will read anything. This is almost true, except if I start a book, and the hero seems about to make a fool of himself, I put down the book. You will have no trouble in getting me to read, but rather to keep me from reading too much. As to how much—the answer is—too much! When? Home, school, anywhere and when I have an extra minute.

I like individual study with reports back to the class, or everyone studying the same thing, approaching it from different ways, and then a general discussion, pooling our information.

I really don't know what I would like to study, except I particularly like things to do with people, their reactions, their actions, and their ideals.

I sincerely hope this is what you wanted—and that it helps you.

Not all of the boys and girls were so perceptive as Dotty, nor did all of them share her insights into their own motivations and actions. Yet most of them took a remarkably objective and dispassionate look at themselves. Such reactions can be of invaluable help to the teacher as he strives to understand his students.

2. THE STUDENT LOOKS AT THE GROUP

Similarly, evaluation can take the form of the student's looking at the progress of the whole class group as one eighth grade did after a few months' work. One student's opinions are worth noting.

CLASS EVALUATION OF FALL QUARTER

I think the group was a little unsure to start the year off. Still they did fairly well in their first assignments. The group I was in was rather slow in starting to work together, but several changes in seating helped. It is hard to tell how the other groups got along as I was not in them.

When we settled down on unit work the groups we divided into were a little slow in getting down to business. The members did not pay attention too well.

However, I think we did pretty well on the whole. A few things should be corrected, such as paying attention and working individually without fooling around.

Most of the class should have learned something about the unit. If they didn't, it was not the fault of the committees.

The class discussions went pretty well most of the time. Their attitude toward the work was pretty good.

I think that for the first quarter it was pretty successful. Many of the faults can easily be corrected this winter.

3. THE GROUP LOOKS AT ITSELF

In many general education classes teachers have group evaluation at the conclusion of a unit, sometimes in writing, more often through discussion. Listed on the board as they are mentioned are the good points of their work on the unit and the bad points, along with suggestions for improvement. At various times during the study of the unit the class evaluates itself on its success in meeting the objectives agreed upon by the students at the beginning of their study.

After one such discussion by some eighth-grade boys and girls of their strengths and weaknesses as a group, the teacher made the following summary of their conclusions and gave each one a copy.

EIGHTH GRADE EVALUATION

On the whole the eighth grade has a friendly, cheerful manner that is most desirable; this pleasantness is usually accompanied by an attitude of co-operation and understanding. These qualities should be strengthened, where necessary, and will probably become more and more evident as time passes.

The helpful attitude which some of us adopt toward others is most admirable. It is very gratifying to see how some of us are always so willing to assist another person, to take up for him if we think he is unfairly put on the spot. This loyalty and sympathy might well become more general, since they are very desirable qualities.

We have a noticeable curiosity about a variety of things and our ideas usually show thought and imagination. Many of us have a clear and pleasing way of expressing ourselves and seem to be quite at ease in front of the group.

We have made much progress in learning to work together well and in planning co-operatively. There has been marked improvement in the procedures we follow in group sessions and in the ways we work with one another.

Along with these very fine strengths there are naturally some weaknesses which we should endeavor to overcome. However, there can be progress and growth only if *all* of us think seriously about our objectives and take an active and co-operative interest in achieving these goals which we think are important.

1. Class discussions still remain too frequently the monopoly of only a few people, chiefly because the rest do not care to contribute or feel they have nothing to offer.
2. While there is a great talent for *talking* things through and verbal planning, there is a lesser desire to *act* and carry through plans. We are all anxious to have things done, but we are reluctant to *do* them.
3. Occasionally our sense of humor is still a little "off-balance," and we are easily amused at some things which are not really funny.
4. There is sometimes a lack of tolerance for other people's ideas and interests; occasionally we are all too quick to make fun of a classmate's suggestion or to reject it because it doesn't interest us particularly.
5. We are still taking too much time to do things. This results from a reluctance to get down to business immediately in group planning and a generally slow-moving way of tackling problems both individually and in groups.
6. There is a general unwillingness to devote some "out-of-general education" time to important projects. Many occasions will require us to do some of this in the future.
7. One of our most serious weaknesses is a lack of attention to care of property and appearance of the room. We are entirely too careless in our handling of books and magazines, and so far there does not seem to be enough pride in our room to want to keep it neat and clean.
8. Another important weakness is our failure to form certain habits of neatness and organization, such as arrangement of notebooks, appearance of papers, passing of papers, etc.

4. THE TEACHER LOOKS AT THE STUDENT

It is important for the teacher to give the students his reactions to their work as individuals and as a class. In this way the students can be guided in the right direction for improvement.

For example, in one situation a teacher made a practice of commenting on students' work, either directly on their paper or on a separate page in the case of oral presentation. The following comments were placed in the folder of one of the boys after he had presented an individual project to the class.

It is very difficult to evaluate your project, Harvey, since there was so little evidence on which to base criticism. I do not believe your work represented any deep research, nor were your sketches of much help. Did you consult with one of the arts staff about your plans?

Although Carroll had already presented a similar project, you could have still done a good job with pointing up certain basic ideas. In addition, you could have given a lot more information. There are many fascinating details you might have explored, such as a comparison of building materials, building methods, and laboring conditions.

I do not feel that you have yet given any indication of your true ability. Remember, too, not to chew gum when reporting to the class.

The eleventh-grade students welcomed such specific and concrete criticisms of their individual efforts, and the teacher had found this a useful and efficient method of making evaluation an on-going process, not a culminating activity at the end of the unit or semester only.

In the same way some eighth-grade committees could occasionally look forward to the teacher's reactions to their presentations and reports.

EVALUATION OF GROUP 1

Your presentation was excellent from the point of view of interest, form, and information. The script was well thought out and well written. You did especially well in carrying out the idea of a radio program from beginning to end. It is little things, like introducing the program, using a station name, having a time signal, mentioning the next program, that make a presentation like yours successful.

Your manner was informal and friendly, and showed an understanding of your material, on the whole. All of you spoke clearly and loudly enough, but a couple of you might give some thought to putting more expression into your speech. You are to be congratulated on your pronunciation of difficult words and names; there were only one or two slips on that score.

The information you included was excellent and well organized; on the whole, I think it gave an adequate and satisfactory picture of your topic. There is, however, some slight question in my mind as to whether everyone in the group has as thorough an understanding as might be desirable.

There were some weaknesses to which you might like to give thought in the future. As you yourselves have pointed out, some time was lost through "fooling around" and a reluctance to keep your mind on the problem at hand. This was evident not only in your group meetings but also in other work situations, when you worked alone or with another person.

In some instances your note taking could have been better, especially in the more "mechanical" aspects of neatness, organization, clarity, etc. This is especially important if a committee is going to assume the responsibility of "pulling things together." Then, too, better notes would mean a better understanding of the topic on your part. Also, it may well be that you placed too heavy a load on the committee of three who wrote the script. Think critically of your personal contribution to the entire project and decide whether you did your best or not and what you can do to improve. As an example, it is always wise to "follow through" with a plan, unless there is an excellent reason for discarding it. I believe that some of you had started a map, but nothing came of it. A good map of your own might have been more attractive and helpful than the smaller wall map you used.

There might have been some more helpful introductory remarks in which someone explained what you had been studying, how you divided the assignments, and what kind of project you had prepared. This type of introduction not only acquaints your audience with certain essential details, but also helps to "set the mood" for the presentation which is to follow.

One very obvious omission was your failure to mention that a member of your group would locate various areas on the map during the recording. As a result, hardly anyone noticed this being done. If the attention of the class had been called to this very helpful aspect of your presentation, it is highly likely that a more intelligent understanding of your topic would have resulted. Another helpful procedure would have been to list new words and names on the board beforehand, so that the class would recognize them upon hearing them. Then, too, pictures would have added effectively to the project. If you had wanted a longer presentation, you might have incorporated some dramatic skits in your radio program—perhaps as added proof of the greatness of these men.

However, these are just suggestions to keep in mind for the future. On the whole you did a fine piece of work, and you should be pleased. You had intelligent leadership, although you often made it difficult for it to operate effectively. In general, it seems that each of you fulfilled your responsibility more or less satisfactorily.

5. THE GROUP LOOKS AT THE STUDENT

In some classes where there is an unusually high quality of rapport among all members—teacher and students—individuals can gain much valuable insight into their own behavior and skills and aptitudes through group discussion and reaction. One teacher has found it possible to have a total group discussion of the good points and weaknesses of each student. She has reported the comment of one boy who said after such a session, "I knew all those things about me but I didn't know everyone else did." In a similar way another class has evolved such *esprit de corps* that committee chairmen can rate committee members without harmful effects to the morale of any individual or the group.

In another class it was decided to have each student evaluate five of his classmates with regard to personality and work habits, with special attention given to points that needed improving.

Here are the five opinions of Billy.

1. *Personality*—appears to be very smart (has knowledge) ; knows how to express himself
   Work Habits—very good
   Improvements—should give others a chance to talk and should show less of his knowledge because he appears to be a "know-it-all"

2. *Good Points*
   Personality—speaks well
   Work habits—does pretty well

   Bad Points
   Personality—1. talks too much to his neighbor
                 2. talks too much in discussion
                 3. sometimes he tries to act comical
   Work Habits—talks too much

3. *Good Points*
   Personality—1. Good speaking ability
                 2. as far as I know he is honest
   Work Habits—expresses himself well

   Bad Points
   Personality—1. needs to improve conversation
                 2. talks too often
   Work Habits—1. doesn't take enough time to think clearly about assignments
                 2. doesn't always have material
                 3. full of ideas but doesn't follow through
                 4. wants things his own way

4. *Good Points*
   Personality—his personality is not so good; he needs to think more of others than of himself
   Work Habits—he is a good worker and knows it

Points to be Improved—needs to understand that other people have feelings too

5. *Good Points*—is a nice boy; is improving greatly

Points that Need Improvement—still talks too much at times; pay more attention when others are talking

Such evaluation as this, while it has its danger signals and should be utilized by only the most sensitive and understanding teacher under the best of circumstances, can serve several valuable purposes. In forthright, objective, unprejudiced manner it can help each boy or girl see himself as others see him. He gains a glimpse of the "self" which faces his classmates and in many ways learns much from this reflection in a mirror. Then, too, these young people can gain a deepened appreciation of the difficulty of the evaluative process and a heightened respect for the judgments which, of necessity, must be made of young people as they move from grade to grade.

6. THE PUBLIC LOOKS AT THE STUDENT

One school has developed an interesting approach to the question of field trips which serves as an excellent example of another kind of evaluation. Students are permitted to make field trips in small groups without a teacher. The committee takes along a brief evaluation sheet to be filled in and returned (in stamped, self-addressed envelope) by the firm or person visited.

Will you please answer the following questions after the survey visit made by my children:

How many children were in the group?
Did they arrive on time for their appointment?
Did they ask intelligent questions?
Was their behavior satisfactory?
Do you approve of this type of education?
Would you welcome other groups of children?

Comments:

Teacher _____

Two replies will serve to illustrate how effective such a procedure is in helping students see themselves as the public sees them.

We at Central Fire Station were most happy to conduct a tour for your pupils through our station.

You sent a letter requesting answers to various questions; these I will answer numerically:

1. There were five (5) pupils.
2. Their attitude and behavior unquestionably was one of the best we have encountered.
3. The questions asked by the group were exceptional for their age. In fact, they cornered some of our men and officers and they had to be rescued by our Chief, who happened to be present.
4. This mode of education in which a student can see first hand is definitely far superior to the type where they have to read it. A picture is worth a thousand words.

Allow me to reiterate that we were most happy to conduct this tour and should any other group from your school desire to visit our station they are most welcome. We are at your service.

This letter was signed by the captain of the fire station. The following letter was returned by the assistant superintendent for the county public schools.

1. How many students were in the group?
   Six
2. Was their attitude and behavior acceptable?
   Yes
3. Did they ask intelligent questions?
   They asked intelligent questions. The questions which they asked me were very clear-cut and penetrating. I only wish that all of the school personnel in the county understood fully the answers to all of the questions which this group of students raised.
4. Do you feel that this experience is good education?
   Yes, good training in civic responsibility
Remarks:
   In our present society one must learn how to conserve the time of a person who is being interviewed and how to get the most information from the time which is used. One must also learn how to proceed in obtaining information about the various phases of his government. The students had thought through their questions very carefully in advance of the conference with me, asked them most intelligently, and raised further questions when any points were not made clear. I thought it one of the best conferences which I have ever held with any group.

D. New Ways of Evaluating Require New Ways of Reporting to Parents

With the breadth of purpose and goal that is typical of general education teaching and the variety of evaluative techniques employed as part of class learning, it becomes well nigh impossible to confine reporting to parents to a single, stereotyped form, embodying the use of letter or number grades. It has become necessary to evolve more effective and satisfying means of communicating with parents the degrees of success and failure which their children are experiencing in working toward their goals and objectives. More and more, too, general education teachers are using several ways of reporting to parents rather than one way only, so that there will be as completely mutual understanding as possible. While general education teachers alone may use these procedures, increasingly we find that all teachers find value in these different techniques. Many schools are adopting them as their standard methods for reporting to parents.

Two procedures that have gained favor with many teachers are the parent conference and the letter to parents. Some teachers use both techniques to supplement each other and schedule them at appropriate intervals throughout the year. There is a great flexibility to such scheduling, for it might be desirable to confer with some parents more frequently than with others.

One teacher, reporting of his use of the parent conference, has said

One semester I substituted parent conferences in lieu of report cards with some of my students. The plan was on a voluntary basis and about 50% of parents participated. This method of reporting helped me understand students better, and I believe allowed me to clarify the program and help parents better understand their children.

The letter to parents is a technique that informs parents not only how Jimmy is doing but also what the entire class has been concerned with and how well the students are achieving their goals. It gives a comprehensive picture of what goes on in a general education class, of Jimmy's strengths and weaknesses in general education and also in his other subject areas.

One such letter was sent to the parents of an eighth grader at the end of the first quarter.

EIGHTH GRADE REPORT—GENERAL STATEMENT

In general education during autumn quarter the eighth grade has focused its attention on three major projects—room decoration, a party for the seventh grade, and unit study. "Interior decoration" of the room is a long-term project, having as its purpose the co-operative planning of an attractive "living" room. It has involved (and will involve) selection and care of plants, designing and making of draperies, ceramics, and other creative art work. Responsibility for specific plans rests with certain groups, and progress, though necessarily slow, has been satisfactory.

The masquerade party was a success, not only in the final result but also throughout its planning stages. It is noteworthy that every member of the class contributed in a very vital way to the success of this project.

The most mature thinking of the group was evident in the discussion and selection of study units, and it was very gratifying to note that the members of the class thought in terms of the entire year and did some very effective long-range planning. Our first unit centers around the Revolutionary War period in the history of our country. For an intelligent understanding of the events of this era, the class thought it wise to give some preliminary attention to the age of discovery, exploration, and settlement. Committee work in these areas has resulted in some fine learning along with a realization of some basic weaknesses in the group's approach to a historical area of study. From the evaluation of their achievement in this committee work the members of the class have reached certain conclusions concerning the ways of working together and means of organizing their work—conclusions which should indicate effective growth in these directions in the future.

The class plans to study next about another people and their way of life, with France being a tentative choice. During spring quarter our unit will be *Sports, Hobbies, and Recreation.*

In the area of skills attention has been centered on analysis of language arts needs of the pupils, with special emphasis on broadening reading interests and developing abilities in oral and written expression. The boys and girls have written three stories this quarter and efforts have been made not only to assist with the so-called mechanics of writing—spelling, punctuation, vocabulary, but also to encourage more interesting and effective ways of expression.

For more satisfying results with research and unit study attention has been given to ways of taking notes effectively, and the students are being encouraged to develop habits of neatness and organization.

In the area of reading it has been thought wise to try to stimulate genuine interest in reading and a desire to share with others one's reactions to the books being read. Attempts have been made to broaden the reading interests of the students, to develop curiosity in new directions. At the same time careful analysis has been made of the reading needs and difficulties of each student, and throughout the year efforts will be made to assist with these needs.

Throughout all our work together there has been uppermost in our minds the need for learning to live together in a co-operative and satisfying fashion. The assumption of responsibility is a major objective—responsibility not only to a group but to one's self, to see that a job is effectively carried through to a satisfying completion. Along with the development of co-operative group action there has been an effort to assist the individual to grow within the area of his own capacities and abilities. In the final analysis this emphasis on *individual growth,* in all directions, is the key to our work together, not only this past quarter, but for the entire year.

Jimmy has made some fine progress in general education this quarter. He has been conscientious and dependable and seems to be quite happy in his eighth-grade group. His attitude has always been one of friendly co-operation.

If anything, he does not attach enough value to his abilities; as a result, he sometimes has a tendency to be overcritical of himself with little real justification. The sooner he recognizes that he has some fine abilities in many directions, the greater will be his progress, I feel sure.

His writing is quite good, with a pleasing creative style. At the same time he tries to give careful attention to the more mechanical aspects, such as punctuation, spelling, capitalization. Jimmy is one of the few people in the class to have a perfect record on our spelling tests.

He is a careful and meticulous worker. His notes for his unit study show a fine understanding of what he read, and as a result he contributed to the understanding of his particular group. While his classroom participation might be more frequent, when he does take part his contributions are valuable.

He has discharged his responsibilities as vice-president of the class very well, on several occasions conducting business meetings when the president was absent. Jimmy has also represented his class faithfully and well on the Christmas Committee.

There is every indication that Jimmy will continue to make gratifying progress this year, especially after he develops some much-needed self-confidence.

The report continued with similar comments from his other teachers concerning Jimmy's progress in their classes.

One school has analyzed in excellent fashion the characteristics of a good written report to parents.

1. Reports should analyze a student, as specifically as possible, in the following ways:
   a. The growth in skills he should be gaining in a particular area of learning.
   b. The growth he is making in relation to his ability.
   c. The achievement he has made in relation to what is necessary for future learning in the same area.
   d. The personal growth a student is making, or failing to make, in co-operativeness, creativeness, thoroughness, resourcefulness, initiative, respect for the rights and needs of others, personal appearance, participation, leadership, problem solving, responsibility, emotional maturity, self-direction, and work and study habits.

2. Reports should be clear and meaningful to parents, students, and teachers.
    a. Specific incidents where the types of behavior described have been demonstrated aid understanding of a very abstract thing—human behavior and the reasons causing certain kinds of behavior.
    b. Illustrations of the ways students could or should behave in given situations are usually helpful to both parents and students.
3. Reports should be written in relation to past reports.
    a. Repetition of the same type of behavior, either good or bad, in several successive reports by any one teacher is not particularly helpful and in many cases is harmful.
    b. Contradictory remarks in successive reports are all right provided there is seemingly some recognition of the contradiction on the part of the writer.
4. Reports should be written not just as a reporting device but also as a teaching aid or motivative device.
5. Reports should be long enough to accomplish their purpose but not long enough to decrease the effectiveness of the entire report.
6. Reports of student's growth should be related and compared to student self-evaluation.

• Evaluation, then, is a continuous and integral part of the learning process. As such, it serves to help students and teachers to clarify purposes, goals, and objectives; it offers opportunities for examining the degree of success in attaining these goals; and it provides a basis for adjusting learning procedures to meet individual differences and the needs of students.

Evaluation to be effective must be planned from the beginning of the study. As plans progress and as work is completed there must be constant checking against objectives. This checking should be done by the students with the help of the teacher.

There must be evaluation of each activity, each group, each individual and of the study as a whole and it must be continuous. Final evaluation of the project is much easier and more understandable if this is done.

Part Three

Looking Ahead with General Education

9

Teachers for

Tomorrow's Citizens

For some time now the role of the teacher in American education has been gradually shifting from that of imparter of knowledge and sole source of intellectual authority to one of intelligent guidance of the learner toward wisdom and maturity. There have been many reasons for this change. Psychological theory has taught us much about the way people learn, the distinction between learning and recitation, the role of motivation in the learning process, and many other relevant issues. As knowledge has increased in all of the areas of human existence, it has not been possible for any one person to encompass within himself a complete fund of information in any given field which he can then pass on to students. The mind of one individual can no longer be the sole fount of wisdom but must accept as helpful partners the vast quantity of instructional materials and resources that can provide the learner with insight and understanding. The time problem—a nine-month school year, five-day week, six-hour day, forty- to fifty-minute periods—has itself forced a change in our approach to teaching. No longer can the history teacher impart to his students all they need or might want to know about world history—or American history—in the space of one year. Not only must choices be made regarding identification and selection of important content, but also we must employ more effective means of teaching and making this content meaningful.

In every class, then, the role of the teacher has become recast to fit more appropriately the new demands for a mature educational approach. Nowhere is this new role more dramatically in evidence than in the general education classroom where the teacher has the responsibility of fitting his students for life as intelligent citizens in a vast democracy, of developing in them an awareness of broad issues faced by men and women in our society, and of providing them with the intellectual tools of inquiry, assessment, and decision that will enable them to deal with these common problems of man and mankind.

The preceding chapters have given glimpses of the various facets of the teacher's role. We need now but to point out and highlight them to show the nature of the teacher's work in a general education class.

A. *Role of the Teacher in the General Education Class*

It should be clear by now that the general education teacher is, in many ways, as much a *student* as those he teaches. He is constantly a student of adolescents and adolescent behavior, of the sociology of his community and nation, of the culture of his society and its implications for education, of the subject disciplines that bear upon areas of study in the general education classroom. If he should ever forget or grow lax in his role as student, he will have lost the source of all creativity and originality and will soon become the automaton teacher whose notes remain static from year to year and whose teaching remains unaffected by the swirling life and times around him.

If, on the other hand, the general education teacher continuously enlarges his own horizons, retains a healthy curiosity about life and humanity, learns more each day about people and things, he will be in an enviable position to serve his students as guide and consultant. For it is as *guide* that the teacher makes his major contribution to effective learning. By using the knowledge he has carefully acquired and is constantly supplementing, he can lead students along those paths most suited to them, challenging the quick and gently but firmly prodding the slow, inspiring vision and stretching aspirations. It is as a guide that he is ever ready to point directions, set goals, suggest alternatives, evaluate results—*with* his students, not for and in spite of them. As a guide, he can assess and use strengths in young people and gauge weaknesses and ways of overcoming them.

As *consultant* for learning, he is a resource person greatly to be prized, familiar with materials, ready with the appropriate reference at the right time, willing to explore new avenues for the acquisition of knowledge. In the roles of guide and consultant the teacher must stand ready to permit students to make mistakes in plans and errors in judgment, for how else can they learn self-control, self-direction, self-motivation? By the same token the teacher must be quick to help students profit from errors and learn not to make the same mistake twice.

Certainly much is to be learned from failure to succeed—if there is a wise teacher who can point to the learnings effectively.

As the teacher serves variously as student, guide, consultant, he is emerging more and more as a *friend* to young people. The role of friend may seem a strange one to those who have considered the relationship between teacher and students as one involving authority, status, impersonality, even fear. However, there is sufficient psychological evidence to support the belief that learning is more effective when the student-teacher relationship is one of mutual respect and the students can look to the teacher for friendly understanding.

Being a friend to students should not be confused with being "one of the gang." The teacher who becomes too chummy with his students, behaves as though he is one of them, is defeating one of his major roles. For it is unlikely that students who want help and guidance will turn to the teacher who seems too much their own age in actions and outlook. The subtle but important dignity of adulthood should at all times be evident and will give strength and support to the teacher who genuinely tries to be a friend to his students.

Finally, it is not possible for a teacher to serve in any of the roles just outlined without seeing himself at all times as an active citizen in his own society. No longer is the ivory tower of the scholar to be desired, the withdrawal from the clamor of civilization, the remoteness of contemplative isolation. Rather it is the men and women who actively participate in the many institutions of which our society consists—civic, religious, political, club, fraternal—that will be the stimulating and provocative kinds of teachers who should be entrusted with the care and nurture of youth. The teacher who has the qualities needed to provoke, stimulate, and inspire the next generation is the one who contributes to the life of his country, who has convictions based on intelligent understandings of the economic, political, and social issues of his times, and who meets and lives with his fellow men in convivial and productive ways.

B. The Kind of Teacher Needed for the General Education Class

It might be well at this point to highlight some of the important characteristics needed by the person who will be largely responsible for the general education of our youth. Many of these have already been illustrated in earlier chapters, and calling attention to these qualities now serves to sum up our feeling about the kind of teacher needed and will help us then look at how we can obtain such teachers through improved higher education.

1. RESPECT

The general education teacher, more than any other, perhaps, should understand and act upon Emerson's dictum—that the secret of education lies in respecting the pupil. There has been an unfortunate tendency in our pedagogical inheritance to look upon respect as a one-way obligation—to expect, require, demand it of students for teachers and other adults, without the corollary of adult respect for youth. The wise teacher recognizes that this respect involves understanding without misplaced sympathy, empathy without identification, and acceptance with or without approval.

Because the general education teacher remains with students for relatively long periods of time and sees them more as total entities than fragmented receptacles for specialized knowledge, he needs a perspective that permits him to understand cause and effect relationships in student behavior, to perceive skills and abilities as relative in depth and scope, to relate personality factors to learning efficiency. Such skills can be acquired and used effectively only if the teacher has a fundamentally healthy respect for the student as a human being worthy of guidance and, where necessary, redirection and rehabilitation.

2. ADAPTABILITY

The nature of the general education class is such that inescapably the teacher must be an adaptable person. The authoritarian—or insecure—person who must know how to account in advance for every minute of his time with students, the rigid person who cannot deviate from advance plans, the inflexible teacher who cannot tolerate intelligent inquisitiveness in his students—these have no place in a general education classroom, if indeed, in any class.

To help young people achieve maturity in decision making, in cooperative action, in wise compromise, requires a teacher who himself can share responsibility for learning, can involve students in planning, can modify procedures on a moment's reflection. Such a person understands clearly the difference between adaptability and a laissez-faire philosophy and is in no danger of allowing permissiveness to deteriorate into chaos. A capacity for rapid and sudden adjustment to changing learning situations and changing moods of students requires intelligence and skill of a very high order.

3. INTEREST AND INVOLVEMENT

Because the general education teacher is responsible for those learnings commonly needed by all youth, he must have a breadth of interest in and familiarity with a wider area on the spectrum of knowledge than do most people. As we have seen, the learnings needed by all youth range from communication and the communication arts to self-understanding, to awareness of the physical world, to an appreciation of the social, economic, and political pressures existing in society today, to name only a few.

A teacher of such students must have a personal interest in the arts and the contribution they can make to creative living as well as to the development of society and culture. He needs to be familiar with the impact of scientific advances upon social adjustment along with political implications of technological progress. He must understand the intricacies of democratic processes with all their attendant strengths and weaknesses. These few examples illustrate the scope of interest needed by the teacher of a general education class.

However, it would be a mistake to assume that interest and knowledge alone are sufficient. Rather, personal involvement in the many aspects of life is a requisite for the general education teacher—involvement as a person and as a citizen. To be a spectator at the game of living, to peer from an ivory tower at the foibles, aspirations, setbacks of society will only serve to separate the teacher from the mainstream of life as it is lived today and make it impossible for him to guide young people wisely.

4. WELL-BALANCED MATURITY

In effect, a sum of the characteristics above adds up to one major requirement—that the general education teacher be a mature person who lives a healthy, well-balanced, productive life of his own. Maturity is not easy to achieve these days, but somehow we must learn to develop in our prospective teachers a mature outlook that involves self-understanding and understanding of others. And we must develop men and women who themselves have hobbies and interests that keep them constantly growing individuals—alert, curious, human beings involved with life, who do not cease learning after they have met an arbitrary college graduation requirement.

5. KNOWLEDGE

Teaching in a general education class presupposes a background of preparation that has placed a high priority on knowledge. The very nature of such a class imposes responsibilities that make great demands upon the intelligence, wisdom, and understanding of the teacher. Because he is dealing with problem areas that can and do embrace content from many disciplines, he must be conversant with a breadth of subject matter not usually required (even though desirable) of a more specialized teacher. Because he works with young people over a relatively long span of time each day, the general education teacher must have a grasp of the twin psychologies of learning and of adolescence in order that the most effective use be made of time for learning. Because general education is concerned with individuals in their societal setting, the teacher must be familiar with the community environment from which his students come and be able to assess this environment and its influence on students within the larger framework of sound sociological understandings.

Above all, the general education teacher should have a realistic understanding of himself—his own motivations, behavior, goals—in order that he can work effectively with boys and girls as they develop toward mature adulthood. Bringing a background of such varied knowledges is no easy task; however, the importance of a firm grasp of these areas cannot be underestimated. Let us look at one or two in more detail.

a. *Broad grasp of content.* With the bewildering multiplication of knowledge that is a commonplace of our generation, it is not possible for any one person to know everything about anything, nor even much about many things. However, the general education teacher can bring three assets to his teaching: (1) a sound grasp of at least two broad content areas; (2) a curiosity about other areas of knowledge; and (3) a firm command of those tools that give us access to knowledge when it is needed.

(1) TWO BROAD CONTENT AREAS. Certainly it is not too much to ask that a teacher working with fundamental common learnings, should have a thorough grounding in the social sciences and language arts. If we remember that he will be teaching these areas as part of an adolescent's general education, the prospect will not be frightening. His will not be the preparation needed by the prospective researcher or by the specialist in Chaucer or Elizabethan literature or Napoleonic France or economic interpretation of history, whom we find teaching in our colleges and graduate schools today. Rather, the secondary school general education teacher will need broad command of those skills of language—reading, speaking, listening, writing—required of everyone; and of those understandings—historical, geographic, economic, and civic—needed by all informed citizens regardless of vocation, profession, or career. With the specialist teacher lies the responsibility of developing depth where needed by individual students pursuing specified future goals.

For example, some high school students may desire and need a course in journalism; and, if possible, it should be offered. However, all students need to develop an awareness of the nature and impact of mass media on American life. With the general education teacher lies the responsibility for helping students with an understanding of the role of the press, radio, and television in modern society and of the impact these agencies have on our everyday life, along with analysis of bias, motivation, governmental and other restrictions, pressures, and the like. No student should leave high school without such understandings if he is to be a citizen capable of intelligent participation in civic life—at local, state or national level; if he is to be a discriminating purchaser and consumer in the market places of society.

(2) OTHER AREAS OF KNOWLEDGE. However, such breadth in two fundamental areas of knowledge is not sufficient. In addition, the general education teacher must bring to his task some acquaintance with the sciences and the arts, along with a firm respect for all knowledge and a healthy curiosity that will lead him to pursue learning as long as he lives. In a sound college program the student can obtain a foundation of understanding in other areas of human wisdom, sufficient to keep him from being ignorant. Furthermore, it is inconceivable that anyone could have a thorough college preparation in the field of the social sciences without, for example, gaining rich dividends in the form of understandings about art and music. How can one study the Renaissance without studying art, literature and science? How can one study ancient civilization without learning of the "glory that was Greece"?

More important, however, than the specific amount of knowledge gained in college, is the attitude that the general education teacher brings to his teaching. If there is an attitude that perceives the inseparability of knowledge, that respects the contribution of science to social engineering, that is filled with a questing spirit, willing to roam whatever pathways beckon for enlightenment—if such an attitude exists, the general education teacher is already well fortified for his task of drawing upon any and all content for the furtherance of his students' education.

(3) TOOLS FOR FURTHER KNOWLEDGE. Finally, to security in certain subject areas and familiarity with and curiosity about others, must be added a skill in acquiring knowledge not at his finger tips. The general education teacher must bring to his class an ability to use tools of research, to locate information, to weigh and evaluate sources, that will permit him to obtain specific knowledges when needed, to guide boys and girls in their search for knowledge, and to educate himself constantly.

Such skill makes it possible for a general education teacher to embark upon his teaching secure in the knowledge that he can cope with the broad problem areas that are the content of general education classes. He may not be able to discourse at length on atomic and hydrogen energy (although he should be conversant with the social and political implications); however, he will know how to guide his students to sufficient understanding of the scientific principles involved, to draw upon the more detailed knowledge some of them are obtaining in their science classes, to recommend materials and resources to students who want specific technical information.

A firm grasp of content, then, involves a broad understanding of the varied content drawn upon in general education classes, a depth awareness of at least two subject areas, and an ability to further learning in all areas on the part of the teacher as well as the students.

b. *An understanding of adolescents and the way they learn.* An understanding of teen-agers is a recognized requirement for all teachers. However, the general education teacher needs a stronger sensitivity to the adolescent than does anyone else. There is an intimate quality about the general education class—an intimacy growing out of time spent together; out of the nature of co-operative planning; out of the stress on the development of the individual to his highest potential. Such an intimate relationship between teacher and students implies more than mere recognition of the nature and needs of adolescents.

What are some of the important understandings that guide a general education teacher in his work with teen-agers? First, there must be a recognition that adolescence is a time of *adjustment,* a time of *ambivalence,* a time of *decision.* The adolescent is having to adjust to himself and to the changes he notes in himself—physiologically and emotionally. He is adjusting to a new perception of his parents and his family group. He is adjusting to standards and expectations of his peer group, while at the same time facing an orientation to the expectations or lack of them that our present-day society has for teen-agers. He tries to meet the demands of his own expanding maturity—but often without the societal outlets for his churning energies. He is adjusting to new feelings and insights regarding the opposite sex.

All of these adjustments are complicated by the ambivalent nature of adolescence. As the teen-ager matures, he strikes out in the direction of independence from adults—but for a few years finds that he welcomes the security that comes from some degree of dependence upon them. He finds puzzling the fact that society expects responsible, adult-like behavior from him but provides no opportunity for the exercise of adult responsibilities. He is not welcome in the labor market; there is little opportunity for participation in civic affairs. The ambivalence of society is nowhere better demonstrated than in the requirement of military service and training for young people, who are not, however, granted the privilege of active participation in the government which they are, in effect, serving and supporting.

Adolescence is a time for decision in many respects, not least of which is that regarding the young person's choice of future occupation. While still a young teen-ager, he must focus on some future goal in order that he can make intelligent curriculum choices in the secondary school. He must make decisions in the realm of ethical behavior, for which he is woefully unprepared.

Along with an understanding of the personal development of adolescents and their problems must be a recognition that teen-agers are a reflection of the society they live in. At no time has this been more vividly demonstrated than in the middle decades of the twentieth century. The society of the 1950's has been an affluent one, yet an insecure one, a complacent and a conformist society that still raised the call for the individualist, the independent mind; the "cultured" society accepting the superficial accoutrements and culture imposed by the mass media without the necessary struggle for understanding and insight and resulting discrimination that comes with true culture.

Caught in the resulting conflict of values, aware of the examples set by an adult society that, in effect, says, "Don't do as we do, do as we say"; unable to find a place of their own, adolescents have indeed embarked on their own quest for identity. Whether it takes the form of hot-rodding or rock 'n' rolling—of fan clubs and idol identification— the activities are thinly disguised efforts at finding themselves, of discovering some meaning for their enforced stay in a kind of no man's land of growing up.

In the midst of these cross-currents the secondary school raises the banner of education—and is ever hurt and startled that not all teen-agers jump quickly for the grab.

C. Implications for the Preparation of General Education Teachers

If we are to have the kinds of teachers needed for an effective job in the general education class, our teacher education program must be one that is peculiarly suited to the needs of these prospective teachers. There are many reasons to believe that the traditional concept of college courses and teacher education is inadequate to handle the task. Rather than focus on names and numbers of courses that would constitute a good sequence of general and professional education, let us look at teacher education in terms of kinds of experiences and instruction that will best fit teachers for the task they face in the secondary school general education class.

First of all, many experiences will be needed to help college students learn the art of studying others. While such experiences might well focus on adults as well as children, great emphasis, for obvious reasons, should be placed upon firsthand contacts with boys and girls of all ages and levels of maturity. The prospective teacher should engage in frequent observations of childhood and adolescent behavior, sometimes concentrating on individuals, at other times studying group behavior and interpersonal relationships. Anecdotal records, for example, could become a familiar and useful technique as students strive to discover needs, to detect patterns of behavior, to seek out causal factors.

Where can such study and observation be done? In general, there might be two sources of contacts with young people. First, there is the formal school experience, which in itself might be dual in nature. Students should have a wealth of varied experience in observation of children in all their school activities—the classroom, the playground, the hallways, assemblies. At the same time, the prospective teacher should be gradually assuming responsibility for the actual guidance of the learning experiences of children, from the participation stage where the college student shares in the teaching process to the self-sufficient level of full responsibility for a teaching assignment. Increasingly we must re-think our usual student teaching practices so that they are no longer a one-time culminating kind of experience coming supposedly after all the pedagogic theory has been learned, but rather become a continuing, ever-expanding source of experience in which theory and practice are inevitably interrelated.

A second source of contact with young people is less formal but in some ways perhaps more yielding of potential riches than the planned kind of experiences. Students should be encouraged to work with boys and girls in a variety of situations and be guided to find just such situations. For example, camp counseling, playground activity, story-telling are only a few of the rich possibilities in this area. In addition, the church offers many opportunities for working with young people through Sunday school teaching and young people's leagues. It is important that all of these activities be considered a part of the prospective teacher's actual college preparation, and college instructors should utilize these experiences to help develop in students some of the basic principles concerning child development and human behavior.

A second area needing attention in a college program is that of community study. To be effective in a general education class a teacher needs great familiarity with the nature and characteristics of the community (or communities) from which his students come, familiarity with its idiosyncracies and needs, its strengths and weaknesses, its people and its machines. While a large part of this information can be gained informally through residence or casual observation, much of it might have to be learned through purposeful study; hence the growing practice of school staffs embarking on community surveys and community study programs.

Four kinds of experiences related to this area deserve special consideration in the teacher education program. First, might be mentioned courses in sociology. Second, there might be actual study of the student's own community from which he comes to college, or of the community of which the college itself is a part, or of a community surrounding a school where the college student is working as a participant or student teacher. Such study could be part of the sociology class or could develop in one of the professional courses.

Third, the student should certainly be encouraged to participate in a wide variety of community activities. A fourth suggestion worth special attention would be experiences involving living in various kinds of communities—rural, industrial, suburban. In the case of the fourth proposal, obviously a student would not be expected to repeat an experience in a kind of community with which he is already familiar, but would be given opportunities to extend his understanding through living in communities somewhat different from his own.

In another direction, the college student needs varied contacts in the field of work and social service. He should be encouraged to work out a program of employment that will give him valuable experiences in business and industry, while not conflicting with the demands of his college program. He should become an active participant in organizational work, becoming familiar with the variety of agencies and organizations that exist in a community for the welfare, improvement, and enjoyment of its citizens. Such participation will also give him helpful experience in the art of human relations and the acquisition of the skills necessary for living in harmony with his fellows.

From what has already been written, it is obvious that the general education teacher needs to have a breadth of outlook on current issues, on contemporary problems, at least a nodding acquaintance with the forces at work in the twentieth century. While a sound course or two on contemporary history or international relations would, of course, be important, there are other courses and other kinds of experiences that would also contribute to the breadth of vision and interest desired. For example, contact with a wide variety of courses in areas like anthropology, social and political science, communications and the communication arts, to mention only a few, should be encouraged. Thought should be given also to the development of facility, written and spoken, in at least one modern foreign language. Such facility is rapidly becoming a requisite for almost every educated person in our age. To obtain firsthand impressions and knowledge, students should be encouraged to travel widely—at home and abroad; to start thinking and living in world terms—before we are all forced to think in interplanetary terms. And what could give more meaning to an understanding of many of the problems and issues that surround the ordinary citizen today than participation in national, state, and local political or governmental activity?

Such involvement would give additional experience to the college student in the area of group dynamics—working with people on common tasks, seeking certain goals, and sharing responsibility. The need for engaging in such co-operative ventures cannot be overemphasized when we remember some of the fundamental tenets upon which our concept of a general education class has been based. In their college classes, then, students should have many opportunities to study group dynamics—concept and theory as well as practical implications; leadership concepts—recent studies as well as visits to business and industry, to become familiar with approaches to leadership training in those areas.

We must remember, though, that we do not learn about co-operative action only by studying about it: we must also participate in experiences of a group nature. Thus it would be well for prospective teachers to engage in many kinds of experiences that require co-operative effort—dramatics, college class activities, dormitory councils, club work, and the like. Of even greater value would be experiences in some college classes that are conducted on a co-operative basis. If it is true that we teach as we have been taught, then we must make every effort to utilize as much as possible those procedures in college that we desire for students in the general education classes. Greater emphasis must be given to a workshop approach to learning, to the informal discussions of the small seminar, to the involvement of the students in the planning of their own work, to the independent pursuit of learning, to self-analysis and self-direction. College teaching must not limit itself to the stereotype of the lecture presentation but must move to the vivid use of the multitude of approaches that lend life and sparkle to learning.

Much attention has been given to the role of the general education teacher in the guidance of young people—educational, vocational, emotional, personal, and social. It is important, therefore, that the pre-service education of these teachers include study of fundamental principles of counseling, interviewing, testing, and the use of projective techniques. There should also be familiarity with the kinds of special services that might be available in schools, services rendered by a psychologist, remedial reading specialist, speech therapist, as well as the librarian, the nurse, the doctor, and the social worker. For one of the major attributes of an effective teacher is the ability to detect a need that he himself cannot meet and to know the resource person best qualified to deal with the situation.

As much as possible college students should have firsthand experiences with counseling. These might include work as camp counselors, direct experiences in the college personnel services, or work experience in personnel departments of various businesses.

There must also be a system of continuous and close individual and group guidance of college students. The impersonal way in which it is sometimes possible to progress through many of our colleges is unfortunate for all students affected, but especially so for the future general education teacher. He needs to experience as a student the kind of attention and guidance that he must later give to his students. And because the needs of the general education teacher are of a much broader nature than those of most college students, someone must be able to see the total picture of the student's progress through college and serve as confidante and mentor.

• **The teacher of tomorrow's citizens faces a challenging and difficult task. He can be no less than the kind of person described in these pages, and he must be given in his own education those insights, knowledges, and skills that will enable him to guide young people toward responsible maturity. The real challenge, then, is the one facing all who are concerned with teacher education, whether at the pre-service level or in-service, whether in graduate school or in on-the-job experiences.**

10

Curriculum Change

and General Education

The process of change is a highly complex one, posing problems of readiness, understanding, adaptability, know-how, and personnel, to mention only a few. In an institution as firmly rooted in society as the public school, change assumes a more formidable aspect than it presents in other areas of our life. All of us have attended schools, and all of us have cherished recollections with perhaps some abiding antipathies. Our reactions to educational modifications will inevitably be colored by these personal feelings, which can run the gamut from "What was good enough for me is good enough for my children" to "I want my children to study all the things I didn't."

Other factors, too, affect our thinking about school programs and educational reform. High tax levies, community mores with regard to certain controversial issues, the degree of respect accorded teaching as a profession—these and many other influences play an important part in people's readiness for change in general and receptivity to changes in particular.

If, then, our schools are to move in desirable directions based upon sound methods and dispassionate appraisal of needs and goals, certain helpful guidelines are needed. It is not our task to define the dynamics of a good curriculum improvement program. However, we would like to highlight certain general principles underlying effective curriculum development before speaking more directly about initiating a sound general education program in our secondary schools.

A. Basic Principles for Curriculum Change

Whenever change is considered in areas as dynamic as the educational process, the people involved might well focus their attention

194

upon three basic areas of concern: (1) identification of goals and objectives; (2) evaluation of present programs; (3) consideration of possible plans for change.

1. ESTABLISHING THE GOALS AND OBJECTIVES OF THE SCHOOL

In a highly complex culture such as ours, where there are relatively few values upon which all people of any community agree, and where such a great diversity of opinion may be found concerning any topic of discussion, obviously the objectives of the school will be controversial. Educational literature is filled with lists of educational objectives for the public schools, not only for the total program, but for any facet of the program including general education, special subject areas, extracurricular activities, and guidance. It is of course impossible for the public schools to achieve all these objectives in a twelve-year period, and even if they could, examination reveals that some of the objectives are mutually incompatible.

In a dilemma such as this, it becomes highly important that when choosing objectives, we should have a list of criteria for their selection. These criteria should be agreed upon by all responsible for the selection. Any process of selection implies the use of criteria. However, they have too seldom been known and understood by all concerned. This has resulted in the use of different criteria by individuals and small groups working on the same problem and thus arriving at mutually incompatible objectives. A detailed discussion of criteria which must be met for the validation of educational objectives may be found in Chapter Eleven of *Fundamentals of Curriculum Development* by Smith, Stanley, and Shores.[1] Some of the more obvious criteria which should be applied to the selection of objectives are: social adequacy, basic human needs, democratic ideals, non-contradiction and consistency, and behavioristic interpretation. Any group charged with the development of educational objectives would do well to have a thorough understanding of these criteria.

The criterion of social adequacy becomes more critical in a society where rapid changes are taking place. In a society which is relatively stable, the educational objectives will automatically be highly consistent with the present social circumstances. However, in a rapidly changing social order, the educational objectives are very likely to reflect practices which are no longer characteristic of the social scene. There may well appear a severe lag between educational objectives and the social circumstances.

This is a condition which those charged with curriculum should

[1] B. O. Smith, W. O. Stanley, and J. H. Shores, *Fundamentals of Curriculum Development* (Yonkers: World Book Company, 1950), Ch. 11.

realize may well exist unless a thorough and continuous study of the social scene is an integral part of curriculum development. In other words, the need for a general education class in a given community may be much greater today than it was around the turn of the century, but the need may not be recognized by those who have not continuously studied the rapidly changing social scene.

The criterion of basic human needs refers to the drives that are characteristic of all people in a given culture. Some of these needs may be biological, such as food, sex, and shelter, while others may be derived from the culture. Among the basic human needs derived from the culture are such things as: the need for proper and acceptable dress, the need for appropriate use of language on various occasions, the need for social status, and the need for personal acceptance. These are a few of the basic human needs which may exist in a given situation; there will certainly be others, and it is highly important that the curriculum objectives of the school take them into consideration.

The criterion of democratic ideals has been discussed at some length in Part One, Chapter Two. However, it appears that there are certain basic democratic ideals which should permeate educational objectives. Among these are: (a) the human being is the factor that is of prime importance; this means that the student is more important than the desk, chair, building, or other physical surroundings; (b) all who are involved reap greater benefits if differences are resolved through discussion and mediation rather than by force; (c) deviations from generally accepted norms must be understood and valued for reasons of enrichment and progress; and (d) unlimited access to information is a prerequisite for the survival of democracy. This is not an exhaustive list but the items mentioned are among the more important ones.

Contradiction and inconsistency are highly prevalent in a fluid society such as ours. However, it is important that education objectives and procedures seek to minimize and eliminate these in so far as possible. Much mental disorder is generated by the fact that individuals are required to play contradictory roles concurrently in our society. Those charged with establishing the goals of the school must be very careful that the educational objectives do not perpetuate this societal characteristic.

The first and foremost phase of curriculum study, then, is the establishment of goals based upon carefully thought-out criteria. This process should be a co-operative venture undertaken by educators, lay people, and students. It may be carried on in many ways—through questionnaires, interviews, discussion meetings, and the like.

2. EVALUATING THE PRESENT PROGRAM

The next step is to determine, in light of established goals, the extent to which the present school program is contributing to the realization of the goals. This requires a thorough look at the *total* school program because some phase of the school program may be contributing to the attainment of several goals and on the other hand more than one phase of the program may be contributing to a single goal. Various kinds of information are important in this phase of curriculum study. It is important to know (a) how parents, teachers, and pupils feel about the degree to which goals are being achieved; (b) what is happening to the graduates of the school; (c) what the holding power of the school is, and (d) the actual level of achievement of students in the various aspects of the program. From this phase of curriculum study it is possible to discover gaps or weaknesses in the school program which are responsible for the inadequate attainment of desired goals.

As information is gathered and plans are being considered, questions like the following can be helpful:

1. How well is the present program meeting the needs of the students and the community?

2. What changes appear desirable to increase the effectiveness of the program?

3. What evidence do we have that the proposed changes will improve the over-all program?

4. How will the proposed changes affect certain human relationships (school-community, teacher-pupil, teacher-administration, pupil-pupil, and teacher-teacher)?

5. How, when, and where is it appropriate to lay the groundwork for a change in program?

6. What effective techniques can be employed to introduce the idea to those who will be concerned?

7. How can the change, both direction and intensity, be controlled once it has been started?

8. What steps can and should be taken to prevent the program from reverting to its former form once the transition has been accomplished?

9. With whom and to what degree does the leadership role belong in the process of curriculum transition?

10. What resources, both human and material, will be needed to assist in an orderly transition? How may they be used most effectively? Are they available?

11. How will the new program be evaluated in order to ascertain whether or not it is achieving desired goals?

This list of questions is not exhaustive; however, it should be comprehensive enough to point out the need for very careful thought and organization when attempting curriculum changes. Many very worthwhile attempts at curriculum revision have failed purely because educators have not devoted adequate prior thought and planning to the above questions.

3. PLANNING FOR CHANGE

Before looking at some of the specifics involved in the possible development of a general education program, let us consider two general ways in which the projected change can be carried out. The nature and needs of a particular school system and the exigencies of the times will determine which approach is preferable.

One approach to effecting change is the system-wide one in which a particular curriculum modification is made in all the schools of the system at the same time. There are some obvious advantages to this approach in terms of administrative detail. Also, there is a certain strength in solidarity. Help can be obtained through mutual sharing of problems and discussion of solutions. Teachers can draw upon the strengths of all their colleagues in a system. An in-service program can have widespread impact.

An example of the introduction of a program of general education on such a large scale is that of the state of Maryland which, in the year 1945, established a twelve-grade system uniformly throughout the state. This addition of one year to the school program provided an opportunity for re-examination of the entire curriculum. Study was done first by an exploratory committee appointed by the State Superintendent, then by representatives from all the counties. Resource units were developed at a workshop held in 1946, and soon after, selected teachers developed a unified general education program. While no county was required to go into the program, by 1952 every county had at least one school using a general education block in the junior high school grades. The impetus for this curriculum change, it can readily be seen, came from the state leadership.[2]

A second way of effecting curriculum change is the "broken-front" approach by which changes are made in specific situations as faculty, students, and parents deem them desirable. Sometimes only one school

---

[2] Grace S. Wright, *Core Curriculum in Public High Schools: An Inquiry into Practices, 1949* (Washington, D.C.: U.S. Office of Education, Bulletin 1950, No. 6), p. 18.

in a system modifies its program. For example, the time schedule often varies from junior high school to junior high school in any given system, as schools work through their own changes regarding length of school periods and number of periods in the school day. Sometimes a change is introduced in only a few classes within a school in somewhat of a pilot approach.

This latter approach of the pilot situation, whether it be in a class or two or in a school or two, has several advantages. It permits school staffs to modify programs in terms of the peculiar needs of certain student bodies or certain community settings. It also has the merit of the action research concept in which faculty members are actively involved in testing out new ideas and appraising results. Such a limited trial situation permits thorough study and analysis of the effectiveness of a particular change before it is introduced more widely.

One disadvantage of the pilot approach is that other teachers in the same school may knowingly or unknowingly undermine the pilot program in their normal contacts with parents and pupils. Many times pupils involved are labeled "guinea pigs" and the teachers are accused of buttering up the administration. The best defense against these unjust criticisms is to bring parents and pupils who are to be affected into all deliberations concerning the experimental units and to make sure that the changed programs can be defended from the standpoint of sound educational practices and research as well as from the standpoint of the emotional well-being of both parents and pupils.

B. Specific Suggestions for Introducing a General Education Class

Assuming that the above study has been done and it has been decided that a general education class would be a desirable direction in which to modify the existing curriculum, there are some specific steps that now need to be taken. Before considering these steps, a word or two about personnel is in order. If the change is to be system-wide, some arrangement must be made for the involvement of faculty members from each of the schools to be affected. If the class is to be introduced into only one school, it would be well to have the entire faculty involved in planning for the change. If there is to be a pilot study approach in only a class or two, care must be taken to keep the entire faculty informed of progress in the planning and to involve all faculty members at important decision-making points.

Although stress has so far been placed on faculty participation, we cannot emphasize enough the desirability of a completely co-operative approach to this curriculum change, including administrative and supervisory staff, special service personnel, faculty, students, parents and other lay persons. As we discuss some of the procedures involved, it will be evident that students and parents must inevitably be involved. Aside from this need for their help, though, there is the value resulting from having all interested parties to the change actively participate in the process. In no other way can there be true readiness for, and understanding of, the new ideas introduced into the educational program and the reasons for them.

1. TIME FOR STUDY

In developing an effective general education class much time is needed for a thoughtful and thoroughgoing study by educators, parents, and students. There should be familiarity with adolescent and societal needs in general. Time must be provided for gathering data regarding the needs, problems, interests, and concerns of the youth group served by the system or school involved. This information can be gathered by the various means discussed in preceding chapters. An analysis of the drop-out situation will be helpful. Attention must also be given to study of the particular community setting of the school and its students; an analysis of community problems and needs as related to the educational program must be made. After this information and all other pertinent data have been gathered, there should be time for study and analysis, leading to a consideration of implications for the general education program that is to be set up.

2. DEVELOPMENT OF A GENERAL EDUCATION PROGRAM

The information that has been gathered and the study of broad adolescent-societal needs should lead next to consideration of the kinds of problem areas that would be most suitable for the general education class. Also, thought must be given to the grade placement of any particular problem areas and to a suggested sequence. Even in situations where it is decided to permit the teacher and class to work in an unstructured situation, suggestions for appropriate scope and sequence can be helpful guides to the teacher in his own thinking and planning.

3. IN-SERVICE EDUCATION

While all this study is going on and plans are being made, thought must also be given to the necessary preparation of teachers for effective teaching in a general education class. Involvement in the curriculum study and planning is a form of in-service education, it is true. However, it would be well to have other definite activities that focus more specifically on helping teachers with the realistic and practical problems encountered in a general education class with characteristics that may be strange to the teachers' experience.

An effective in-service program might involve visits to other schools where similar programs are in operation, wide reading, discussion groups, use of resource persons, viewing of films, and the like. Any and all procedures that offer a broad background of knowledge and understanding are to be recommended.

Often overlooked in any in-service preparation is the need to provide similar experiences for parents and other lay people. In fact, thought might be given to a joint program of parent-teacher education, at least in certain respects, so that the general education class can be introduced in an atmosphere of readiness and understanding. All along the way, too, students should be involved as much as possible. They can be helpful in some of the studies of youth and community needs that are undertaken. Some students can join teachers and parents in visits to other schools that have general education classes. Other ways will come to mind for keeping them in direct contact with the planning that is taking place.

4. A CAUTION OR TWO

If the suggestions outlined in this chapter are followed, there should be a minimum of misunderstanding and antagonism to the proposed introduction of a general education class. However, we are not suggesting that all will inevitably proceed without problems or setbacks. Any change that involves social processes and relationships is a highly volatile experience, subject to unforeseen currents and dynamic interplay.

Some words of caution are in order:

1. Temper your idealism with realism. Almost every human endeavor has its setbacks and moments of discouragement. Don't let them override the more frequent and more lasting successes.

2. Don't rest on your laurels, once the general education class is introduced. You have only made a start. The same effort must be put into careful nurturing of its health and growth as went into bringing it to birth.

3. Make careful plans for continuous evaluation of the effectiveness of your new program. And *do* make intelligent plans! Find appropriate evaluative procedures for the particular goals and objective you are trying to assess. Remember, a pencil-and-paper test

of factual information will produce little or no evidence regarding the development of attitudes, appreciations, skills, and basic understandings.

Much more could be written in the way of advice and suggestions. For example, we have not touched directly on the role of the administrator in developing an effective general education class; but our point of view on his role can be deduced from all that we have suggested. Nor have we spoken about the need to provide sufficient and appropriate materials for a general education class; but again, any intelligent approach to curriculum change could not overlook this essential consideration. We have merely attempted to point out general guideposts for effective curriculum change and to suggest specific paths for the introduction of a general education class into the secondary school program.

• If two school systems can do it, if twenty can, if two hundred and more can, why not more? If so many schools across the country have found a general education class to be a promising direction for the improvement of the educational program of the secondary school, then perhaps more of us might find promise along this path. Or perhaps more careful analysis of this particular approach may lead us to as yet unidentified patterns and processes of sound education. What of the future? In our next and final chapter, let us turn our attention to the unknown.

11

A Forward Look

It would be a rash person, indeed, who would attempt to predict the pattern, the process, the content of the secondary school curriculum in the United States in the coming decades. Out of the welter of alternative suggestions, some conflicting, some reinforcing of each other, there is no easily discernible trend that one can confidently point to and say, "That is the answer." Perhaps we would have it no other way, if we are to remain true to our tradition of uniformity of goal through diversity of means.

Although we may not be able to predict with certainty, we can and should play some important hunches in the light of intelligible evidence. Our hunches can be based upon a stern assessment of the present, honest examination of the past, serious appraisal of the possible future based on available projections, with a willingness to go out on a limb as a result of ensuing conclusions.

A. Growth and Present Status of General Education Classes

The idea of a secondary school general education class like the one described in this volume is relatively new in the history of educational thought. Until the past few decades the program of the secondary school was conceived in terms of subject divisions evolving out of the concept of the academic disciplines of knowledge that can be traced back to Alexandrine times. It was believed that there were certain fixed bodies of knowledge, an understanding of which should mark the educated man.

With the coming of the twentieth century new insights emerged in the realm of psychological theory regarding human growth and development and ways of learning. At the same time the sociologist was

203

contributing his understandings and hypotheses regarding the adolescent in modern society. In addition, the secondary school during the 1920's and 1930's was rapidly becoming a school for *all* American youth, not just a select few.

As a result of the impact of all these influences, educators began searching for ways in which secondary schools could better implement these new ideas and beliefs and more effectively meet the needs of all youth in our society. The general education class was one result of the experimentation and research and can be said to have had its genesis in the experimental ferment stimulated by the Eight-Year Study.[1] As the idea has developed in different parts of the country, it has taken various forms and has had varying emphases. Some classes never moved beyond the stage of meaningful synthesis of two or more subject areas; some focused on a social orientation in problem selection; while others emphasized adolescent needs as an approach to content.

In one form or another, however, the idea of a block of time devoted to certain common learnings and utilizing a process in which students assume a great deal of responsibility for their own learning has gained wider and wider acceptance during the past two decades. Various studies have been made of the incidence of general education classes in our secondary schools. Because of the varied definitions used to describe these classes it is difficult, if not impossible, to indicate degrees of growth for the problem-centered kind of class that we are concerned with. However, certain generalizations can be made.

It seems that in the past ten years the number of schools using a block-of-time approach to general education has increased. The greater incidence of such classes occurs at the junior high school level, with more of them found in the seventh and eighth grades than in the ninth. In a study by Wright[2] in 1956–1957, she found that almost one-fifth of the sampled schools had some kind of block-time class. Of these schools 12 per cent had classes that seem to correspond to the kind of general education concept suggested in the present volume.

While this number is relatively small, it is sizable enough when one considers the newness of the idea. A new approach to curricular

[1] A study of secondary school curriculum in the 1930's under the auspices of the Progressive Education Association involving thirty schools and two hundred colleges, in the course of which interesting curriculum changes were made in an effort to determine the relationship between curriculum patterns and later success in college. For a complete description see Wilford M. Aiken, *The Story of the Eight-Year Study* (New York: Harper & Brothers, 1942) and *Thirty Schools Tell Their Story* (New York: Harper & Brothers, 1943).

[2] Grace S. Wright, *Block-Time Classes and the Core Program in the Junior High School* (Washington, D.C.: U.S. Office of Education, Bulletin 1958, No. 6), pp. 5, 15.

content and method cannot be expected to sweep away immediately the traditions of centuries. If one takes the long perspective, it is rather gratifying to see the progress that has been made in twenty-five years. It is gratifying, too, to find that a start has been made in attempting to evaluate the effectiveness of general education classes.

B. Research Supporting General Education

Before citing any of the research evidence, it would be well to point out that not very much research has been done to date. What has been done is so sketchy as to yield results that are not sufficiently reliable or comprehensive. It must also be kept in mind that one cannot always tell the specific nature of the general education classes involved in a given study. They may consist of a block of time in which one teacher teaches two subjects, or in which fusion of content occurs, rather than truly adolescent-societal problem-centered classes.

Another caution is that for the most part the evaluative instruments have been testing limited goals and ones that are not sufficiently representative of the broad scope of general education aims and objectives. There is a great need for the development of instruments that will focus upon attitude-formation, skills of critical thinking and research techniques, human relations skills, and the like. It is not enough to discover whether general education students read better and faster and write more effectively than those students in traditionally organized classes.

With these cautions in mind, let us look at the results of some of the studies. Wrightstone and Forlano [3] conducted an investigation in which ninety-four pupils in a ninth-grade general education curriculum were matched with ninety-four pupils from a subject-centered curriculum on the basis of sex, intelligence, chronological age, reading level, arithmetic level, and socioeconomic background. After a year of instruction, achievement of the two groups was measured with a co-operative test of reading comprehension, co-operative test of social abilities, co-operative mathematics test, and the Wrightstone Scale of Beliefs. The general education group was superior to the nongeneral education group in gains in English, social studies abilities, mathematics abilities, and had developed more satisfactory civic beliefs.

In another study by Wrightstone [4] standardized tests were ad-

[3] J. Wayne Wrightstone and George Forlano, "An Evaluation of the Experience Curriculum at Midwood High School," *High Points* (December, 1948), 30:35–42.

[4] J. Wayne Wrightstone, "An Appraisal of Experimental High School Practices" (New York: Bureau of Publications, Teachers College, Columbia University, 1936).

ministered in three experimental high schools, using general education organization, and in three conventional high schools in New York City. Results obtained indicated that the experimental schools were superior in teaching and developing literature facts, work skills in the social sciences, civic beliefs, and science beliefs.

Forlano[5] studied social acceptance in a vocational high school in New York City among general education and nongeneral education students. The Ohio Social Acceptance Scale was administered to both general education and nongeneral education groups at the beginning and end of a school term. The results indicated a significant increase in acceptance scores and a significant decrease in rejection scores within the general education groups. The opposite was true among the nongeneral education students. This study involved seventy-eight general education and nongeneral education students and the amount of change in scores was significant at the .001 level of confidence.

For the Kalamazoo Public Schools[6] a study was made of the rate of growth of seventh, eighth, and ninth grade general education pupils in the areas of reading, language ability, work study skills, and basic social processes. Standardized tests were used to measure growth. It was found that grades seven, eight, and nine made gains beyond expectations in reading and work study skills; grades eight and nine made better than expected gains in reading; and grade seven made better than expected gains in basic social processes.

In an effort to show that general education students learn basic skills, Kelley and Beatty[7] matched general education and nongeneral education pupils in grades seven through nine. Through the use of standardized tests, it was discovered that general education pupils demonstrated achievement superior to nongeneral education pupils in the areas of language, reading, and arithmetic.

Reiner, Hauber, and Weitz[8] found that in selected academic high schools in Brooklyn, general education students were significantly above their age norm in reading. In a later study of the same academic high

[5] George Forlano, "Measuring the Quality of Social Acceptability in Some Ninth Grade Core and Non-Core Classes," *High School Journal* (October, 1954), 38:12–16.

[6] Kalamazoo Public Schools, "How Much Did They Grow?" (Kalamazoo, Michigan: Public Schools Bulletin Number 164, September, 1952, mimeographed).

[7] Arthur C. Kelley and Robert E. Beatty, "Here's Proof That Core Program Students Learn Basic Skills," *School Executive* (February, 1953), 72:54–55.

[8] William Reiner, Katherine W. Hauber, and Leo Weitz, "A Study of the Introduction of the Core Program in Selected Academic High Schools" (Brooklyn: Board of Education of the City of New York, 1953, mimeographed).

schools Reiner [9] found through standardized testing that general education pupils were achieving beyond expectations in reading and work study skills. He also found that exceptionally bright students were making significant gains in reading.

Capehart, Hodges, and Berdan [10] conducted a study at Oak Ridge, Tennessee, in which they matched pupils from three tenth-grade general education classes with a like number of pupils enrolled in the school's regular curriculum. The general education pupils made greater gains in effectiveness of expression, work study habits, and in establishing self-confidence. There was no significant difference in gains between the general education and control groups on mechanics of expression and improvement of civic beliefs. In a second study [11] by the same investigators, general education pupils were found to excel in gains in the acquisition of skills and knowledges in English and in the development of critical thinking.

Through the use of standardized tests, Schwartz [12] compared fifty general education experienced pupils with a like number of non-general education experienced pupils in grades seven and eight. He found that general education experienced pupils were more proficient in natural science background, correctness in writing, quantitative thinking, and in reading natural science. He also found that among tenth graders general education pupils had better grades than non-general education pupils.

In a number of studies, Burge,[13] Miller,[14] and Toops,[15] general education pupils have shown reading ability and reading gains superior to nongeneral education pupils. Fair [16] found that the general

[9] William Reiner, "A Second Report of the Evaluation of Pupil Growth in the Core Program in Two Academic High Schools, 1952–53" (Brooklyn: Board of Education of the City of New York, 1953, mimeographed).

[10] Bertis E. Capehart, Allen Hodge, and Norman Berdan, "An Objective Evaluation of a Core Program," *School Review* (February, 1952), 60:84–89.

[11] Bertis E. Capehart, Allen Hodge, and Robert Roth, "Evaluating the Core Curriculum: A Further Look," *School Review* (October, 1952), 61:406–412.

[12] Bernard Schwartz, "An Investigation of the Effects of a Core Program by Comparing Core-Experienced and Non-Core Experienced Students in Various Factors" (Yardley, Pa.: Pennsbury High School, 1954, mimeographed).

[13] Anne Burge, "English Class Uses Social Studies Reading," *Clearing House* (October, 1947), 22:105–107.

[14] Helen R. Miller, "Unified Studies: A History-English Powerhouse," *Clearing House* (October, 1949), 24:103–105.

[15] Myrtle Dewey Toops, "Working in the Core Program in Burris Laboratory School" (Muncie, Indiana: Ball State Teachers College, 1955).

[16] Jean E. Fair, "The Comparative Effectiveness of a Core and a Conventional Curriculum in Developing Social Concern," *School Review* (May and September, 1954), 62:274–282.

education class was superior in developing a democratic position toward social goals and policies.

Hill [17] compared the mathematics and science achievement of students graduating from a Florida high school which has general education, with achievement of graduating seniors throughout the state. He found that the achievement of students graduating from the school with general education classes had been consistently and significantly above state norms for a period of twenty-two years. This study involved approximately 1,200 students.

The foregoing evidence is obviously incomplete and merely indicative of a general tendency. However, it is representative of the research that has been done that supports the general education idea. Certainly it should be reassuring to those who are fearful of the new and the different and should stimulate more of us to be ready to move in the direction of general education classes for secondary school students.

C. Problems Related to the General Education Class

Before venturing a look at the future, it would be well to point out first some of the questions and problems related to the general education class that need our attention if such a class is to be as effective as possible, and if the idea is to become widespread in our secondary school programs. Four such problems deserve careful consideration.

1. DEVELOPMENT OF MATERIALS

One of the greatest handicaps faced by teachers of general education classes is the paucity of appropriate materials. The wide variety of problems studied and the nature of these problems necessitate a vast quantity of materials of many kinds and of differing maturity levels. Since general education problems are not usually limited to a particular "subject" emphasis but cut across subject boundaries, no one textbook can be adequate. Rather, there is a need for the development of books and other materials that use a broadly integrated approach; for example, books that really utilize geographic, historical, economic, and political information in a truly related way in the development of concepts and understandings in the area of the social sciences; or books that place science knowledge in the context of the social sciences; or books that use literature to illuminate history and science. We have not yet begun to tap the possibilities in these directions.

Even more pressing is our need for materials that deal with per-

[17] Thomas J. Hill, "Less Math, Science? Look at the Record," *Journal of the Florida Educational Association* (February, 1958), 35:15.

sonal-social problems of adolescents, that will help students look at themselves in their societal setting; that will focus directly on the developmental tasks of young people and give them understandings about the apparent mysteries of maturing. More should be done, too, with the development of simple projective materials that general education teachers can utilize for guidance purposes as well as for study of various problem areas.

Then, too, there is still the urgent need for books and materials of varying reading levels that will be suitable for the teen-age maturity span. We cannot expect the adolescent slow reader to be content with reading material that was written for the third or fourth grader.

As we move toward the development of more suitable materials for general education classes, it is to be hoped that we can become more flexible and imaginative in our approach. Can we exploit to better advantage the possibilities inherent in pamphlet, leaflet-type publications? Can we discover ways of using soft-cover materials for more ephemeral kinds of information?

While important steps have already been taken to provide suitable materials for general education classes, much remains to be done.

2. SCOPE AND SEQUENCE

Another problem that has troubled all curriculum makers is the familiar one of scope and sequence. The general education class poses its own questions in this respect. What should be the scope of content dealt with in the general education class? To what extent should some learnings be dealt with in separate classes? Should the scope vary with different grade levels?

Even more difficult is the question of sequence. Should a definite sequence of problem areas be spelled out for each grade? To what extent should the order of learning units be left to the discretion of the teacher and students? Should sequence relate closely to the developmental patterns of each particular class or can an appropriate sequence be suggested for all classes at a given level?

All of these questions, of course, presuppose a general education class that has a basic structure already determined, within which teacher and students operate on a relatively flexible basis. However, whether the general education class is thus structured or left unstructured for the teacher and students to evolve together, the principles underlying the above questions are the same and need critical attention. Much thought needs to be given to the criteria by which a manageable scope and effective sequence of learning experiences in the general education class are determined.

3. RELATIONSHIP TO REST OF SCHOOL PROGRAM

Considerable thought needs to be given to the relationship between the general education class and the other aspects of the total school program. In addition to the general education class, there are some other class offerings that are part of the general education of young people—for example, physical education and mathematics. In what ways can these areas be effectively taught to make them consistent with the philosophy of the general education class? Would it be wise to have the general education teacher also teach mathematics, if he is qualified? Should the teachers of the various general education areas meet frequently to correlate work where possible, as well as to share knowledge and understandings about the students they teach?

Similarly, what should be the relationship between the general education class and the specialized classes, especially at the senior high level? How can modern language be utilized effectively in the general education class? What contributions can journalism, speech, and home economics make to the general education of adolescents? What can the general education class contribute to these specialized areas?

Questions like these and many others need to be pondered by the curriculum makers of tomorrow. They may find that the general education class can be considered the hub of the school program with the other classes emerging out of it and flowing back into it in a two-way-spoke arrangement that will somehow provide some hitherto unattainable unity in the educational life of our young people. In any event, the problem is worthy of our best thinking; the solution may be more original than now seems apparent to us.

4. UNDERSTANDING OF PARENTS AND COMMUNITY

The twin problems of readiness and understanding are as important to the success of a general education program as to any other undertaking. Readiness, of course, plays a major role in determining the effectiveness with which a general education class can be introduced into a school or a system.

However, understanding plays a continuous role, since efforts must be made constantly to help parents and other lay people comprehend what is going on in the classroom and the school. In this connection communication proves to be the key, and many programs have stood or fallen because of the kind of communication between school and community.

While this matter of communication is by no means limited to the question of general education classes, some thought should be given to the special problems involved in developing public understanding. It is difficult for people who have known only departmentalized education from their own experience to comprehend a more highly integrated approach to learning. The tendency is to cling to the old labels because they are familiar, even when not completely understood themselves. In the same way it is difficult for many people who have known only a chronological approach to historical content to understand and accept a problem or process or era orientation. Or, consider the parents who knew only the "rod-and-fear" school of discipline; the thought of treating young people with some degree of respect as we attempt to develop self-discipline is a bewildering and disturbing idea. For adults who remember being told what to read, what to believe, what to do, it is not easy to accept a philosophy that involves the learner in the process of reaching decisions regarding what or how he is to learn.

Since the general education class is in so many ways different from the experiences of most adults, its philosophy and point of view can be rather shattering to their security and self-concept. And so, we very much need to uncover more and more effective ways of communicating to others what we are trying to do and how we are attempting to achieve our goals.

There are, of course, other problems that deserve our attention —problems of evaluation, of scheduling, of grading and reporting to parents, for example. It is to be hoped that as we move ahead with educational progress in the second half of this century, we arrive at more and more satisfying solutions to our problems through intelligent and unemotional analysis and study.

D. The Future of General Education

The direction that secondary education will take during the rest of this century will be determined in part by factors beyond the control of educators. Should a third world war develop, its impact upon education would be profound and unpredictable. Any shattering decline in our economy would have an inevitable influence upon our schools. Further discoveries and inventions leading to an interplanetary world could produce results that at present we can scarcely visualize.

However, barring any such unusual circumstances, the future of our school programs and of the place of general education in them rests in the hands of all of us who can, through wisdom and foresight, modify education in desirable and promising directions or through default permit our schools—programs, organizational patterns, methods, and physical facilities—to evolve in haphazard fashion, out of necessity, convenience, or submission to pressures of one sort or another.

Any attempt to move consciously into certain promising directions should, it seems to us, start with a realistic and thorough appraisal of our society and its probable needs in the coming decades. Only then can rational decisions be made regarding the kind of education citizens should have in keeping with such needs. It is not within the scope of this volume to attempt any detailed analysis of American society and the world scene during the remaining half of the present century. However, for the sake of example, we might suggest certain trends as we see them that will need to be taken into consideration by the educational planners of the future.

1. ASSESSMENT OF NEEDS OF OUR SOCIETY

As we look at the world around us and the role that the United States is coming to assume in relation to its neighbors, it seems to us that we are facing a future that is going to make many severe demands upon our citizenry. Only a few of these demands need be touched upon here.

a. *A call for informed leadership-followership skills.* More than ever before in our history we are faced with the need for developing leaders who have the look of greatness about them. In order to cope with the exigencies of national and international affairs our leaders of tomorrow must have the brilliance to grasp and assimilate ideas, concepts, movements, ideologies, happenings, with speed and perception; the intelligence to acquire and use an informed body of knowledge against which to assess these ideas and events; and the wisdom to draw conclusions and make decisions that will have implications and repercussions for millions of mankind.

These leaders need to be creative both as individuals and as members of various groups responsible for analysis and decision making; creative in the sense of being able and willing to be bold, imaginative, daring, capable of charting new paths and pursuing them fearlessly. With such creativity must be combined a flexibility that prevents the hardening of positions into rigid impasses, while at the same time it avoids the bad taste of compromise for expediency alone.

A leadership that is informed, creative, flexible, brilliant, is one that of necessity uses the method of intelligence in all its deliberations, a method that must be free of the taint of special interest, influence peddling, and the like. No longer can we rely on the limited vision of the political hacks, the local bosses of narrow interests, and the remnants of political leadership bequeathed to us from an earlier era of relative peace and security. The times call for men and women of broader vision, greater courage, the long perspective. And such leaders may not be easy to find. We must bestir ourselves to discover ways and means of nurturing such people in our midst and encouraging their appearance upon the national and world stage.

At the same time we must not overlook the need for an intelligent, comprehending followership. More than ever we need citizens who are capable of critical thinking, not blind conformity; who can challenge and inspire the imagination of leaders and stretch their talents to the utmost, rather than uneducated followers who impede progress through lack of knowledge, through attrition of others' skills, through emotional attachment to biased causes.

Perhaps the education of citizens to be intelligent followers is a far more imposing and challenging task than that of citizens to be daring leaders. Certainly it involves educating large masses of people in such a way that each individual is given as much help and opportunity as possible. A large number of our followers will be drawn from the ranks of the poor in spirit, faint of heart, economically handicapped, emotionally unstable, or low in intelligence. It would be the height of folly to encourage such people to leave the halls of learning before they had been taught minimal skills and understandings of citizenship and human relations. Somehow we must find ways of educating all American youth so that they remain under the guidance of the school until they can assume some degree of mature responsibility for and participation in family and community life.

Before leaving the question of leadership-followership we must point out that, in reality, a very large number of men and women at one time or another serve as leaders and followers. We may lead in certain areas of competence but yield leadership to others where our own skills are few or our interests are uninvolved. In effect, education must try to develop in each individual the ability to assume capable leadership when called upon and the wisdom to be informed and co-operative followers during the larger part of our existence.

It should also be pointed out that the concept of followership does not mean unquestioned acceptance of people and ideas. There is need for informed and responsible opposition by people who know how to accept defeat gracefully and abide by majority decisions.

b. *Impact of technology and automation on our social and economic life.* For several decades now, modern technology has posed many problems for mankind and set many needs. The currently accelerated pace of discovery and invention is moving us sooner than we may be ready for it into an age of automation. Already we have felt the impact of some of the problems, like those of technological unemployment. There seem to be certain other issues, however, that have developed a little more subtly and that may overwhelm us before we have even begun to think about how to deal with them.

For example, there are some students of the social scene who predict the possibility of a new class consciousness in our country with our population falling into two broad categories—the professional, white-collar, highly skilled group and the moderately skilled, unskilled, and service group. The latter group, if current trends continue, will probably have more and more leisure time, as the work week decreases. The members of the former group will, in all likelihood, find increased demands being made on their time and energy.

What can we do to help large numbers of people use their new-found leisure in positive, healthful, safe, productive, creative ways? How can we help the overburdened members of the professions and their fellows maintain a healthy equilibrium in their lives between work and leisure? How can we prevent the rise of an obvious "class system" with all its attendant ills? What can we do to retain our respect for the worth of the individual and help him maintain a sense of self-dignity in the face of the encroachment of machines and their apparent dwarfing of the human being and rendering him impersonal and almost powerless?

All of these questions and many more must be faced squarely as we move into the strange new world of technocracy.

c. *The exigencies of the space age.* Not only are we moving into an era of automation but it now seems possible that some people living today will be the first inhabitants of the new interplanetary space age. The prospect of conquering space, apparently man's last frontier, is an exciting, yet frightening one. The exploration of new worlds, the possible discovery of new kinds of life, new civilizations, will inevitably create new problems to be dealt with, new skills and perceptions to be called into play.

Will mankind have to relive its history on a universal and interplanetary stage? Have we learned nothing in our long struggle and up-to-the-present failure to achieve peace among the peoples of one world? Must we repeat the rivalry for possession of new lands, new wealth? Must conquest be our only means of coming to terms with other life on other planets, as has been true in our own history of relations with the native Indians of the Americas? Must worlds fight worlds, as nations have fought nations? Will the same problems of over-population, disease, crime, and the like have to be nibbled away at, little by little? Or have we achieved some maturity as peoples on earth, a maturity that will enable us to learn from mankind's history and approach the problems and challenges of new worlds with foresight and intelligence?

d. *The unfinished business of democracy.* Perhaps it is chauvinistic of us to think on so broad a scale as interplanetary existence when we have still so much unfinished business here at home and among our neighbors on earth. It is easy to identify some of our more pressing needs as a people—adequate and attainable housing for all; improved intergroup relations; abolition of delinquency—juvenile and adult, to mention only a few. While, as a democracy, we have made greater strides than any of our predecessors or contemporaries in achieving the good life for all, candor compels us to admit to the weak spots in our way of life. Pride and compassion must force us to deal with our weaknesses more realistically and more successfully in the future than we have in the past.

Nor can we overlook the need to cope more intelligently with the vagaries of our twentieth century economy; to handle in more mature fashion the uneasy marriage maintained by labor and management in today's life; to resolve in satisfying ways the apparently confused state of male-female responsibility and role in American society. And so we could continue our listing of current domestic needs with which the people of the United States must cope, if we are to have the stability and wisdom for living with our neighbors on earth and afar.

e. *Need for creative thinkers and daring individuals.* Once again we are faced with times that try men's souls. Will we have the raw courage, the revolutionary spirit, the intelligent daring of our forefathers who accepted the challenge of eighteenth-century times and gave birth to a new nation, destined for greatness? Indeed, will courage, spirit, intelligence on the part of a few suffice for the trials ahead of us? Probably not.

Now, if ever, we need vast numbers of men and women who are truly creative thinkers, daring individuals who are willing to be different but who can temper their difference with common sense. Above all, we need the creative person who is creative in positive directions; and we must learn to distinguish the truly talented, the genius who will become a part of mankind and work for its betterment, from the pseudo individualist who exists for self and cult. Each generation, it seems, has its beatniks, its nihilists, and the like. While they add color to society and a leaven of novelty and even humor, we must be careful to recognize when their influence may move outward in ever-widening circles of negativism and defeatism.

2. PREDICTIONS FOR GENERAL EDUCATION

The new world a-comin' would seem to suggest a need for the emergence of a modern version of the Renaissance Man. Certain it is that all of us must be equipped in as many ways as possible to deal with the needs and problems just suggested. No longer can we "let George do it." And so the focus of the future must inevitably be upon the general education of our people.

We venture to suggest some of the directions we believe our educational programs will be taking in the next several decades.

We believe that the secondary school, grades seven through twelve, will focus more and more upon general education, thus making the American public school a truly common school in its entirety and leaving specialization to post-secondary years.

We believe that the content of the secondary school curriculum will in a very real sense become meaningful in terms of twentieth-century needs and pressures and that we will take a fresh look at the criteria by which we judge what makes the educated man.

We believe that the process of education will utilize more effectively the knowledge we have been gaining from anthropology, sociology, psychology, and various other disciplines and that, as a result, we will better help people gain the wisdom, skills, attitudes, and appreciations needed to attain the goals of democracy and peace.

We believe that we are moving toward a greater synthesis of knowledge, a greater appreciation of the oneness of knowledge, and that our new insights will be reflected in our school programs and our approaches to the teaching-learning situation.

We believe that the real revolution in American education is still ahead of us and that the tremors of the various forward-looking movements of the twenties and thirties were but mild portents of greater things to come.

We believe that the ideas developed in this volume (to which we can lay no original claim) will be helping to point directions for whatever changes will occur and that whether the kind of class described herein will be a part of our school program in 1975 or 1990 is uncertain and even irrelevant.

• **If we are to be true to our own belief in creativity, we would certainly hope that the concerted intelligence and imagination and inspiration of all American people will call forth newer and more appropriate educational philosophies and programs that will be consistent with the needs of mankind. Our faith in the future is abundant. We hope that our readers share it with us.**

Bibliography

Bibliography

Books and Pamphlets

Aiken, Wilford M. *The Story of the Eight-Year Study*. New York: Harper, 1942.

Alberty, Harold B. *Reorganizing the High School Curriculum*. New York: Macmillan, 1947.

Alexander, William M., and Paul M. Halverson. *Effective Teaching in Secondary Schools*. New York: Rinehart, 1956.

Alexander, William M., and John Galen Saylor. *Modern Secondary Education, Basic Principles and Practices*. Rev. ed. New York: Rinehart, 1959.

Association for Supervision and Curriculum Development. *Preparation of Core Teachers for Secondary Schools*. Washington, D.C., 1955.

Bostwick, Prudence, and Chandos Reid. *A Functional High School Program*. New York: Hinds, Hayden and Eldredge, 1947.

Caswell, Hollis L. *The American High School*. Eighth Yearbook of the John Dewey Society. New York: Harper, 1946.

Chiara, Clara R. *The Core*. Kalamazoo, Mich.: School of Graduate Studies, Western Michigan College, 1956.

Chisholm, Leslie L. *The Work of the Modern High School*. New York: Macmillan, 1953.

Doane, D. *The Needs of Youth*. New York: Bureau of Publications, Teachers College, Columbia University, 1942.

Douglass, Harl R. *The High School Curriculum*. New York: Ronald Press, 1947.

Faunce, Roland C., and Nelson L. Bossing. *Developing the Core Curriculum*. Rev. ed. Englewood Cliffs, N.J.: Prentice-Hall, 1958.

Flaum, Laurence S. *The Activity High School*. New York: Harper, 1953.

Gilchrist, Robert S., Wilbur H. Dutton, and William L. Wrinkle. *Secondary Education for American Democracy*. Rev. ed. New York: Rinehart, 1957.

Giles, H. H., S. P. McCutchen, and A. N. Zechiel. *Exploring the Curriculum*. New York: Harper, 1942.

———. *Teacher-Pupil Planning*. New York: Harper, 1941.

Gwynn, J. Minor. *Curriculum Principles and Social Trends*. Rev. ed. New York: Macmillan, 1950.

Harap, Henry. *Social Living in the Curriculum*. Nashville, Tenn.: George Peabody College for Teachers, 1952.

Hayden, Miriam A. *The Core in Curriculum*. New York: New York University, The Center for Human Relations Studies, 1953.

219

Hock, Louise E. *Using Committees in the Classroom.* New York: Rinehart, 1958. (Rinehart Education Pamphlets)

Keller, Franklin J. *The Comprehensive High School.* New York: Harper, 1955.

Koos, Leonard V. *Junior High School Trends.* New York: Harper, 1955.

Krug, Edward A. *Curriculum Planning.* Rev. ed. New York: Harper, 1957.

Leonard, J. Paul. *Developing the Secondary School Curriculum.* Rev. ed. New York: Rinehart, 1957.

Lurry, Lucile L., and Elsie J. Alberty. *Developing a High School Core Program.* New York: Macmillan, 1957.

Marani, Jean Victoria. *A Technique for Determining Problem Areas for General Education in the Secondary School.* Unpublished doctoral dissertation. Ohio State University, 1958.

McConnell, C. M., E. O. Melby, C. O. Arndt, and L. J. Bishop. *New Schools for a New Culture.* Rev. ed. New York: Harper, 1953.

Miel, Alice. *Cooperative Procedures in Learning.* New York: Bureau of Publications, Teachers College, Columbia University, 1952.

Mudd, Dorothy. *A Core Program Grows.* Bel Air, Md.: Board of Education of Hartford County, 1949.

National Education Association. Educational Policies Commission. *Education for All American Youth.* Washington, D.C.: The Association, 1944.

———. Educational Policies Commission. *Education for All American Youth— A Further Look.* Washington, D.C.: The Association, 1952.

National Society for the Study of Education. *Adapting the Secondary-School Program to the Needs of Youth.* Fifty-Second Yearbook, Part I. Chicago: University of Chicago Press, 1953.

———. *The Integration of Educational Experiences.* Chicago: University of Chicago Press, 1958.

Newsom, A. Carolyn. *Preparing Teachers for Core Programs in High Schools.* Unpublished doctoral dissertation. Ohio State University, 1954.

New York City Board of Education. *Developing a Core Program in the Junior High School Grades.* New York: The Board. (Curriculum Bulletin, 1957– 58 Series, No. 12.)

New York City Board of Education. *Guide to Curriculum Improvement in Grades 7–8–9.* New York: The Board, 1957. (Curriculum Bulletin, 1955–56 Series, No. 10.)

Noar, Gertrude. *Freedom to Live and Learn.* Philadelphia: Franklin Publishing and Supply Co., 1948.

———. *The Junior High School.* Englewood Cliffs, N.J.: Prentice-Hall, 1953.

North Central Association of Colleges and Secondary Schools. *General Education in the American High School.* Chicago: Scott, Foresman, 1942.

Ohio State University. *The Core Curriculum in the High School.* Columbus: Ohio State University, 1948.

———. *A Description of Curricular Experiences. The Upper School.* Columbus: Ohio State University, 1952.

———. *How to Develop a Core Program in the High School.* Columbus: Ohio State University, College of Education, 1949.

———. *Preparing Core Teachers for the Secondary Schools.* Columbus: Ohio State University, College of Education, 1949.

———. *The University School; Its Philosophy and Purposes.* Columbus: Ohio State University, 1948.

———. *Utilizing Subject Fields in High School Core-Program Development.* Columbus: Ohio State University, College of Education, 1950.

Ovsiew, Leon, and others. *Making the Core Work.* New York: Metropolitan School Study Council, 1951.

Parrish, Louise, and Yvonne Waskin. *Teacher-Pupil Planning for Better Classroom Learning.* New York: Harper, 1958.

Pierce, Paul R. *Developing a High School Curriculum.* New York: American Book, 1952.

Reiner, William. "A Second Report of the Evaluation of Pupil Growth in the Core Program in Two Academic High Schools, 1952–53." Brooklyn: Board of Education of the City of New York, 1953.

Reiner, William, Katherine W. Hauber, and Leo Weitz. "A Study of the Introduction of the Core Program in Selected Academic High Schools." Brooklyn: Board of Education of the City of New York, 1953.

Romine, Stephen A. *Building the High School Curriculum.* New York: Ronald Press, 1954.

Saylor, John Galen, and William M. Alexander. *Curriculum Planning.* New York: Rinehart, 1954.

Schwartz, Bernard. "An Investigation of the Effects of a Core Program by Comparing Core-Experienced and Non-Core-Experienced Students in Various Factors." Yardley, Pa.: Pennsbury High School, 1954.

Smith, B. O., William O. Stanley, and H. J. Shores. *Fundamentals of Curriculum Development.* Rev. ed. Yonkers, N.Y.: World Book Company, 1957.

Stratemeyer, Florence B., and others. *Developing a Curriculum for Modern Living.* Rev. ed. New York: Bureau of Publications, Teachers College, Columbia University, 1957.

Thirty Schools Tell Their Story. New York: Harper, 1942.

Toops, Myrtle D. *Working in the Core Program in Burris Laboratory School.* Muncie, Ind.: Ball State Teachers College, 1955.

University School, Ohio State University, Class of 1938. *Were We Guinea Pigs?* New York: Henry Holt, 1938.

Van Til, William. *A Social Living Curriculum for Post-War Secondary Education.* Unpublished doctoral dissertation. Ohio State University, 1946.

Wiles, Kimball. *Teaching for Better Schools,* 2nd ed. Englewood Cliffs, N.J.: Prentice-Hall, 1959.

Wright, Grace S. *Block-Time Classes and the Core Program in the Junior High School.* Washington, D.C.: U.S. Government Printing Office, 1958. (U.S. Office of Education Bulletin, 1958, No. 6.)

———. *Core Curriculum Development Problems and Practices.* Washington, D.C.: Federal Security Agency, Office of Education, 1952.

———. *Core Curriculum in Public High Schools.* Washington, D.C.: Federal Security Agency, Office of Education, 1950.

Wrightstone, J. Wayne. "An Appraisal of Experimental High School Practices." New York: Bureau of Publications, Teachers College, Columbia University, 1936.

Zapf, Rosalind M. *Democratic Processes in the Secondary Classroom.* Englewood Cliffs, N.J.: Prentice-Hall, 1959.

Periodical Literature

Adkins, Arthur. "What About the Core Curriculum?" *High School Journal,* May, 1954.

Adler, R., and M. Peters. "General Mathematics and the Core Curriculum." *Math Teacher,* March, 1953.

Alberty, Harold B. "A Proposal for Reorganizing the High School Curriculum on the Basis of a Core Program." *Progressive Education,* November, 1950.

Bartlett, Hall. "More Light on the Core." *Social Education,* March, 1957.

Bayles, Ernest E. "Let's Take a Look at Core." *University of Kansas Bulletin of Education,* November, 1954.

Berger, Donald W. "Planning in the Core Class." *Educational Leadership,* January, 1951.

Besvinick, Emma M. "The Planning and Operating of a Good Core Program." *Clearing House,* December, 1953.

Bishop, Leslee J. "Planning Patterns in a Core Program." *Educational Leadership,* April, 1955.

Bossing, Nelson L. "What Is Core?" *School Review,* April, 1955.

———. "Development of the Core Curriculum in the Senior High School." *School Review,* May, 1956.

Brandes, Louis G. "The Core Curriculum in the Secondary Schools." *Progressive Education,* February, 1952.

———. "Status of Core Curriculum in Secondary Schools." *California Journal of Secondary Education,* November, 1951.

Broad, T. H. "How Can the Experience-Centered Curriculum Be Developed?" *The Bulletin of the National Association of Secondary School Principals,* May, 1949.

Brochick, A. "Core Studies, A Concept." *The Bulletin of the National Association of Secondary School Principals,* January, 1950.

Brooks, John J. "Esprit D'Core-Human Relations in the Core Curriculum." *The Bulletin of the National Association of Secondary School Principals,* March, 1955.

Burge, Anne. "English Classes Use Social Studies Reading." *Clearing House,* October, 1947.

Burnett, Raymond W., and Bernice D. Burnett. "Core Programs in Action." *Education,* January, 1953.

Butterweck, Joseph S. "Core Curriculum—The Ideal." *School and Society,* October 4, 1952.

——— and Katharine H. Spessard. *The Unified Curriculum: A Case Study, Grades 7–8.* New York: Rinehart & Company, Inc., 1960.

Buttle, F. J., and J. E. Berry. "Core Curriculum and the Library." *High School Journal,* October, 1957.

Capehart, Bertis E., Allen Hodge, and Norman Berdan. "An Objective Evaluation of a Core Program." *School Review,* February, 1952.

Capehart, Bertis E., Allen Hodge, and Robert Roth. "Evaluating the Core Curriculum: A Further Look." *School Review,* October, 1953.

Chiara, Clara R. "The Core Teacher's Major—Youth." *School Review,* November, 1955.

Cramer, Roscoe V. "Common Learnings Program in the Junior High School." *The Bulletin of the National Association of Secondary School Principals,* April, 1951.

———. "How Effective Is the Core Curriculum in the Junior High School?" *The Bulletin of the National Association of Secondary School Principals,* April, 1954.

Cummins, Evelyn W. "Grouping: Homogeneous or Heterogeneous?" *Educational Administration and Supervision,* January, 1958.

Davison, Paul A. "Initiating the Core Curriculum from the Principal's Viewpoint." *Education,* January, 1953.

Deans, Helen E. "The Language Arts Enrich the Core Program." *School Review,* April, 1955.

———. "Student Self-Evaluation in a Core Program." *Social Studies,* March, 1954.

Deaton, Joseph C., Sr. "A Core-Organized School in Action." *California Journal of Secondary Education,* March, 1952.

Dexter, George. "Fundamental Skills in a Core Program." *Educational Leadership,* December, 1954.

Education, January, 1953. Entire issue.

Edwards, Karl D. "Meeting the Needs of Youth through a Core Program." *University of Kansas Bulletin of Education,* February, 1954.

———. "The Program for the Preparation of Core Teachers at the University of Kansas." *University of Kansas Bulletin of Education,* February, 1957.

Fair, Jean E. "The Comparative Effectiveness of a Core and a Conventional Curriculum in Developing Social Concern." *School Review,* May and September, 1954.

Fawcett, Harold P. "Mathematics and the Core Curriculum." *The Bulletin of the National Association of Secondary School Principals,* May, 1954.

Fickes, James A., and Lucile L. Lurry. "Preparing Core Teachers—A Joint Responsibility." *Educational Leadership,* November, 1953.

Forlano, George. "Measuring the Quality of Social Acceptability in Some Ninth Grade Core and Non-Core Classes." *High School Journal,* October, 1954.

Freyer, Ralph. "How to Make a Core Program Work." *Thirty-Ninth Annual Schoolmen's Week Proceedings.* Philadelphia: University of Pennsylvania, 1952.

Gales, Raymond F. "The Progress of Students and Graduates of a Core Curriculum." *School Review,* October, 1955.

Gibboney, Richard A. "A Rationale for the Societal-Personal Needs Core." *Phi Delta Kappan,* March, 1957.

Gravitt, Bernard C. "Don't Be Afraid to Try It!" *Kentucky School Journal,* January, 1952.

———. "Reviewing an Experience with Core Curriculum." *Kentucky School Journal,* December, 1952.

Hand, Harold C. "The Case for the Common Learnings Program." *Science Education,* February, 1948.

Harap, Henry. "Improvement of the Core." *High School Journal,* October, 1956.

Harvill, Harris. "Eight Advantages of the Core Organization." *Social Education,* January, 1954.

———. "Nature of the Core Curriculum." *Social Education,* May, 1954.

———. "Origins of the Core Concept." *Social Education,* April, 1954.

Hauber, Katherine W. "The Experimental Core Program in the High Schools of New York City." *High Points,* January, 1953.

Henderson, Richard L. "Conversation." *Educational Leadership,* March, 1958.

Hill, T. J. "The Core Idea." *The Bulletin of the National Association of Secondary School Principals,* October, 1957.

———. "Less Math, Science? Look at the Record." *Journal of the Florida Educational Association,* February, 1958.

Hock, Louise E. "From One Core Teacher to Another." *Social Education,* May, 1957.

———. "The Core of the Matter." *Social Education,* April, 1957.

Hoppe, Arthur. "The Core in Junior High School." *Bulletin of the School of Education,* Indiana University, July, 1957.

Jackson, David M. "Development of a Measure of Orientation toward Core and Subject Curriculum Theories." *School Review,* September, 1956.

Jurjevich, Joseph C. "Methods and Results in a Junior High Core Class." *Educational Leadership,* May, 1957.

———. "What Do Parents Say about Experimentation in Our Schools?" *Education,* March, 1958.

Kahn, K. "Guidance Function of Core." *High Points,* March, 1957.

Kalamazoo Public Schools. "How Much Did They Grow?" *General Information Bulletin,* Kalamazoo Public Schools, September, 1952.

Kelley, Arthur C., and Robert E. Beatty. "Here's Proof That Core Program Students Learn Basic Skills." *School Executive,* February, 1953.

Kelly, Earl C. "Why Become a Core Teacher?" *Educational Leadership,* February, 1955.

Kitching, Eugene. "The Education of the Core Teacher." *Florida School Bulletin,* March, 1954.

Klohr, Paul R. "An Upward Extension of Core." *Educational Leadership,* May, 1953.

Knife, William G. "Can You Put a New Program in an Old Classroom?" *School Executive,* February, 1953.

Knox, Opal A. "Core Program in Action." *Wisconsin Journal of Education,* May, 1953.

Krug, Edward A., Clifford S. Liddle, and Quentin F. Schenk. "Multiple-Period Classes in Wisconsin." *Educational Leadership,* March, 1954.

Langer, Ruth. "Core Resource Teacher and Coordinator Becomes an Institution in St. Paul." *The Bulletin of the National Association of Secondary School Principals,* March, 1958.

Leeds, Willard L. "Core Classes in Action." *Education,* January, 1953.

Little, Thomas C. "Two-Hour Periods: Plan of Transition to a Core Program." *Clearing House,* March, 1951.

Mennes, Arthur H. "The Effectiveness of Multiple Period Curricular Practices in High School English and Social Studies." *Journal of Educational Research,* September, 1956.

———. "Pupils Evaluate Democratic Practices in Multiple Period Classes." *California Journal of Secondary Education,* March, 1957.

———. "What Students Think of Integrated Curricular Practices in High School English and Social Studies." *School Review,* December, 1954.

Mickelson, John M. "What Does Research Say about the Effectiveness of the Core Curriculum?" *School Review,* Summer, 1957.

Miller, Helen R. "Unified Studies: A History-English Powerhouse." *Clearing House,* October, 1949.

Miller, Irving. "A Core-Class Unit." *High Points,* February, 1953.

Mudd, Dorothy. "Core Program Uses Evaluation." *Educational Leadership,* November, 1950.

Mumma, Richard A. "The Needs of Secondary-School Teachers in a Reorganized Curriculum." *Educational Administration and Supervision,* January, 1951.

Nettleton, Leon D. "Guidance Role of the Core Teacher." *Social Education,* February, 1957.

Preston, R. C., and E. T. Reddin. "Status of the Curriculum." *Review of Educational Research,* June, 1957.

Reid, Chandos. "Instructional Materials and Problem-Centered Teaching." *Teachers College Record*, October, 1950.

Riccio, Anthony C. "Group Guidance—A Step Toward the Core." *Educational Administration and Supervision*, January, 1958.

Romine, Stephen A. "Needed! Pre-Service Teacher Training for the Core Curriculum." *Education*, November, 1950.

Rothman, Philip. "Core Curriculum—New Frontier." *Journal of Educational Sociology*, September, 1954.

Saylor, Galen. "Core Programs in American Secondary Schools." *Educational Leadership*, February, 1949.

Smith, John H. "Why a Core Based on Adolescent Needs?" *Educational Administration and Supervision*, February, 1957.

Spitznas, J. E. "Core Curriculum: Form or Process?" *School Review*, November, 1947.

Storen, Helen F. "Personal Problems and Social Values as Core Content." *Educational Forum*, May, 1957.

———. "Relation of Method to Content in the Core Curriculum." *High Points*, December, 1956.

Strom, Ingrid M. "The Role of Literature in the Core Curriculum." *Bulletin of the School of Education*, Indiana University, May, 1958.

Taub, Irene S. "Ten Years with the Core Curriculum." *Social Education*, January and February, 1955.

Thomas, Harrison C. "Core Programs in the New York City Academic High Schools." *High Points*, February, 1953.

Toops, Myrtle D. "The Core Program Does Improve Reading Proficiency." *Educational Administration and Supervision*, December, 1954.

Vars, Gordon F. "Problems of a Beginning Core Teacher." *Educational Leadership*, October, 1951.

Wright, Grace S. "Core Curriculum: Why and What." *School Life*, February, 1952.

———. "Ten Years of Research on the Core Program." *School Review*, December, 1956.

Wrightstone, J. Wayne. "Evaluating the Effectiveness of an Integrated Ninth Grade Curriculum." *Teachers College Journal*, November, 1947.

Wrightstone, J. Wayne, and George Forlano. "An Evaluation of the Experience Curriculum at Midwood High School." *High Points*, December, 1948.

Index

Evanston Township High School, general education program of, 35–40

F

Fear, "effective" learning and, 24
Freedom, defined, 22

G

General education (*see* Education, general)
General education classes
assumptions underlying, 9, 15
bases for, 16–26
democratic ideals, 20–22
nature of adolescence, 24–26
psychological theory, 22–24
societal needs, 16–20
defined, 9
distinction between other general education aspects of school program and, 11–12
essential aspects of, 9
evaluation of (*see* Evaluation)
examples of, 31–53
growth of, 203–205
identifying problems for study in, 66–70, 72–83
individual study and, 94–97
introducing, suggestions for, 199–202
materials for use in, 121–123
nature of, 8–10
objectives of, 32
orientation (getting acquainted), 57–62
as part of curriculum, 10
problem-solving approaches in, 83–103
problems related to, 208–211
relationship to rest of school program, 210
resources, 123–130
scheduling of, 12–13
scope of, 209
sequence of, 209
sharing findings in, 97–98

General education classes (*cont.*)
starting, 57–71
status of, 203–205
subject matter in, 13–15
teachers (*see* Teachers)
Getting acquainted (*see* Orientation)
Goals, school, establishing, 195–196
Guidance
evaluation as aid in, 158
individual, lack of, in the schools, 7
individual differences and, 106–121

I

Identification, problem, in general education classes, 66–70, 72–83
Individual differences, 3, 10
adapting teaching procedures to, 105–106
challenge of, meeting the, 104–130
guidance and counseling and, 106–121
In-service education, of teachers, 200–201

K

Knowledge, need of, on part of teachers, 185–189

L

Language, development of skill in correct usage of, 146
Learning
"effective," 23, 24
resources for (*see* Resources)

M

Materials, general education, 121–123
development of, 208–209
Maturity, as major requirement of teachers, 185

O

Organizing, for study of unit, 86–89
Orientation, 57–62